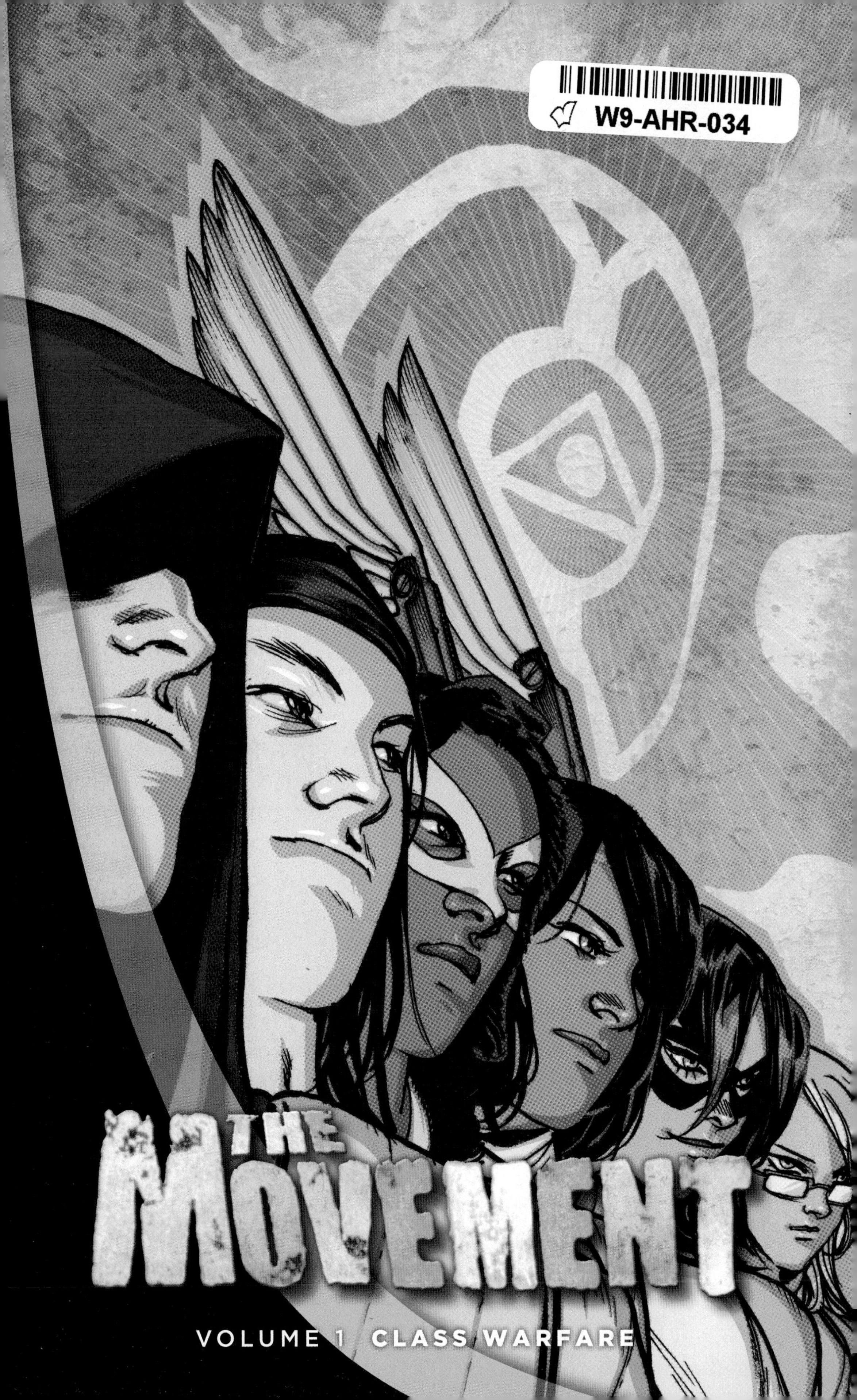
THE MOVEMENT
VOLUME 1 CLASS WARFARE

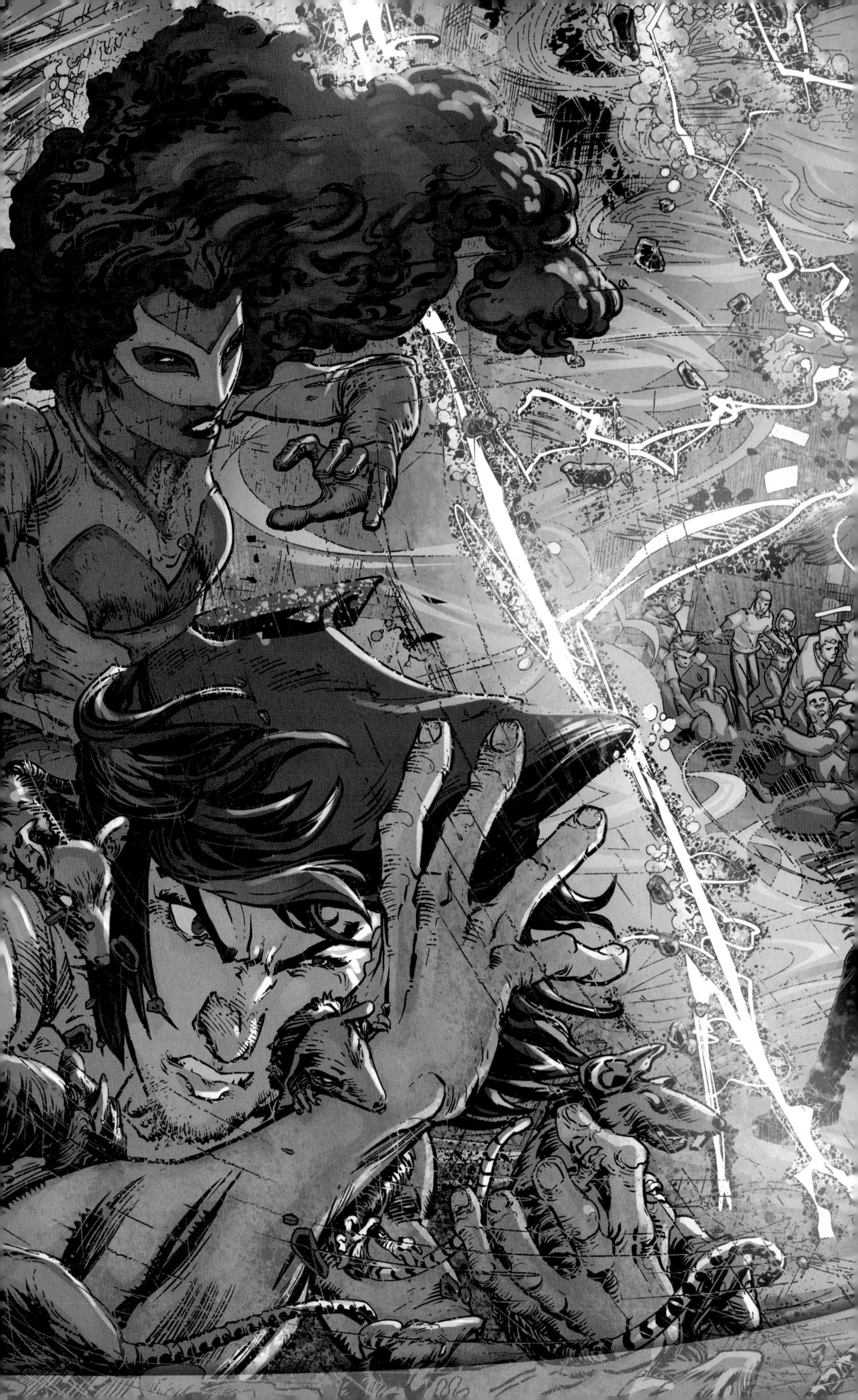

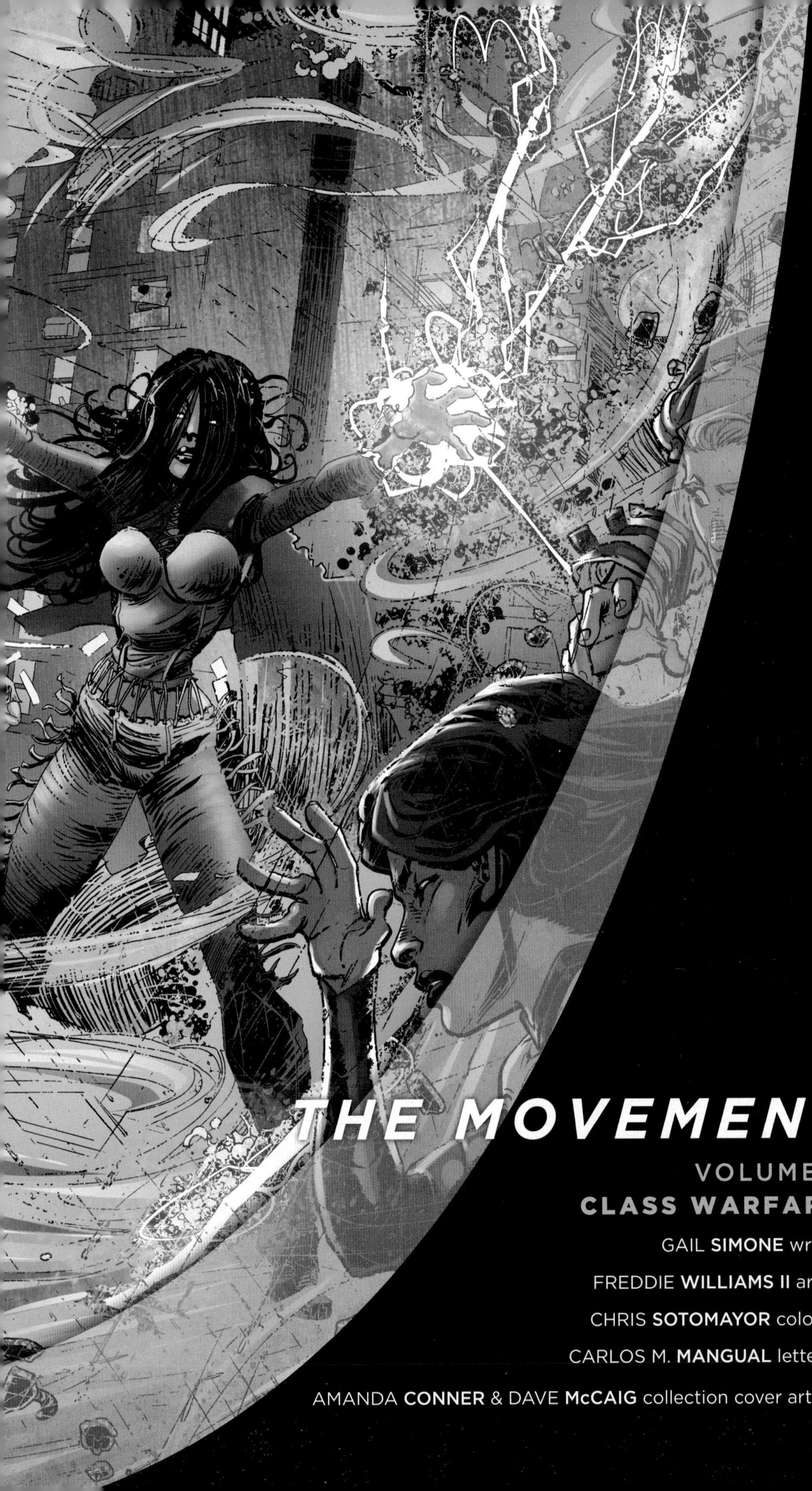

THE MOVEMENT

VOLUME 1
CLASS WARFARE

GAIL **SIMONE** writer

FREDDIE **WILLIAMS II** artist

CHRIS **SOTOMAYOR** colorist

CARLOS M. **MANGUAL** letterer

AMANDA **CONNER** & DAVE **McCAIG** collection cover artists

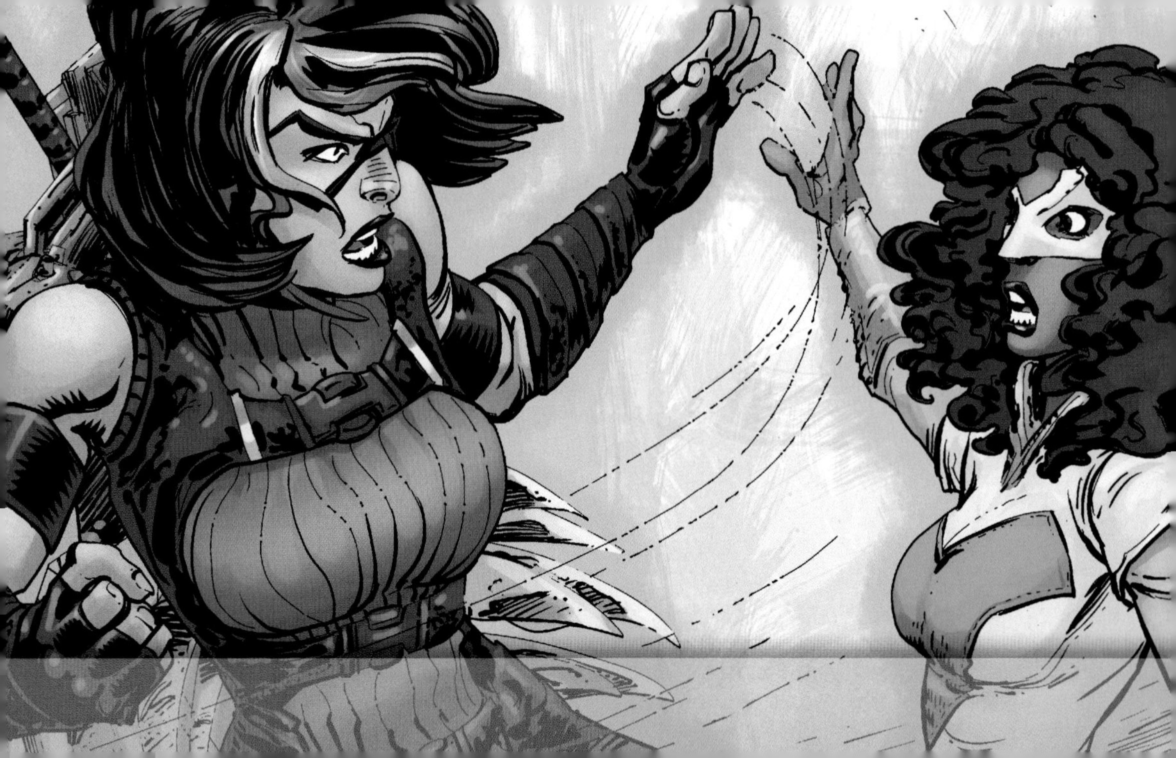

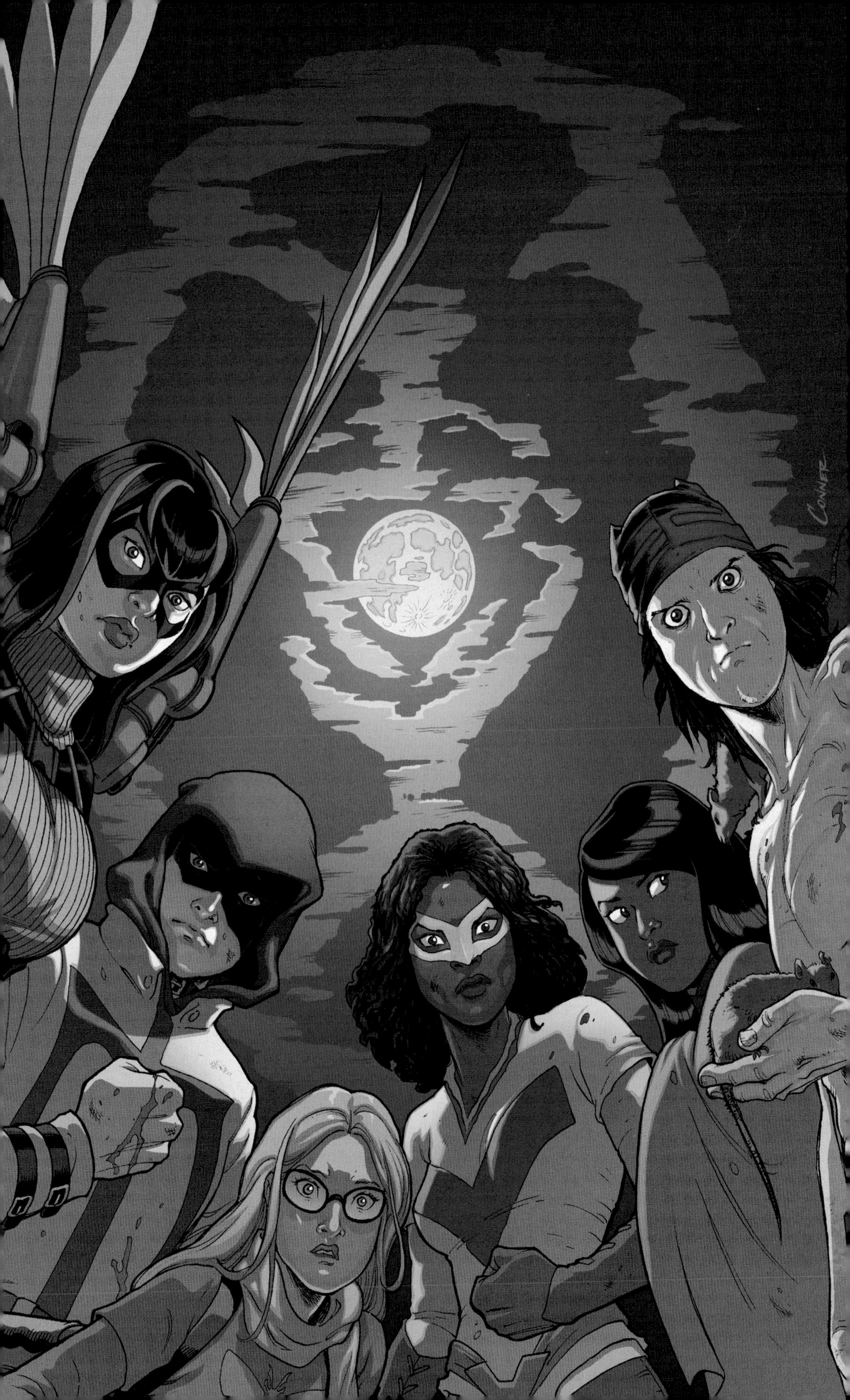
CONNER

The Movement #1 cover by Amanda Conner & Dave McCaig

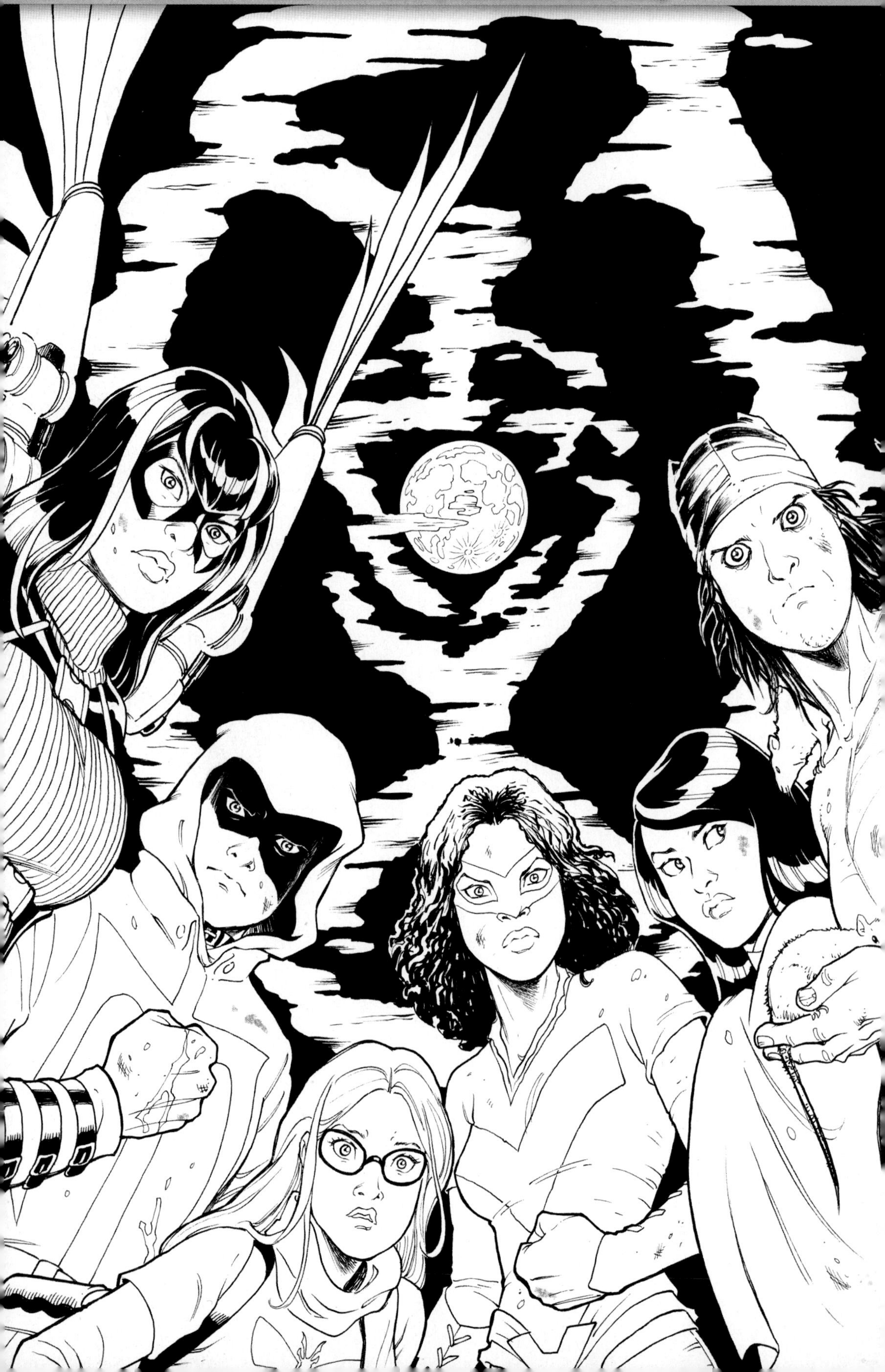

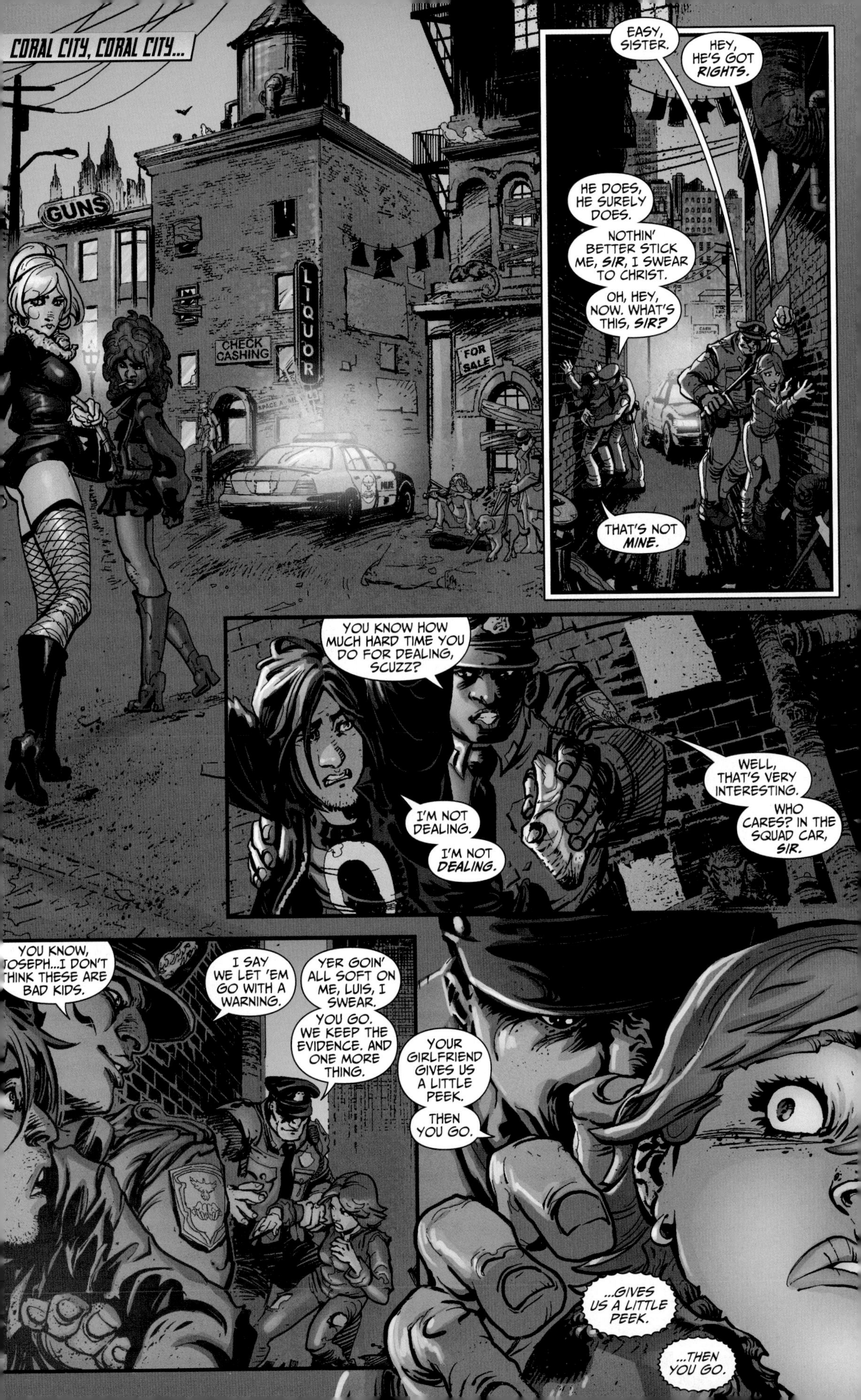
CORAL CITY, CORAL CITY...
GUNS
CHECK CASHING
LIQUOR
FOR SALE
EASY, SISTER.
HEY, HE'S GOT RIGHTS.
HE DOES, HE SURELY DOES.
NOTHIN' BETTER STICK ME, SIR, I SWEAR TO CHRIST.
OH, HEY, NOW. WHAT'S THIS, SIR?
THAT'S NOT MINE.
YOU KNOW HOW MUCH HARD TIME YOU DO FOR DEALING, SCUZZ?
I'M NOT DEALING.
I'M NOT DEALING.
WELL, THAT'S VERY INTERESTING.
WHO CARES? IN THE SQUAD CAR, SIR.
YOU KNOW, JOSEPH...I DON'T THINK THESE ARE BAD KIDS.
I SAY WE LET 'EM GO WITH A WARNING.
YER GOIN' ALL SOFT ON ME, LUIS, I SWEAR.
YOU GO. WE KEEP THE EVIDENCE. AND ONE MORE THING.
YOUR GIRLFRIEND GIVES US A LITTLE PEEK.
THEN YOU GO.
...GIVES US A LITTLE PEEK.
...THEN YOU GO.

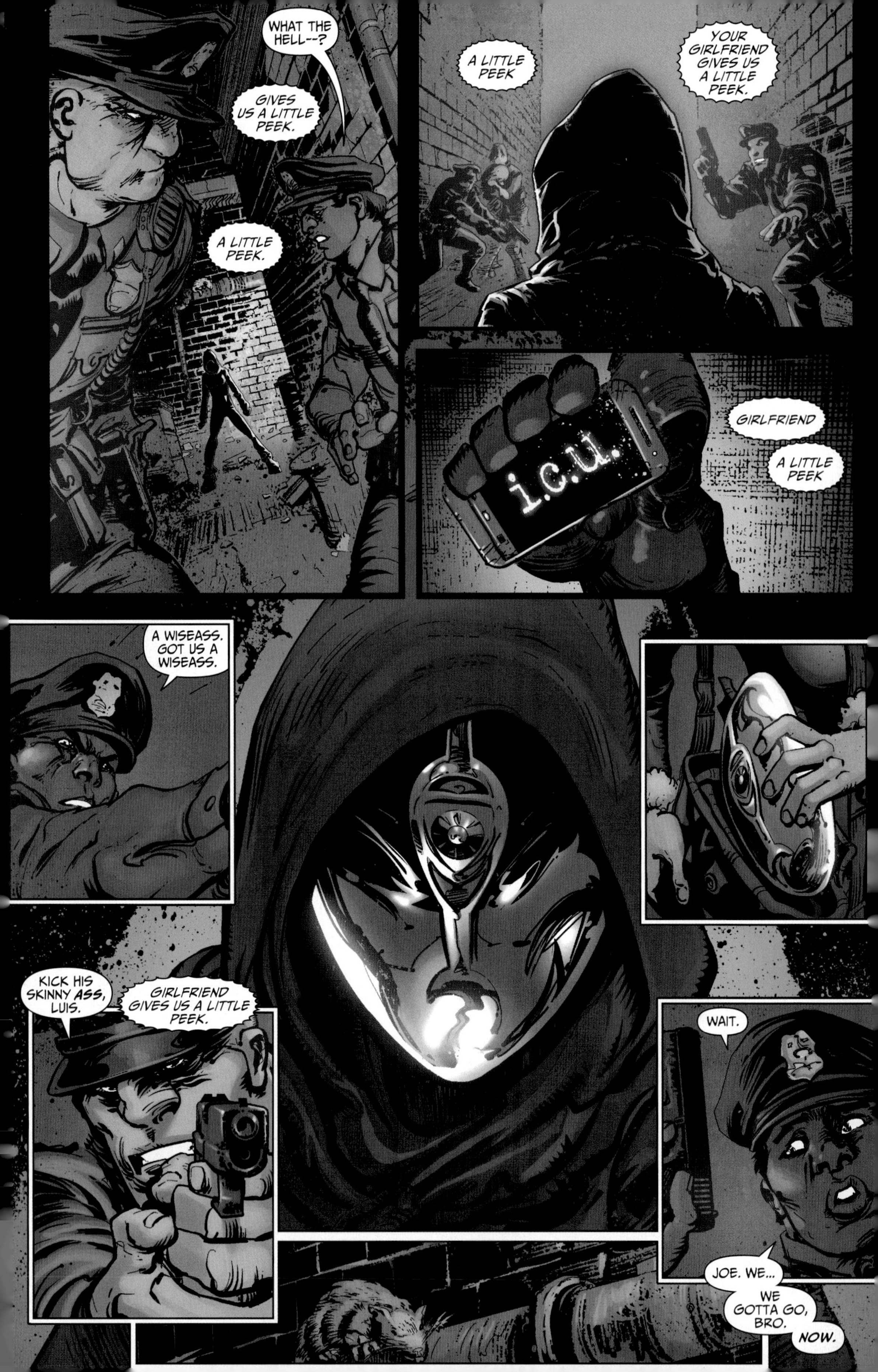

WHAT THE HELL--?
GIVES US A LITTLE PEEK.
A LITTLE PEEK.
A LITTLE PEEK
YOUR GIRLFRIEND GIVES US A LITTLE PEEK.
i.c.u.
GIRLFRIEND
A LITTLE PEEK
A WISEASS. GOT US A WISEASS.
KICK HIS SKINNY ASS, LUIS.
GIRLFRIEND GIVES US A LITTLE PEEK.
WAIT.
JOE. WE...
WE GOTTA GO, BRO.
NOW.

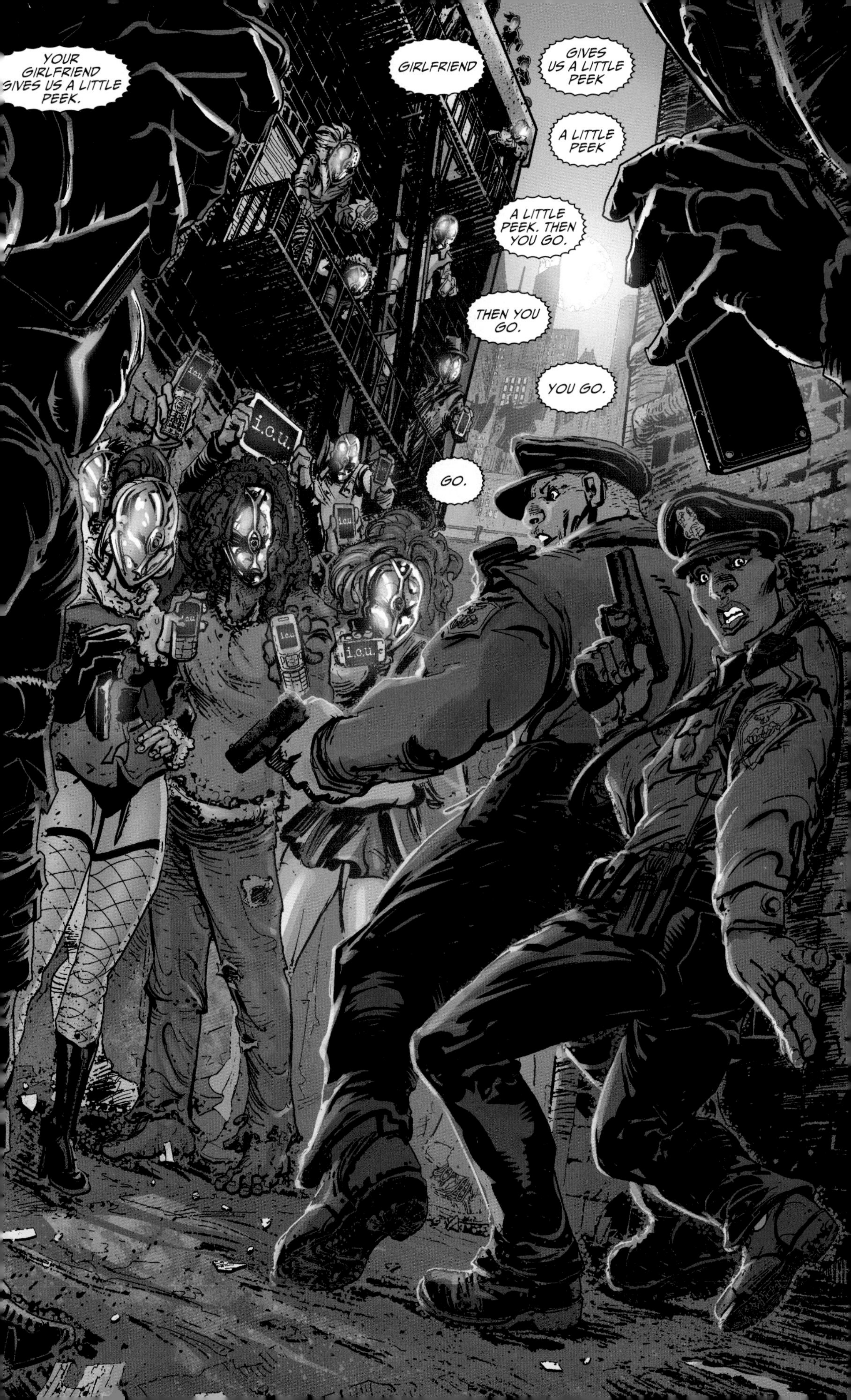
YOUR GIRLFRIEND GIVES US A LITTLE PEEK.
GIRLFRIEND
GIVES US A LITTLE PEEK
A LITTLE PEEK
A LITTLE PEEK. THEN YOU GO.
THEN YOU GO.
YOU GO.
GO.
i.c.u.

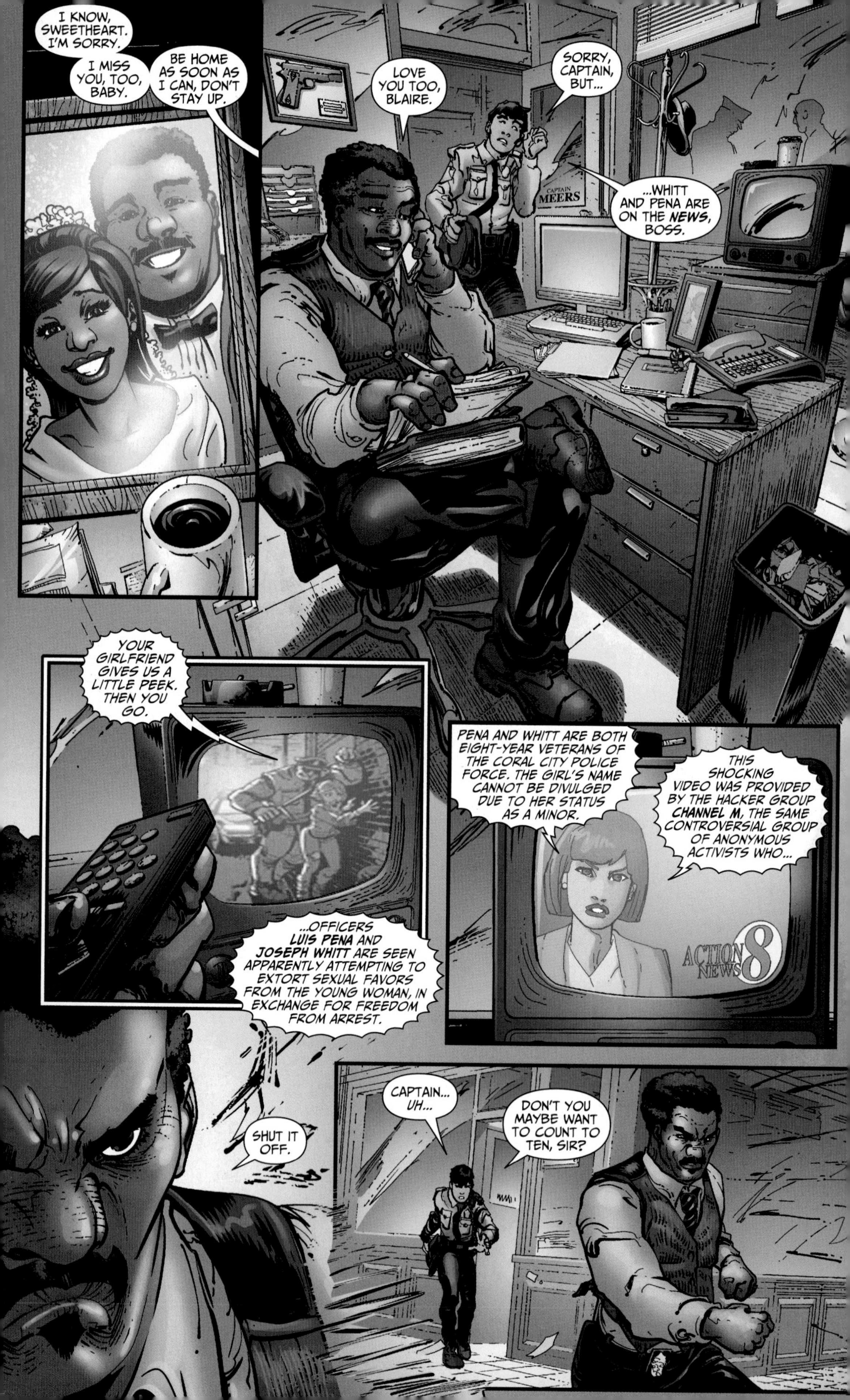
I KNOW, SWEETHEART. I'M SORRY.
I MISS YOU, TOO, BABY.
BE HOME AS SOON AS I CAN, DON'T STAY UP.
LOVE YOU TOO, BLAIRE.
SORRY, CAPTAIN, BUT...
CAPTAIN MEERS
...WHITT AND PENA ARE ON THE NEWS, BOSS.
YOUR GIRLFRIEND GIVES US A LITTLE PEEK. THEN YOU GO.
...OFFICERS LUIS PENA AND JOSEPH WHITT ARE SEEN APPARENTLY ATTEMPTING TO EXTORT SEXUAL FAVORS FROM THE YOUNG WOMAN, IN EXCHANGE FOR FREEDOM FROM ARREST.
PENA AND WHITT ARE BOTH EIGHT-YEAR VETERANS OF THE CORAL CITY POLICE FORCE. THE GIRL'S NAME CANNOT BE DIVULGED DUE TO HER STATUS AS A MINOR.
THIS SHOCKING VIDEO WAS PROVIDED BY THE HACKER GROUP CHANNEL M, THE SAME CONTROVERSIAL GROUP OF ANONYMOUS ACTIVISTS WHO...
ACTION NEWS 8
SHUT IT OFF.
CAPTAIN... UH...
DON'T YOU MAYBE WANT TO COUNT TO TEN, SIR?

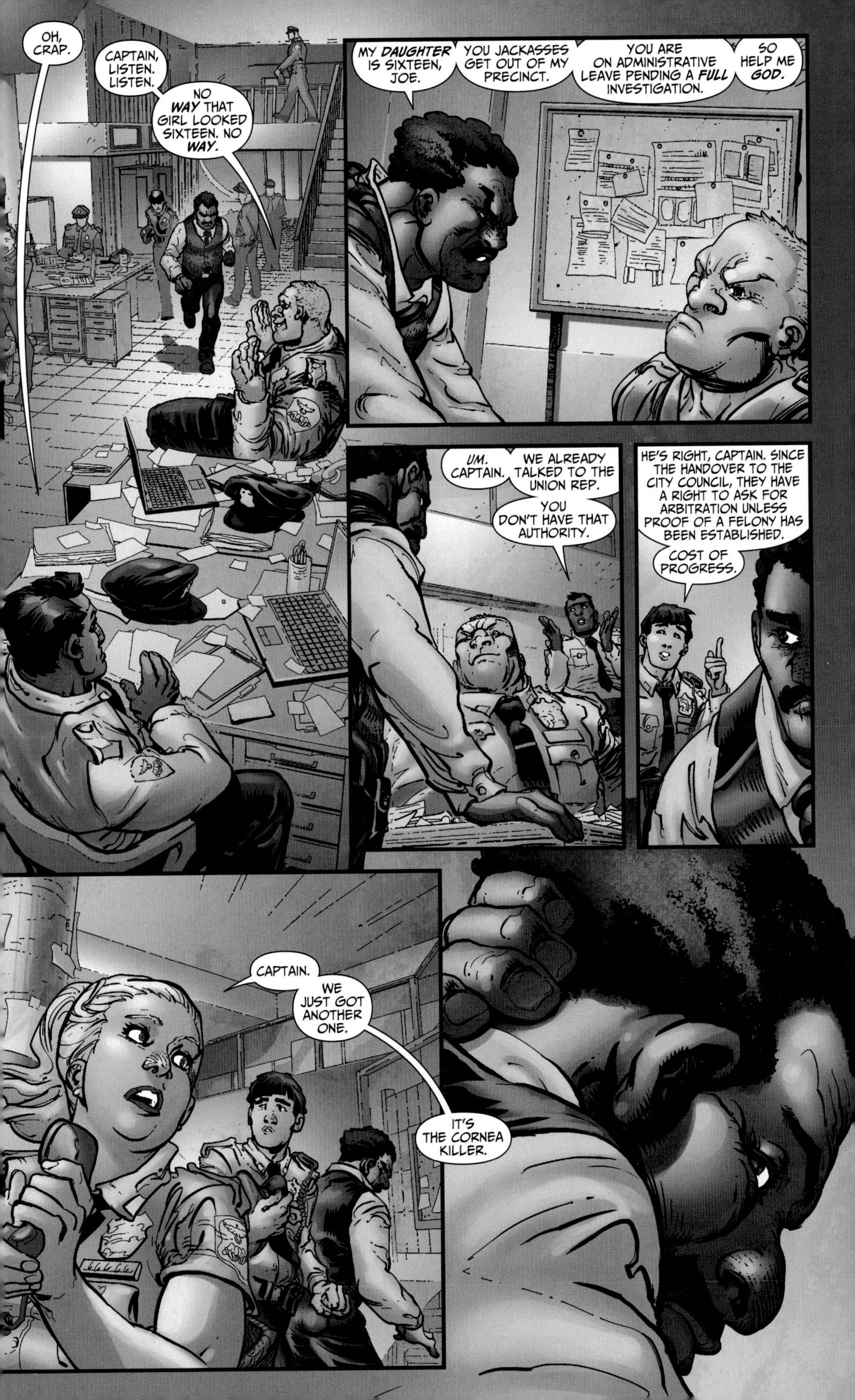
OH, CRAP.
CAPTAIN, LISTEN. LISTEN.
NO WAY THAT GIRL LOOKED SIXTEEN. NO WAY.
MY DAUGHTER IS SIXTEEN, JOE.
YOU JACKASSES GET OUT OF MY PRECINCT.
YOU ARE ON ADMINISTRATIVE LEAVE PENDING A FULL INVESTIGATION.
SO HELP ME GOD.
UM. CAPTAIN.
WE ALREADY TALKED TO THE UNION REP.
YOU DON'T HAVE THAT AUTHORITY.
HE'S RIGHT, CAPTAIN. SINCE THE HANDOVER TO THE CITY COUNCIL, THEY HAVE A RIGHT TO ASK FOR ARBITRATION UNLESS PROOF OF A FELONY HAS BEEN ESTABLISHED.
COST OF PROGRESS.
CAPTAIN.
WE JUST GOT ANOTHER ONE.
IT'S THE CORNEA KILLER.

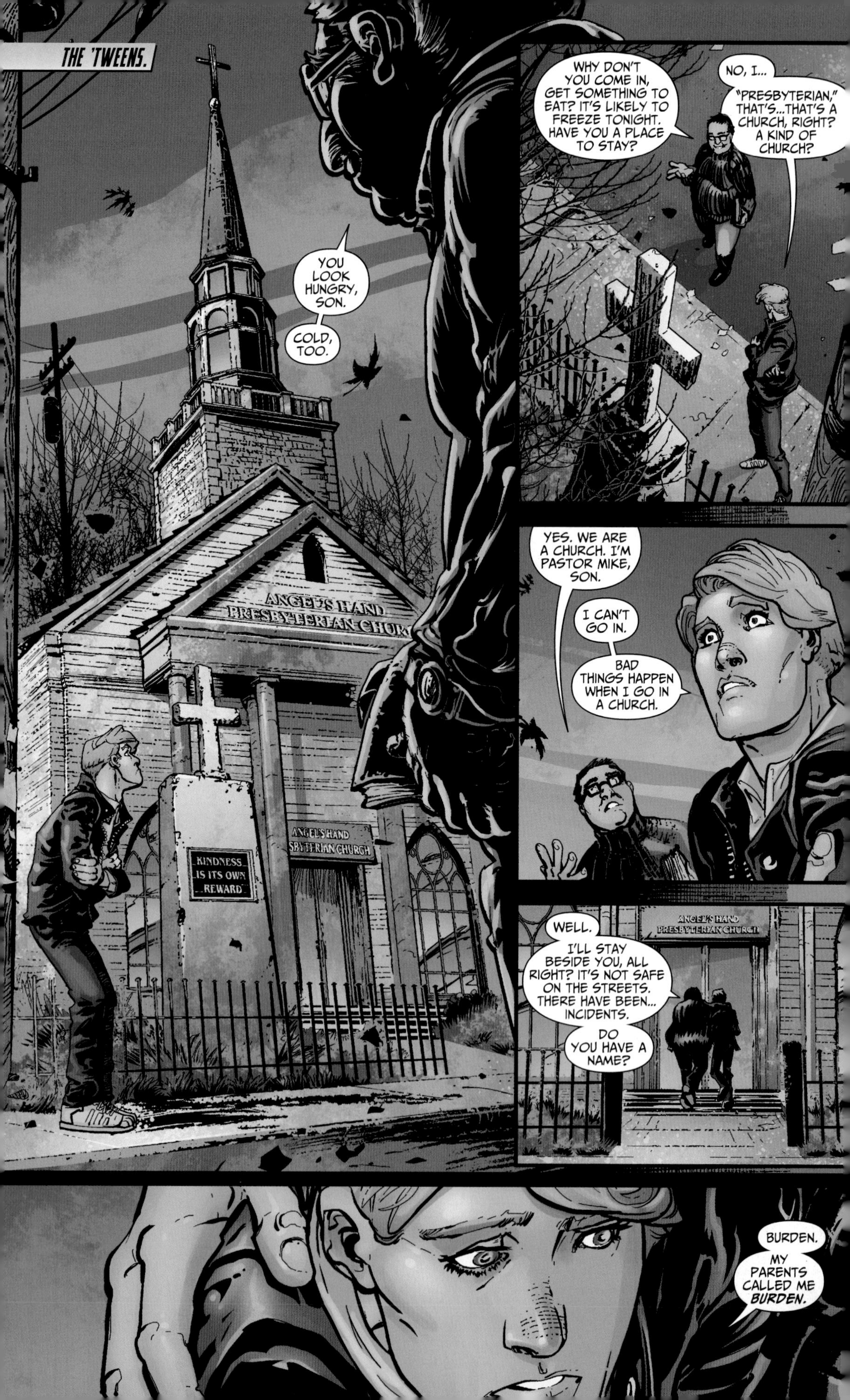
THE 'TWEENS.
YOU LOOK HUNGRY, SON.
COLD, TOO.
ANGEL'S HAND PRESBYTERIAN CHURCH
ANGEL'S HAND PRESBYTERIAN CHURCH
KINDNESS IS ITS OWN REWARD
WHY DON'T YOU COME IN, GET SOMETHING TO EAT? IT'S LIKELY TO FREEZE TONIGHT. HAVE YOU A PLACE TO STAY?
NO, I...
"PRESBYTERIAN," THAT'S...THAT'S A CHURCH, RIGHT? A KIND OF CHURCH?
YES. WE ARE A CHURCH. I'M PASTOR MIKE, SON.
I CAN'T GO IN.
BAD THINGS HAPPEN WHEN I GO IN A CHURCH.
ANGEL'S HAND PRESBYTERIAN CHURCH
WELL.
I'LL STAY BESIDE YOU, ALL RIGHT? IT'S NOT SAFE ON THE STREETS. THERE HAVE BEEN... INCIDENTS.
DO YOU HAVE A NAME?
BURDEN.
MY PARENTS CALLED ME *BURDEN.*

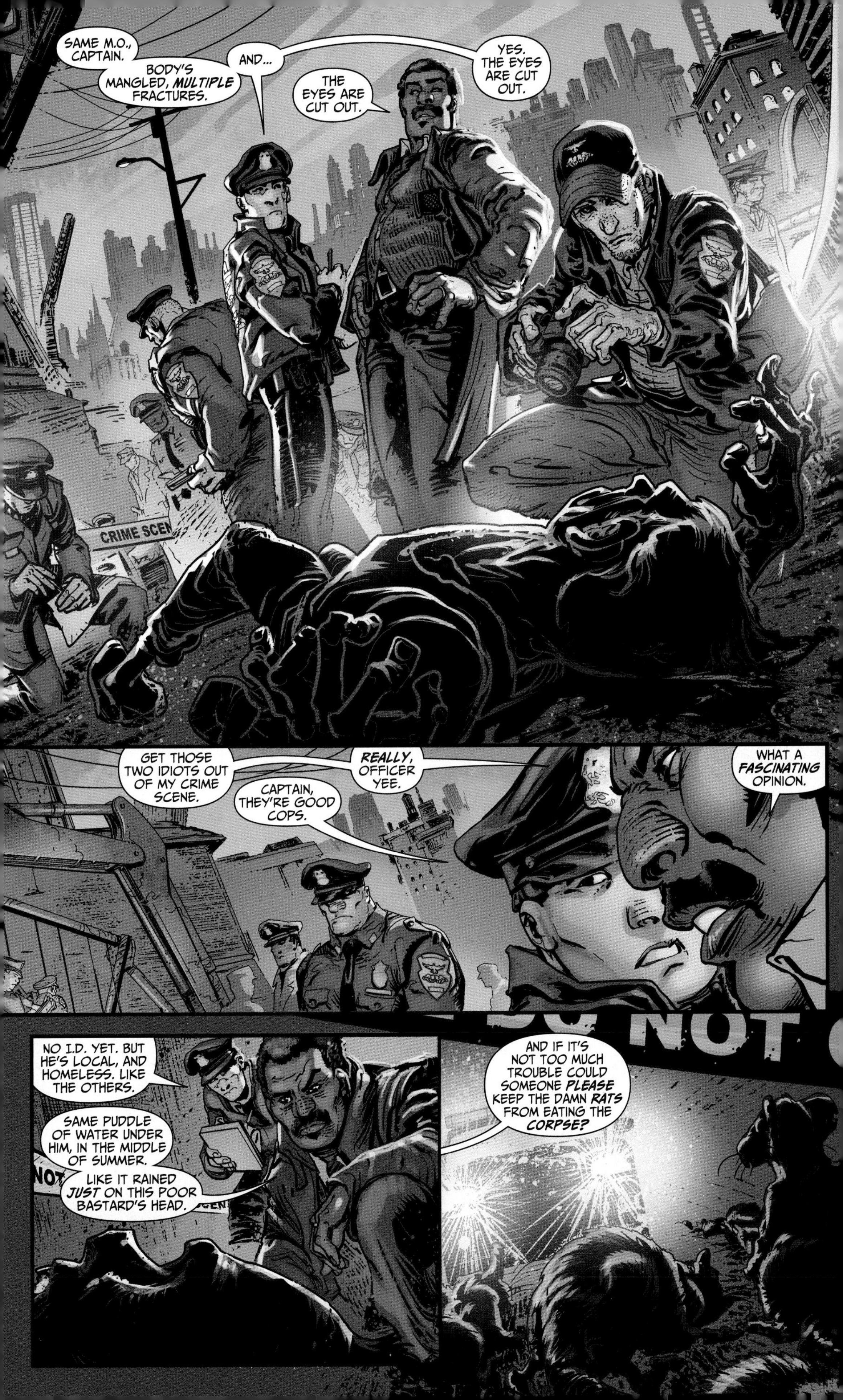

SAME M.O., CAPTAIN.
BODY'S MANGLED, *MULTIPLE* FRACTURES.
AND...
THE EYES ARE CUT OUT.
YES. THE EYES ARE CUT OUT.
CRIME SCEN
GET THOSE TWO IDIOTS OUT OF MY CRIME SCENE.
CAPTAIN, THEY'RE GOOD COPS.
REALLY, OFFICER YEE.
WHAT A *FASCINATING* OPINION.
NOT
NO I.D. YET. BUT HE'S LOCAL, AND HOMELESS. LIKE THE OTHERS.
SAME PUDDLE OF WATER UNDER HIM, IN THE MIDDLE OF SUMMER.
LIKE IT RAINED *JUST* ON THIS POOR BASTARD'S HEAD.
AND IF IT'S NOT TOO MUCH TROUBLE COULD SOMEONE *PLEASE* KEEP THE DAMN *RATS* FROM EATING THE *CORPSE?*

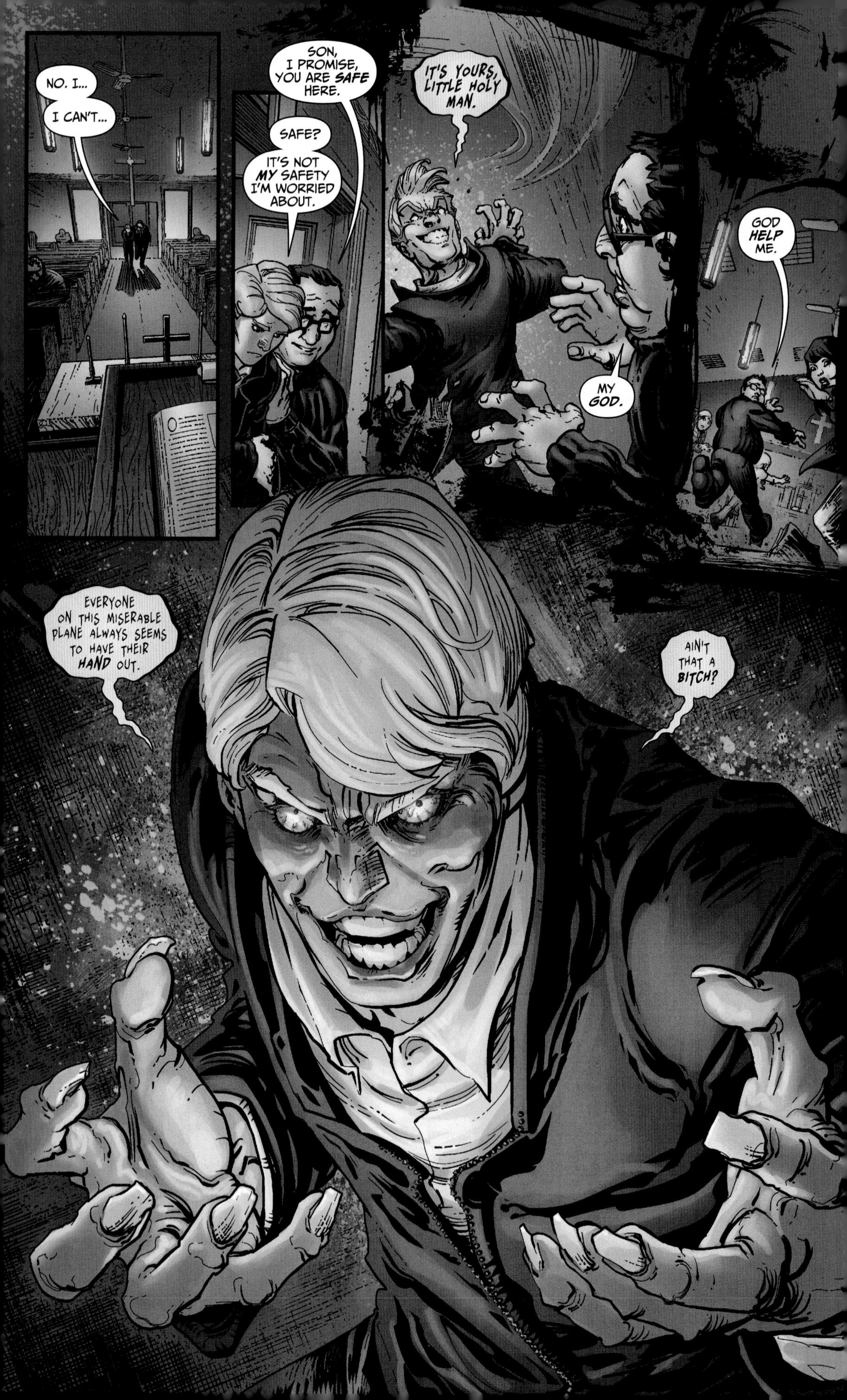
NO. I...
I CAN'T...
SON, I PROMISE, YOU ARE SAFE HERE.
SAFE?
IT'S NOT MY SAFETY I'M WORRIED ABOUT.
IT'S YOURS, LITTLE HOLY MAN.
MY GOD.
GOD HELP ME.
EVERYONE ON THIS MISERABLE PLANE ALWAYS SEEMS TO HAVE THEIR HAND OUT.
AIN'T THAT A BITCH?

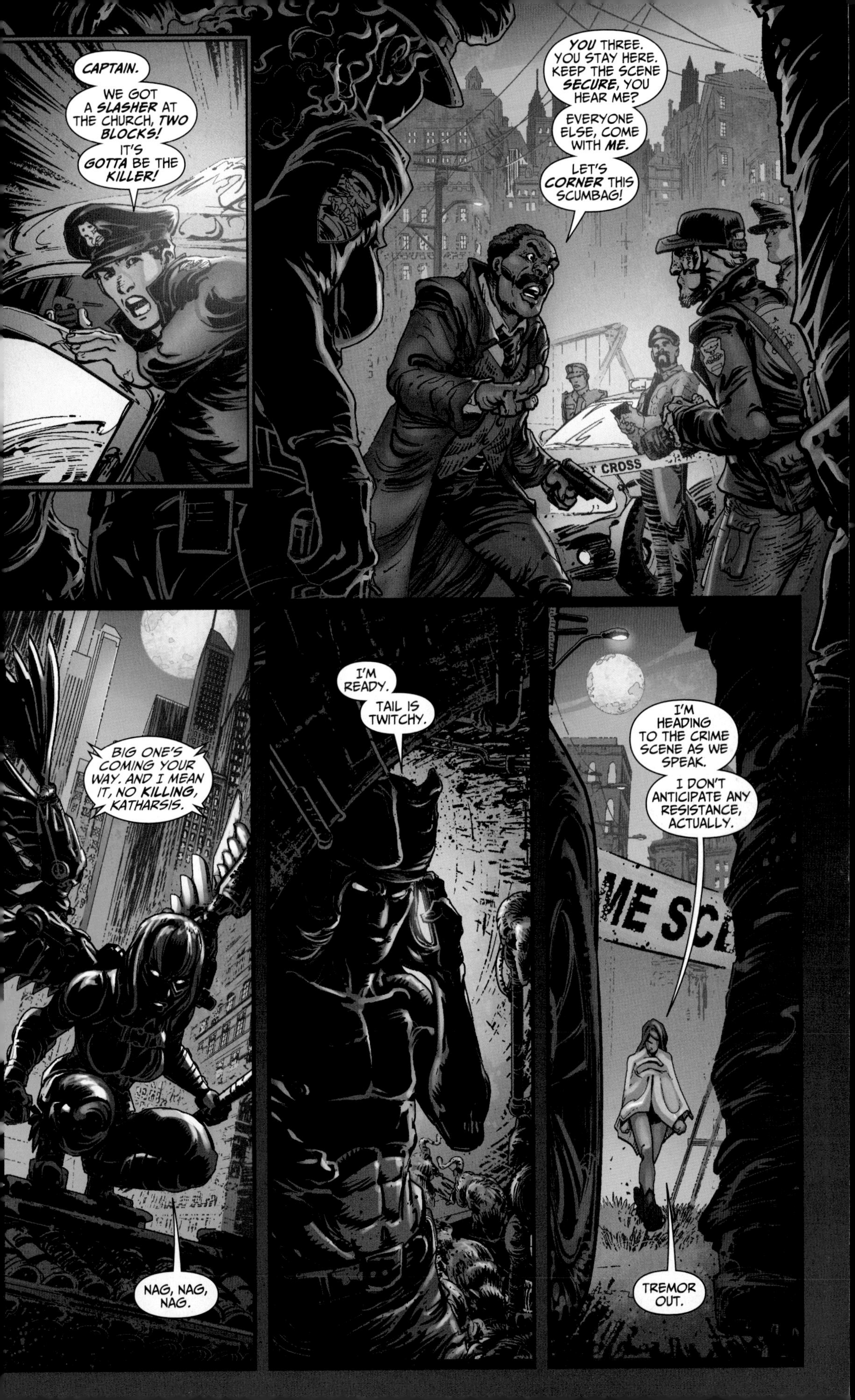
CAPTAIN.
WE GOT A SLASHER AT THE CHURCH, TWO BLOCKS!
IT'S GOTTA BE THE KILLER!
YOU THREE. YOU STAY HERE. KEEP THE SCENE SECURE, YOU HEAR ME?
EVERYONE ELSE, COME WITH ME.
LET'S CORNER THIS SCUMBAG!
CROSS
BIG ONE'S COMING YOUR WAY. AND I MEAN IT, NO KILLING, KATHARSIS.
NAG, NAG, NAG.
I'M READY.
TAIL IS TWITCHY.
I'M HEADING TO THE CRIME SCENE AS WE SPEAK.
I DON'T ANTICIPATE ANY RESISTANCE, ACTUALLY.
TREMOR OUT.

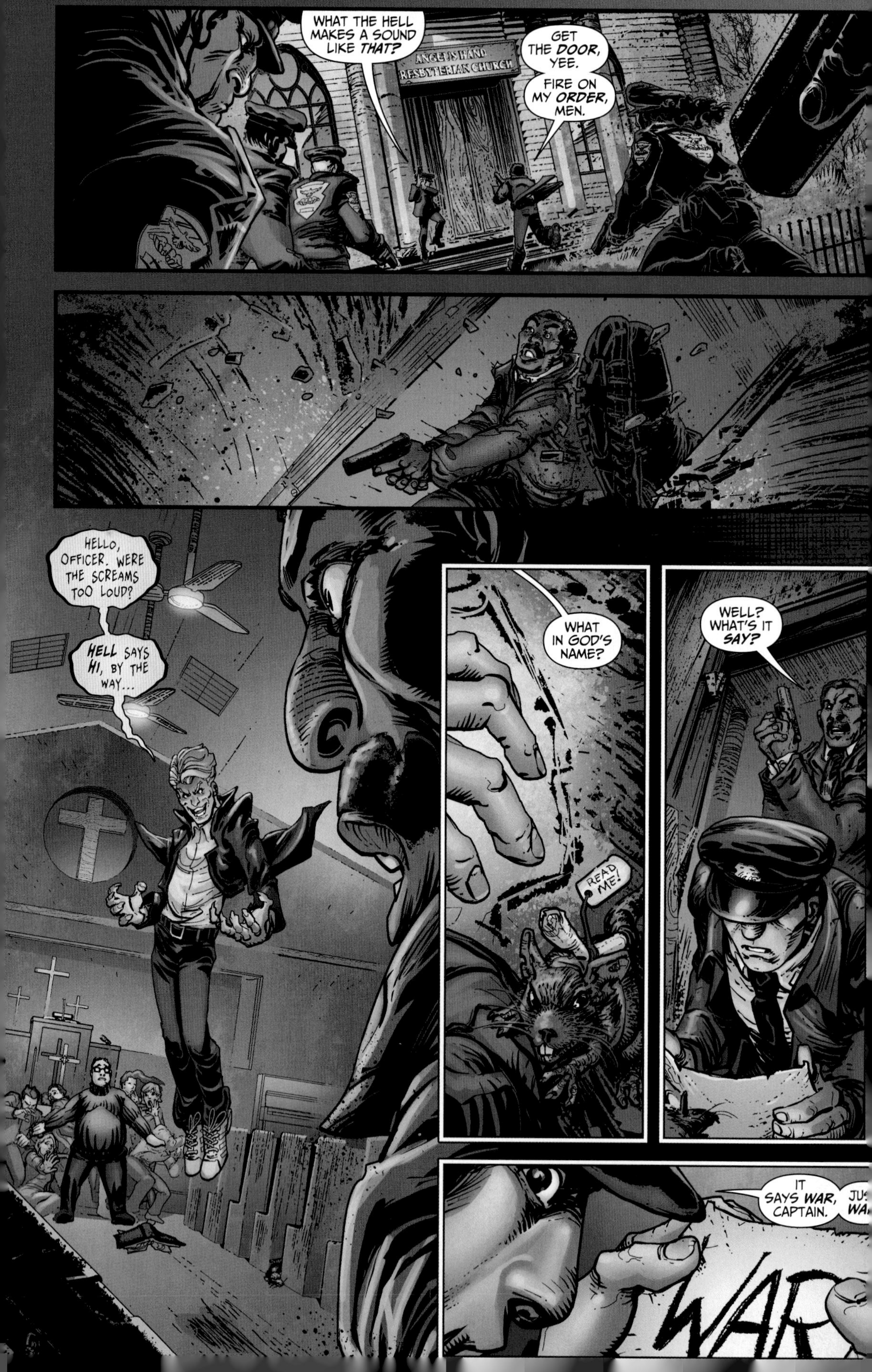
WHAT THE HELL MAKES A SOUND LIKE THAT?
ANGEL'S HAND PRESBYTERIAN CHURCH
GET THE DOOR, YEE.
FIRE ON MY ORDER, MEN.
HELLO, OFFICER. WERE THE SCREAMS TOO LOUD?
HELL SAYS HI, BY THE WAY...
WHAT IN GOD'S NAME?
READ ME!
WELL? WHAT'S IT SAY?
IT SAYS WAR, CAPTAIN.
WAR

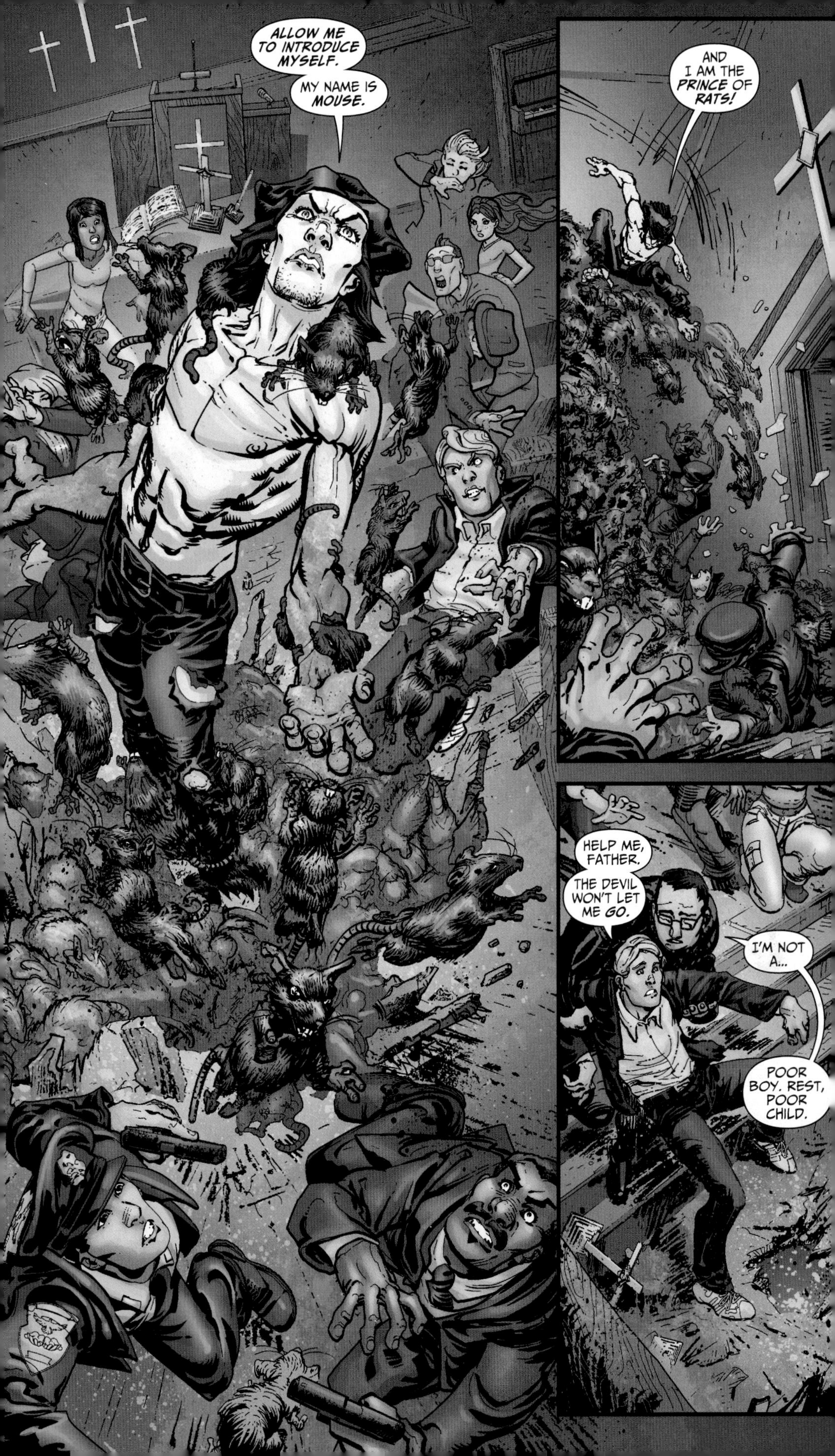
ALLOW ME TO INTRODUCE MYSELF.
MY NAME IS MOUSE.
AND I AM THE PRINCE OF RATS!
HELP ME, FATHER.
THE DEVIL WON'T LET ME GO.
I'M NOT A...
POOR BOY. REST, POOR CHILD.

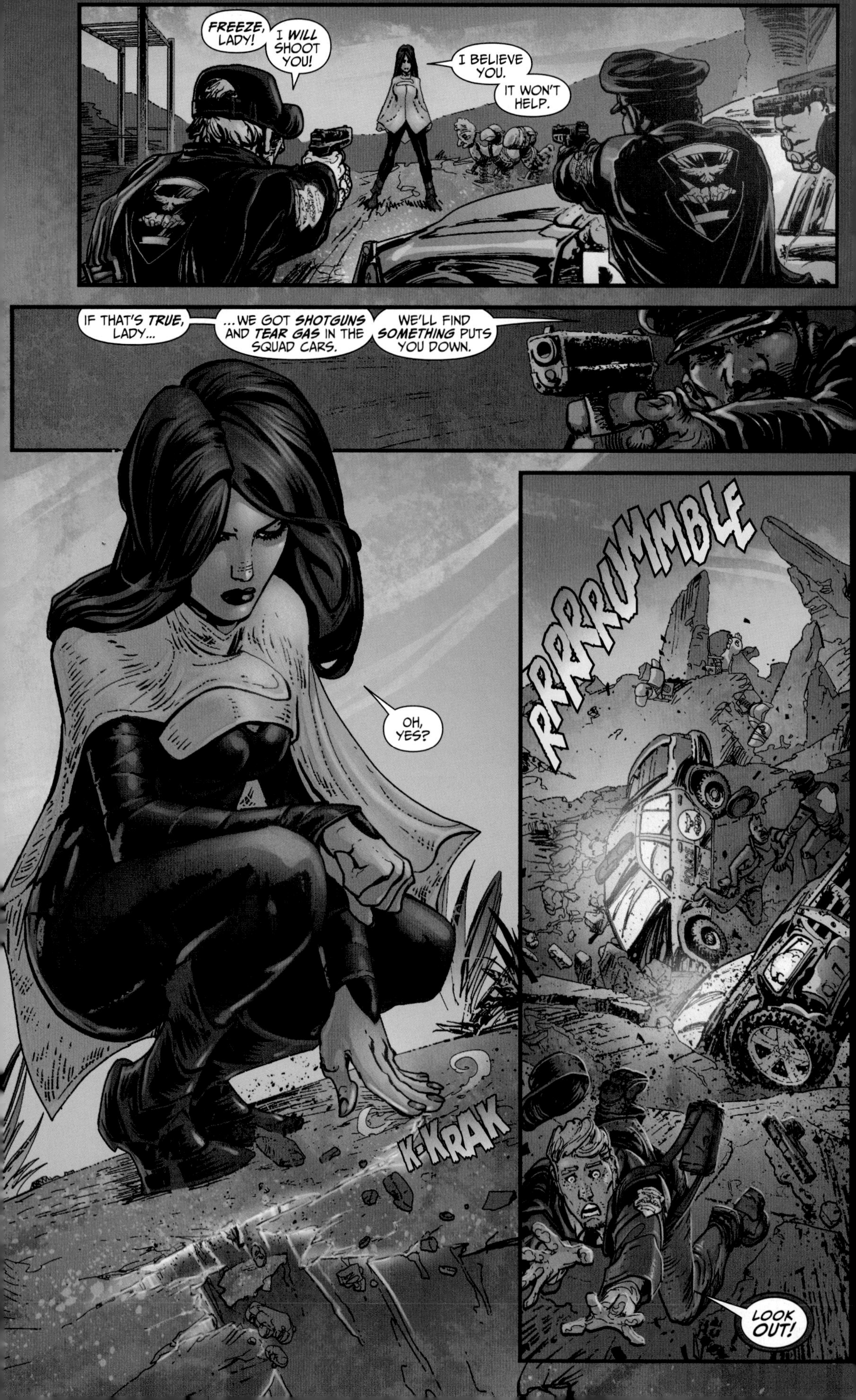
FREEZE, LADY!
I WILL SHOOT YOU!
I BELIEVE YOU.
IT WON'T HELP.
IF THAT'S TRUE, LADY...
...WE GOT SHOTGUNS AND TEAR GAS IN THE SQUAD CARS.
WE'LL FIND SOMETHING PUTS YOU DOWN.
OH, YES?
K-KRAK
RRRRUMMBLE
LOOK OUT!

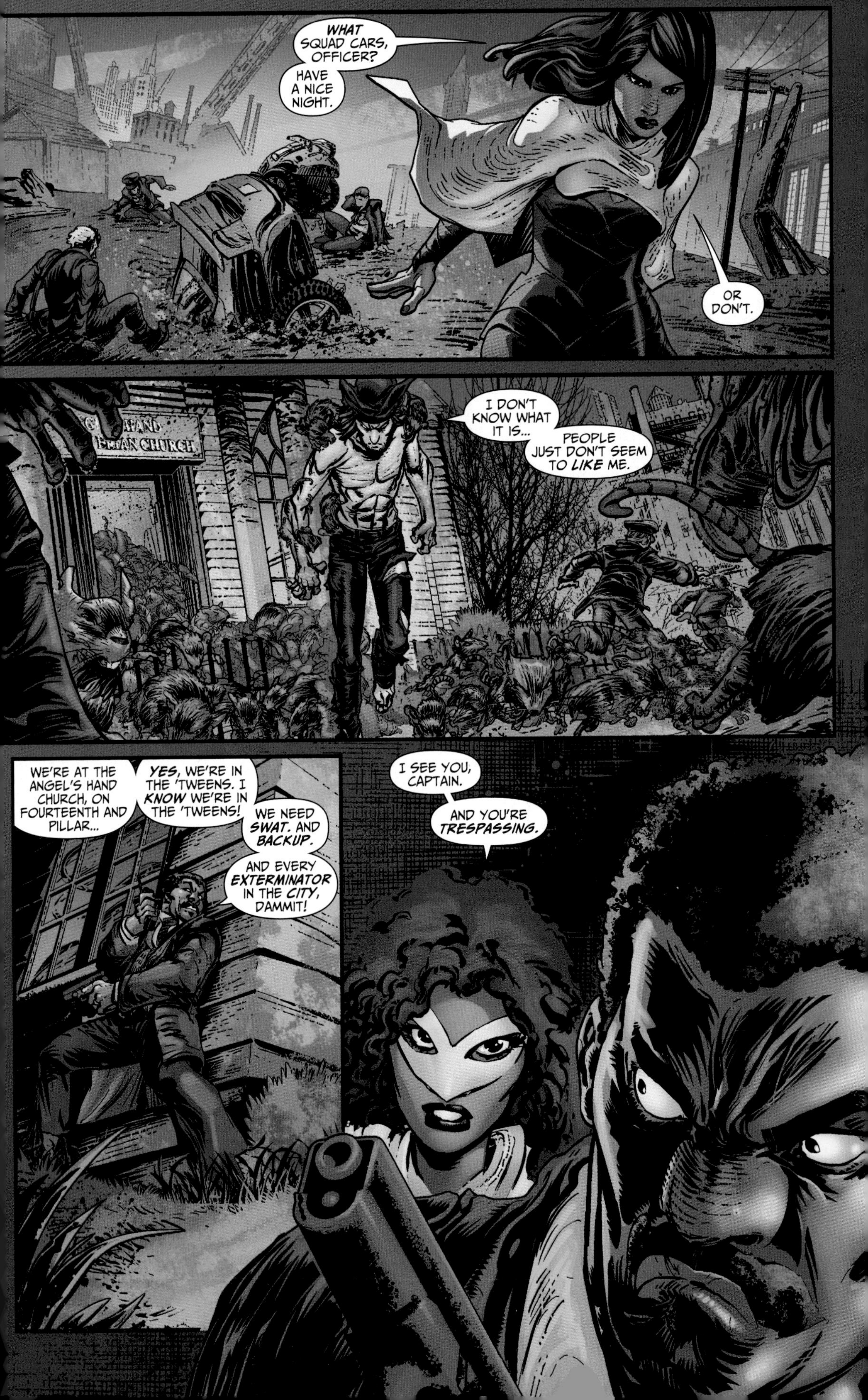
WHAT SQUAD CARS, OFFICER?
HAVE A NICE NIGHT.
OR DON'T.
I DON'T KNOW WHAT IT IS...
PEOPLE JUST DON'T SEEM TO LIKE ME.
WE'RE AT THE ANGEL'S HAND CHURCH, ON FOURTEENTH AND PILLAR...
YES, WE'RE IN THE 'TWEENS. I KNOW WE'RE IN THE 'TWEENS!
WE NEED SWAT. AND BACKUP.
AND EVERY EXTERMINATOR IN THE CITY, DAMMIT!
I SEE YOU, CAPTAIN.
AND YOU'RE TRESPASSING.

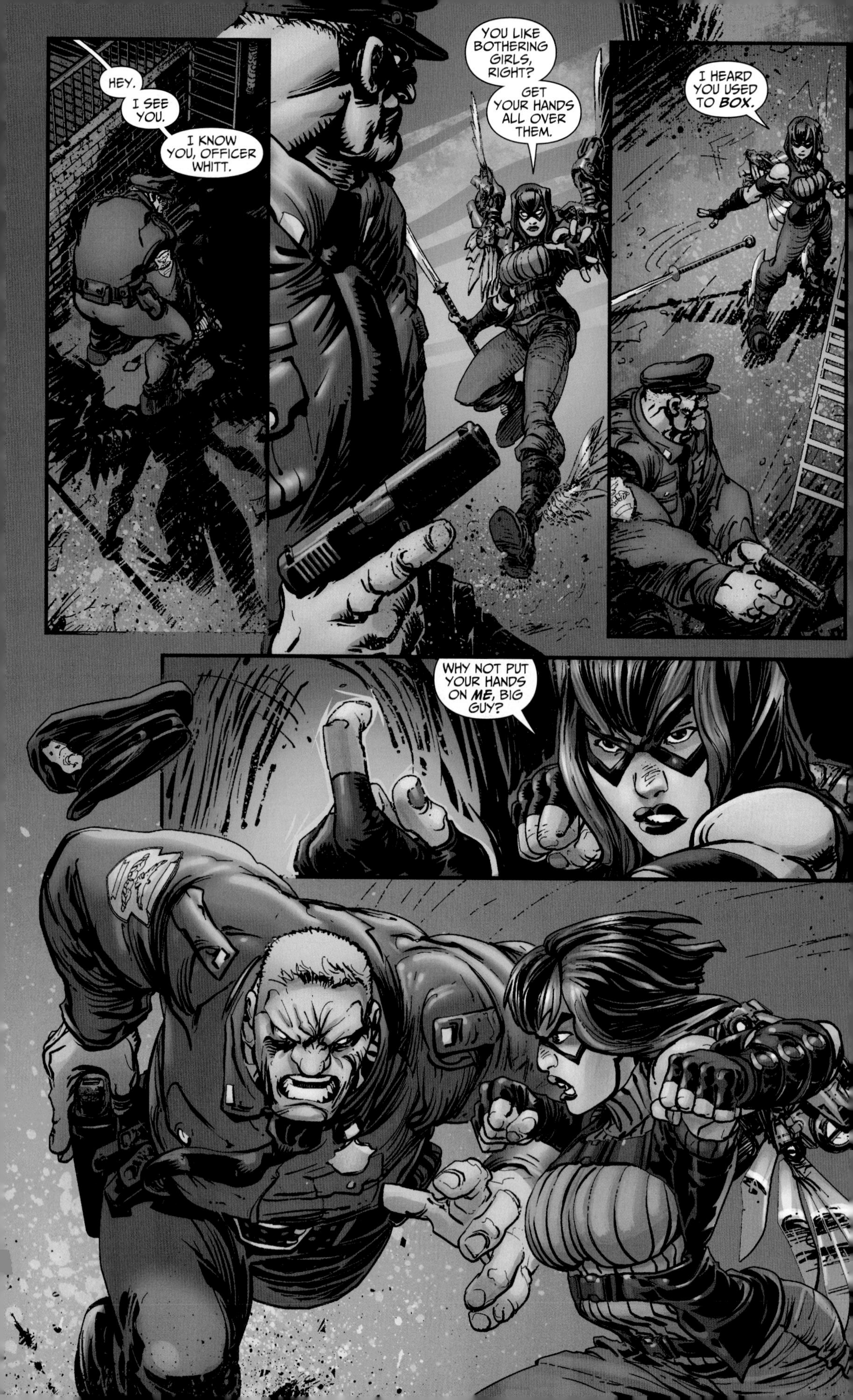
HEY.
I SEE YOU.
I KNOW YOU, OFFICER WHITT.
YOU LIKE BOTHERING GIRLS, RIGHT?
GET YOUR HANDS ALL OVER THEM.
I HEARD YOU USED TO **BOX.**
WHY NOT PUT YOUR HANDS ON **ME**, BIG GUY?

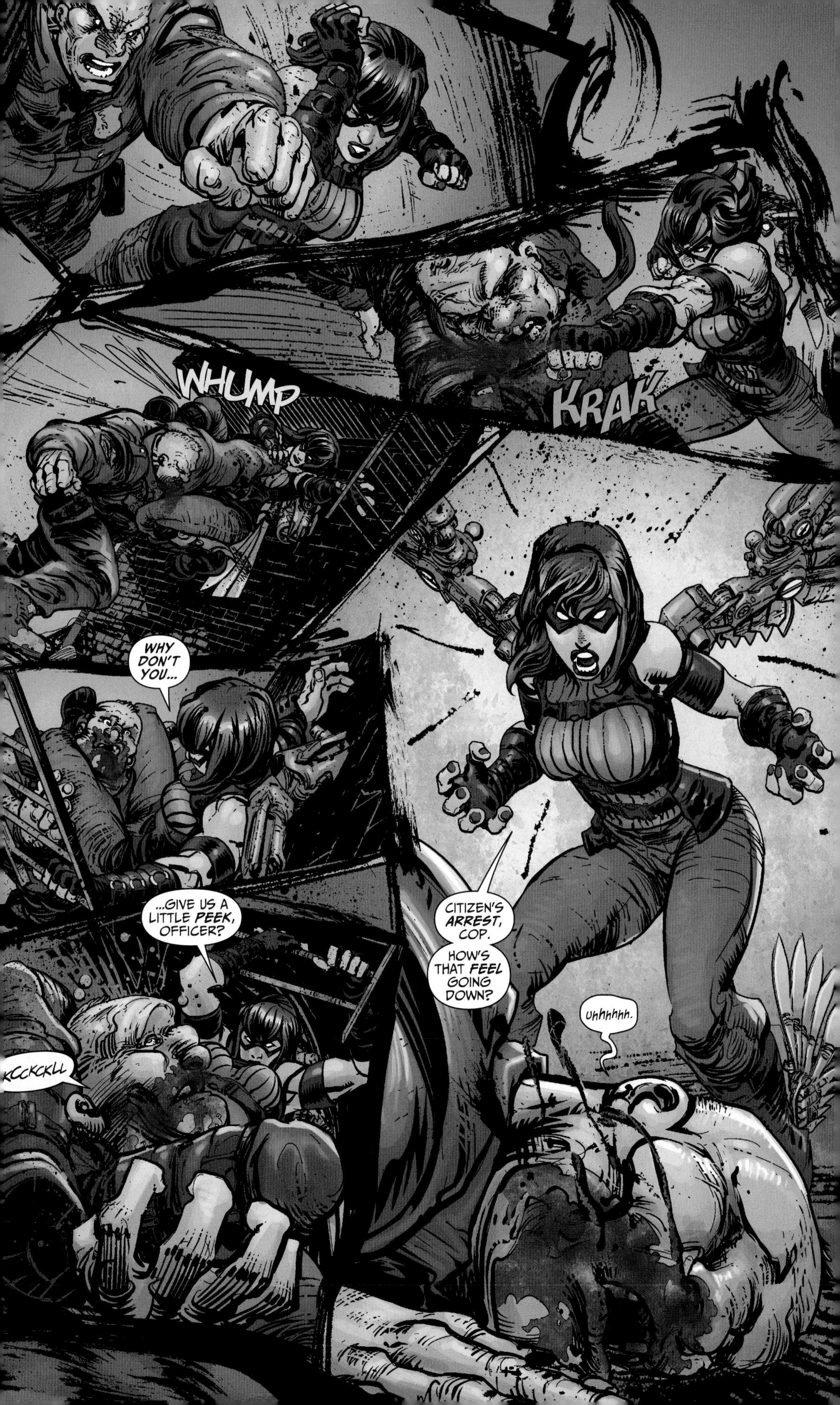
WHUMP
KRAK
WHY DON'T YOU...
...GIVE US A LITTLE PEEK, OFFICER?
KCCKCKLL
CITIZEN'S ARREST, COP.
HOW'S THAT FEEL GOING DOWN?
uhhhhhh.

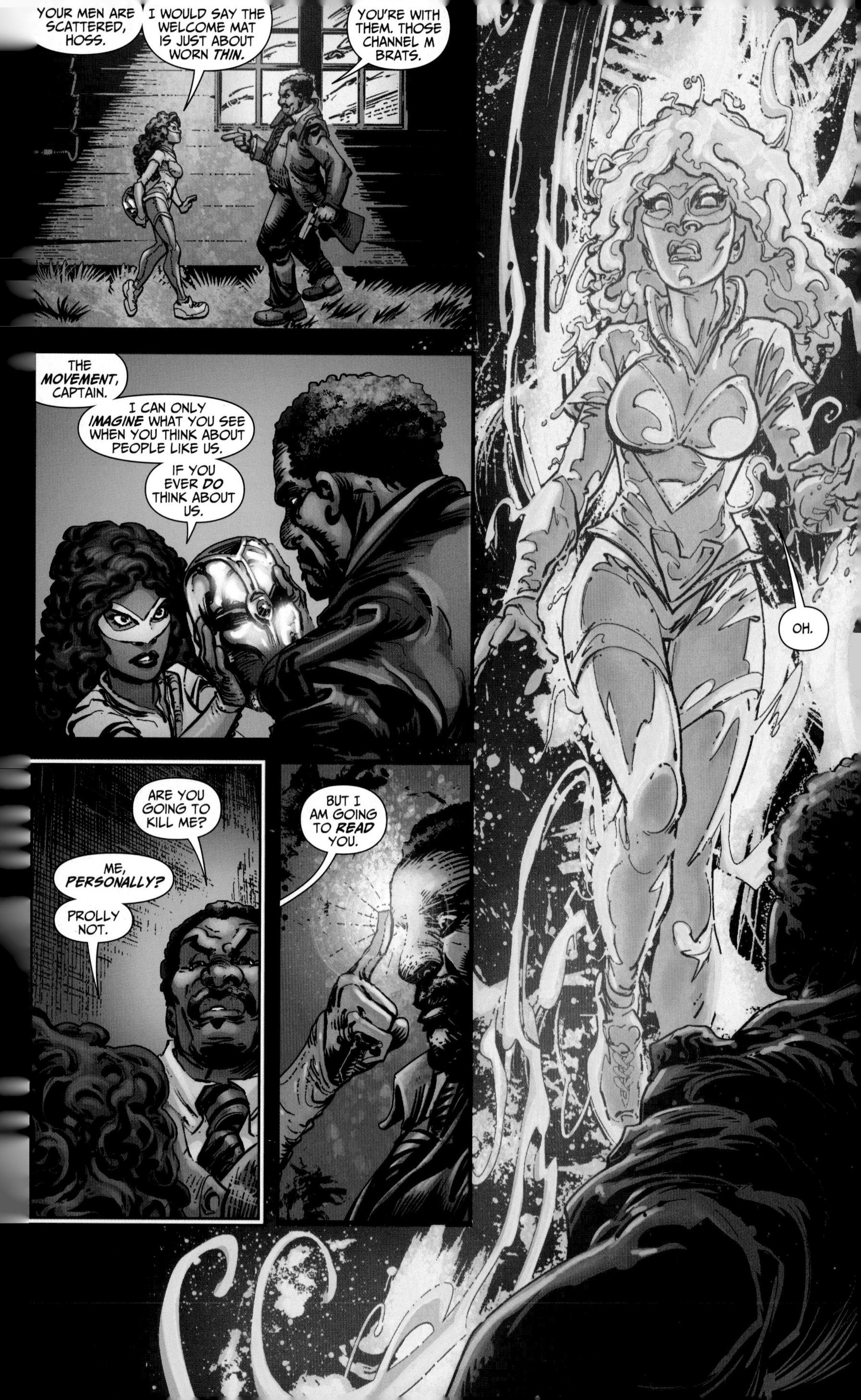
YOUR MEN ARE SCATTERED, HOSS.
I WOULD SAY THE WELCOME MAT IS JUST ABOUT WORN *THIN*.
YOU'RE WITH THEM. THOSE CHANNEL M BRATS.
THE *MOVEMENT*, CAPTAIN.
I CAN ONLY *IMAGINE* WHAT YOU SEE WHEN YOU THINK ABOUT PEOPLE LIKE US.
IF YOU EVER *DO* THINK ABOUT US.
ARE YOU GOING TO KILL ME?
ME, *PERSONALLY?*
PROLLY NOT.
BUT I AM GOING TO *READ* YOU.
OH.

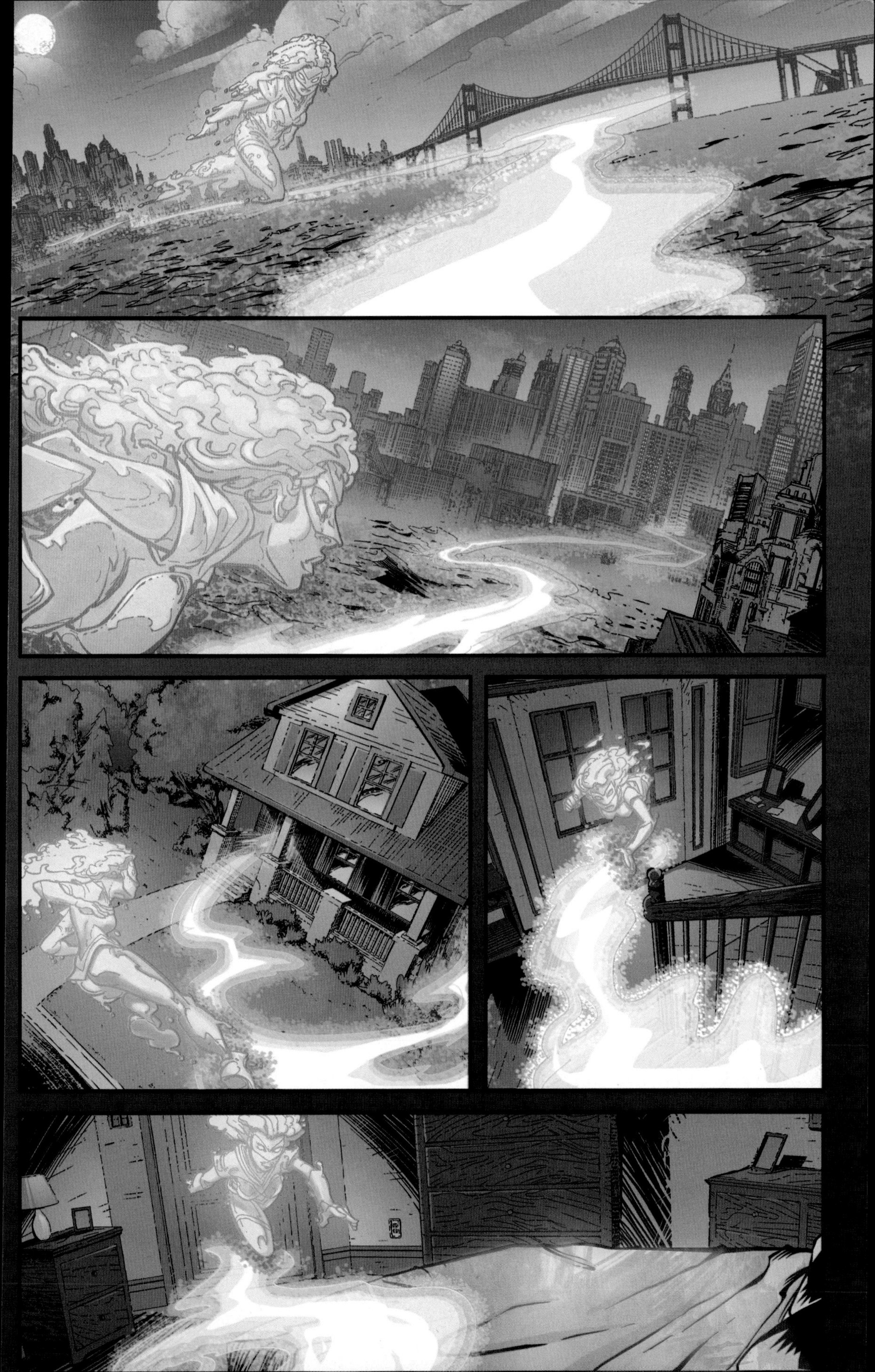

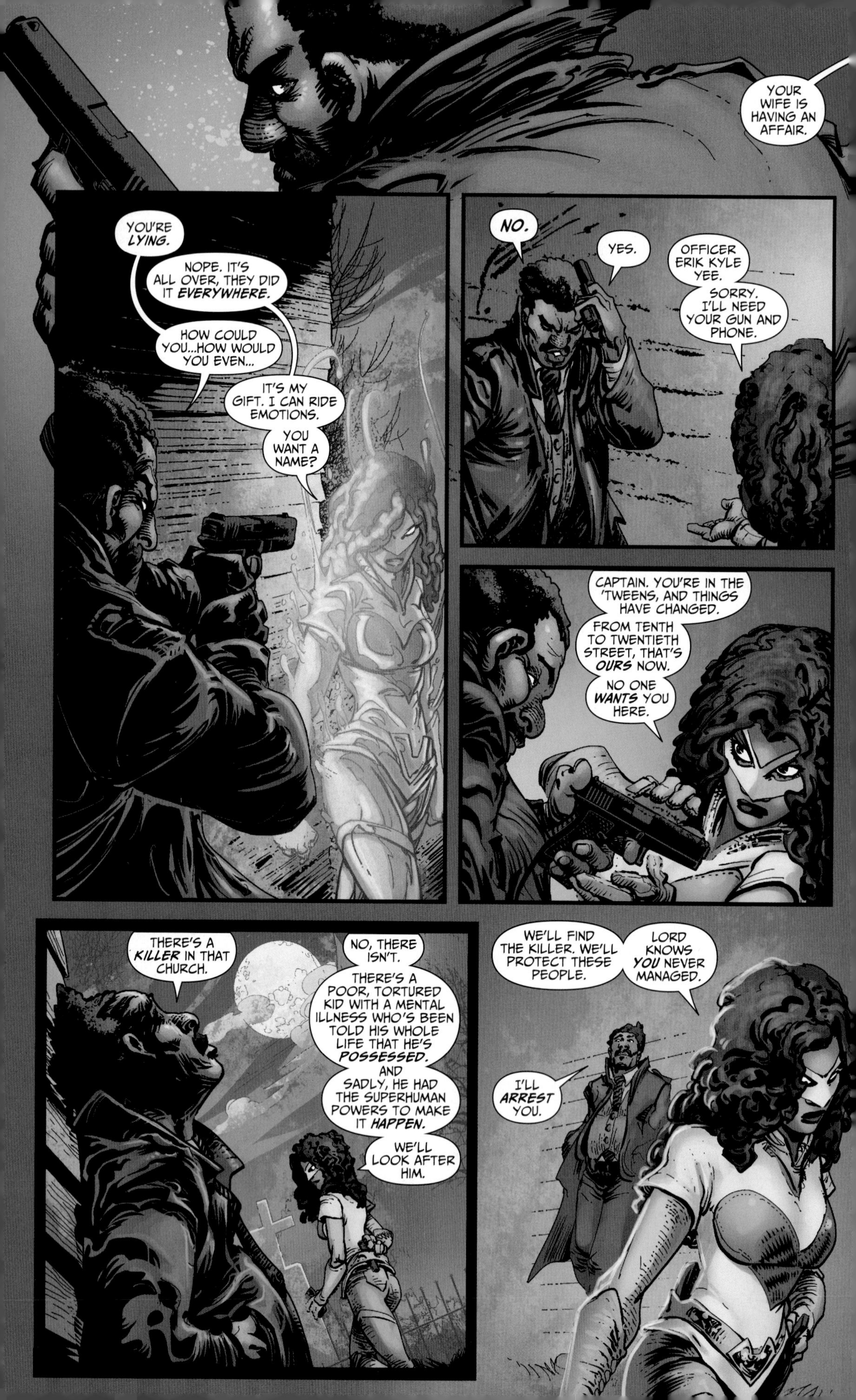
YOUR WIFE IS HAVING AN AFFAIR.
YOU'RE LYING.
NOPE. IT'S ALL OVER, THEY DID IT EVERYWHERE.
HOW COULD YOU...HOW WOULD YOU EVEN...
IT'S MY GIFT. I CAN RIDE EMOTIONS.
YOU WANT A NAME?
NO.
YES.
OFFICER ERIK KYLE YEE.
SORRY. I'LL NEED YOUR GUN AND PHONE.
CAPTAIN. YOU'RE IN THE 'TWEENS, AND THINGS HAVE CHANGED.
FROM TENTH TO TWENTIETH STREET, THAT'S OURS NOW.
NO ONE WANTS YOU HERE.
THERE'S A KILLER IN THAT CHURCH.
NO, THERE ISN'T.
THERE'S A POOR, TORTURED KID WITH A MENTAL ILLNESS WHO'S BEEN TOLD HIS WHOLE LIFE THAT HE'S POSSESSED.
AND SADLY, HE HAD THE SUPERHUMAN POWERS TO MAKE IT HAPPEN.
WE'LL LOOK AFTER HIM.
WE'LL FIND THE KILLER. WE'LL PROTECT THESE PEOPLE.
LORD KNOWS YOU NEVER MANAGED.
I'LL ARREST YOU.

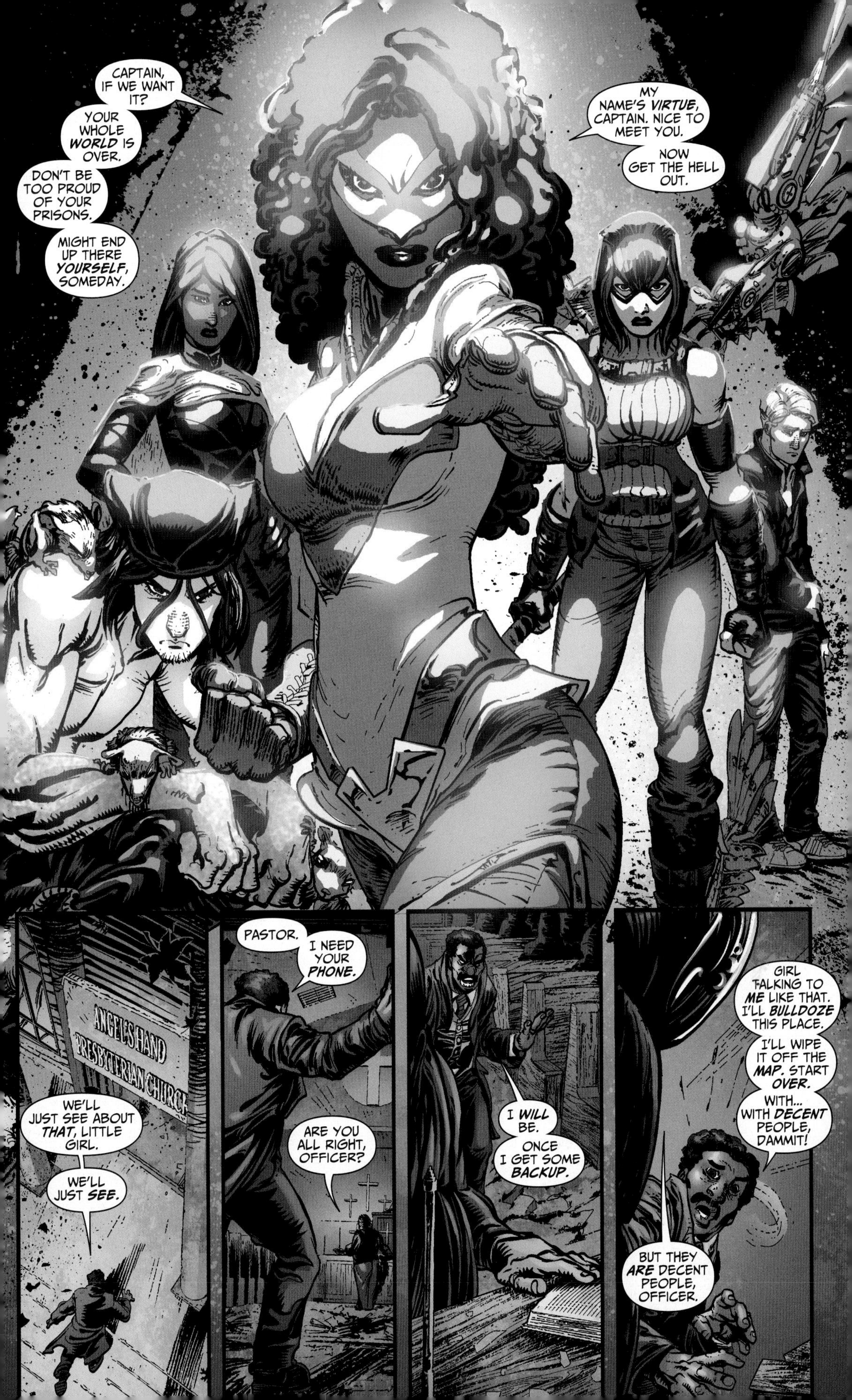
CAPTAIN, IF WE WANT IT?
YOUR WHOLE WORLD IS OVER.
DON'T BE TOO PROUD OF YOUR PRISONS.
MIGHT END UP THERE YOURSELF, SOMEDAY.
MY NAME'S VIRTUE, CAPTAIN. NICE TO MEET YOU.
NOW GET THE HELL OUT.
ANGELS HAND PRESBYTERIAN CHURCH
WE'LL JUST SEE ABOUT THAT, LITTLE GIRL.
WE'LL JUST SEE.
PASTOR.
I NEED YOUR PHONE.
ARE YOU ALL RIGHT, OFFICER?
I WILL BE.
ONCE I GET SOME BACKUP.
GIRL TALKING TO ME LIKE THAT. I'LL BULLDOZE THIS PLACE.
I'LL WIPE IT OFF THE MAP. START OVER.
WITH... WITH DECENT PEOPLE, DAMMIT!
BUT THEY ARE DECENT PEOPLE, OFFICER.

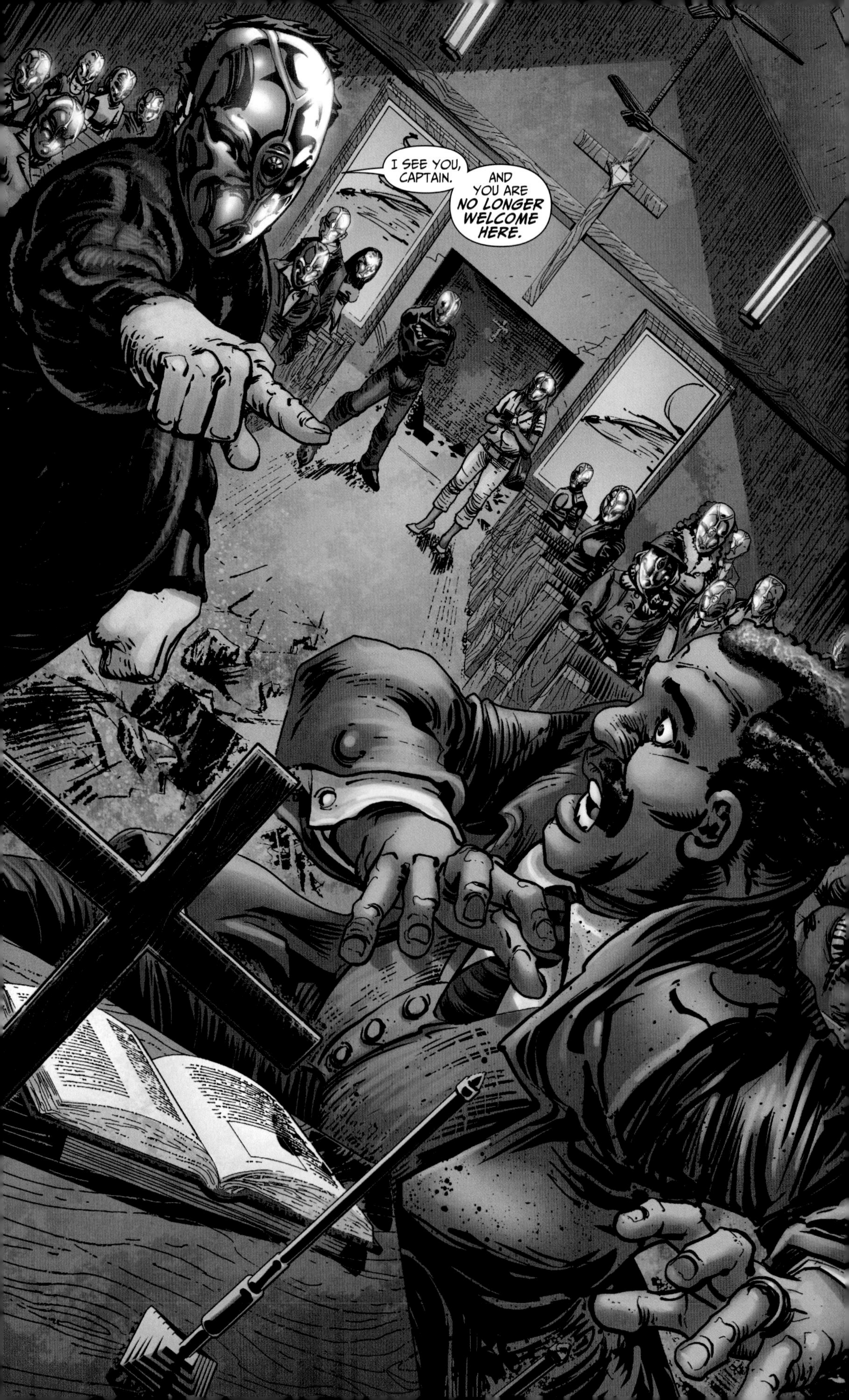
I SEE YOU, CAPTAIN.
AND YOU ARE NO LONGER WELCOME HERE.

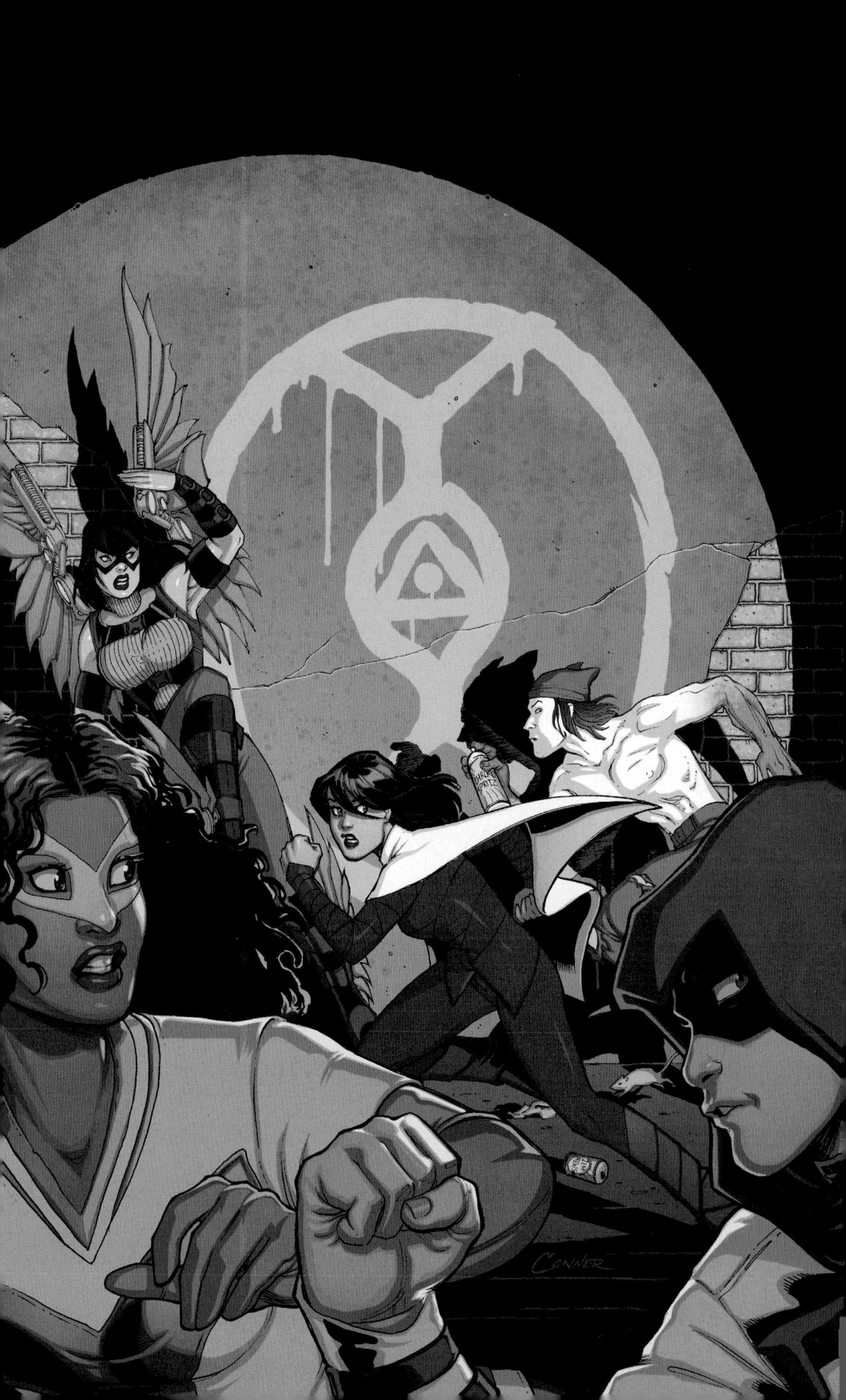
CONNER

The Movement #2 cover by Amanda Conner & Dave McCaig

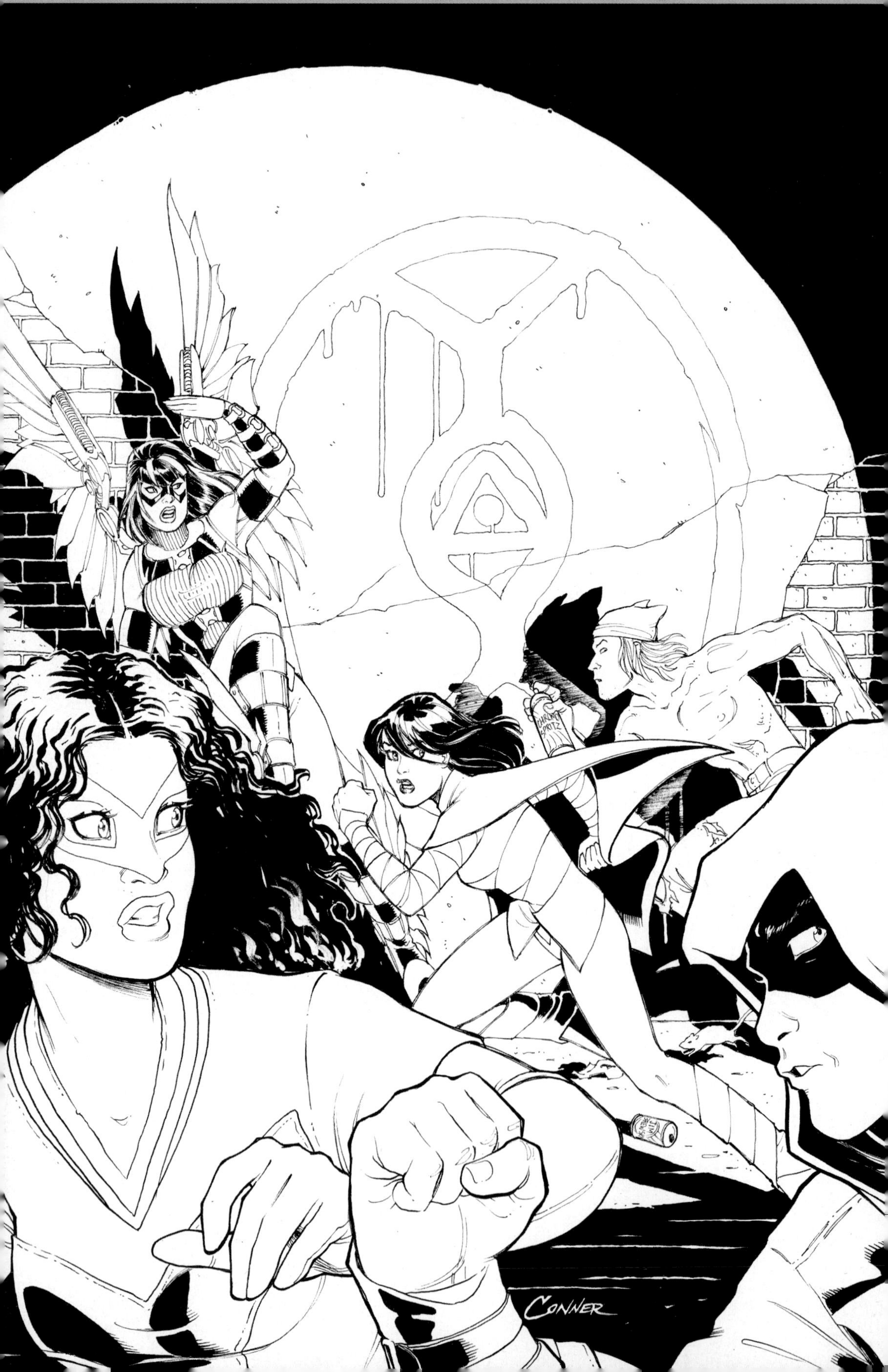
CONNER

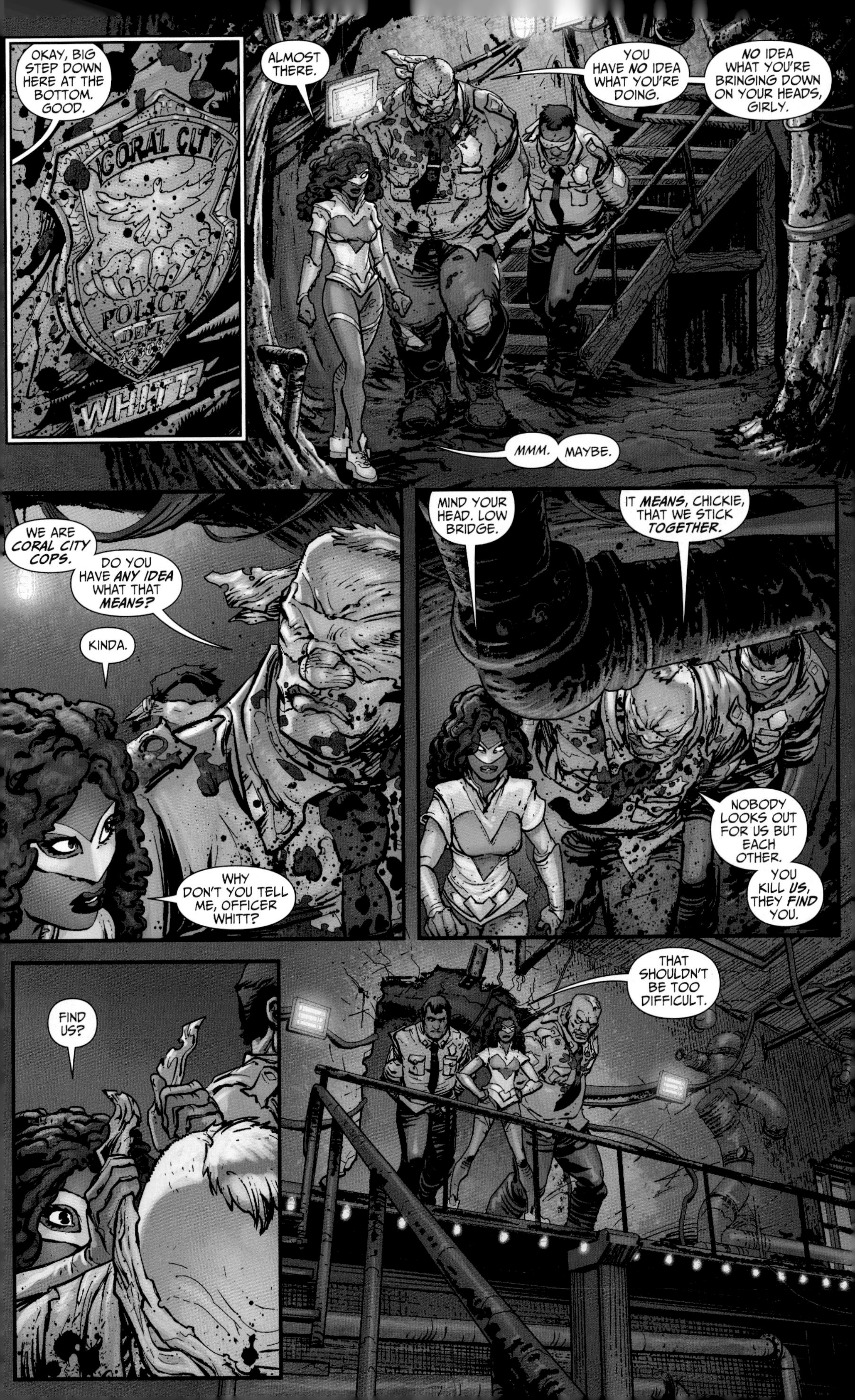
CORAL CITY
POLICE
DEPT.
42303
WHITT
OKAY, BIG STEP DOWN HERE AT THE BOTTOM. GOOD.
ALMOST THERE.
YOU HAVE *NO* IDEA WHAT YOU'RE DOING.
NO IDEA WHAT YOU'RE BRINGING DOWN ON YOUR HEADS, GIRLY.
MMM.
MAYBE.
WE ARE *CORAL CITY COPS*.
DO YOU HAVE *ANY IDEA* WHAT THAT *MEANS?*
KINDA.
WHY DON'T YOU TELL ME, OFFICER WHITT?
MIND YOUR HEAD. LOW BRIDGE.
IT *MEANS*, CHICKIE, THAT WE STICK *TOGETHER*.
NOBODY LOOKS OUT FOR US BUT EACH OTHER.
YOU KILL *US*, THEY *FIND* YOU.
FIND US?
THAT SHOULDN'T BE TOO DIFFICULT.

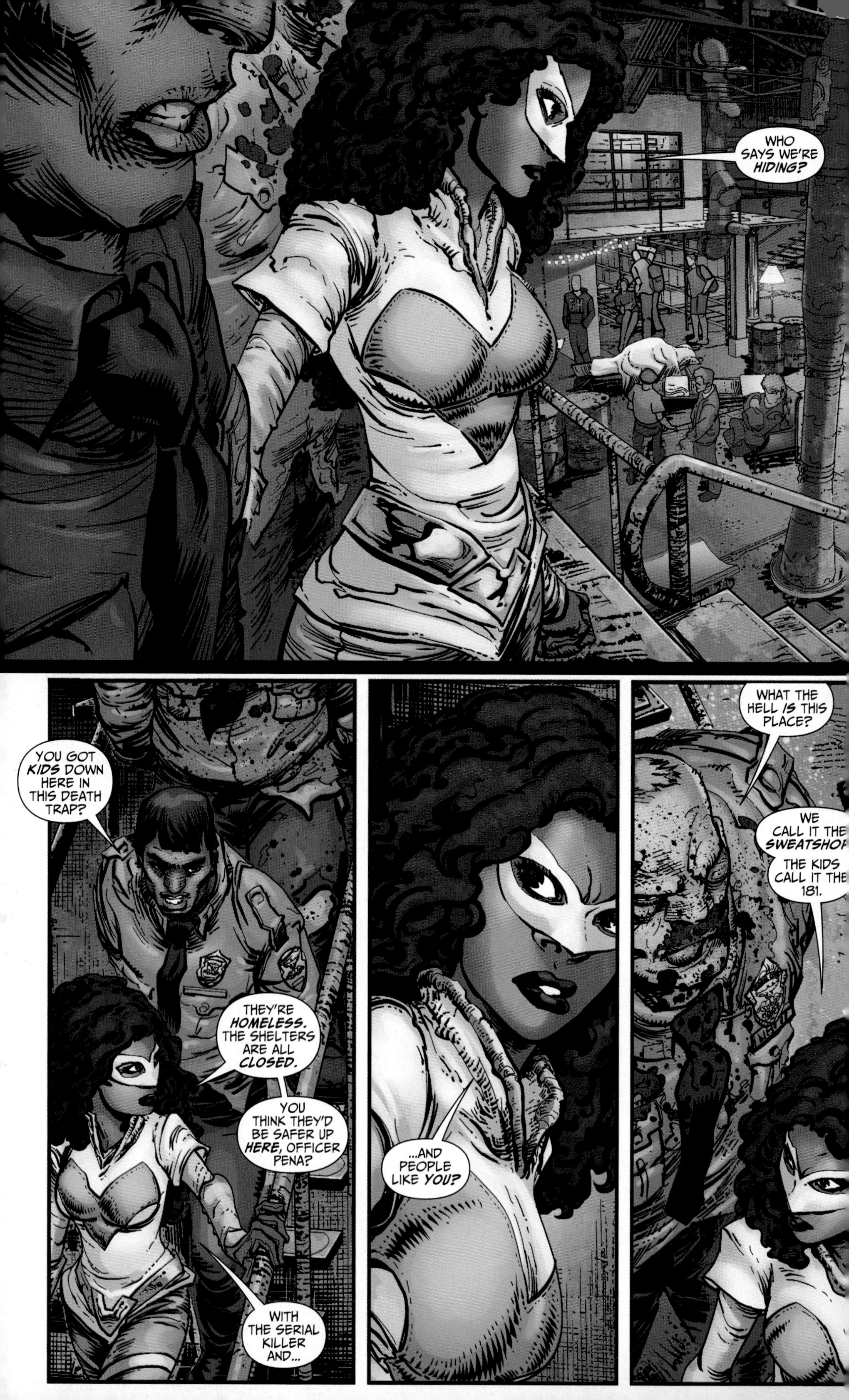
WHO SAYS WE'RE *HIDING?*
YOU GOT *KIDS* DOWN HERE IN THIS DEATH TRAP?
THEY'RE *HOMELESS.* THE SHELTERS ARE ALL *CLOSED.*
YOU THINK THEY'D BE SAFER UP *HERE,* OFFICER PENA?
WITH THE SERIAL KILLER AND...
...AND PEOPLE LIKE *YOU?*
WHAT THE HELL *IS* THIS PLACE?
WE CALL IT THE *SWEATSHOP*
THE KIDS CALL IT THE 181.

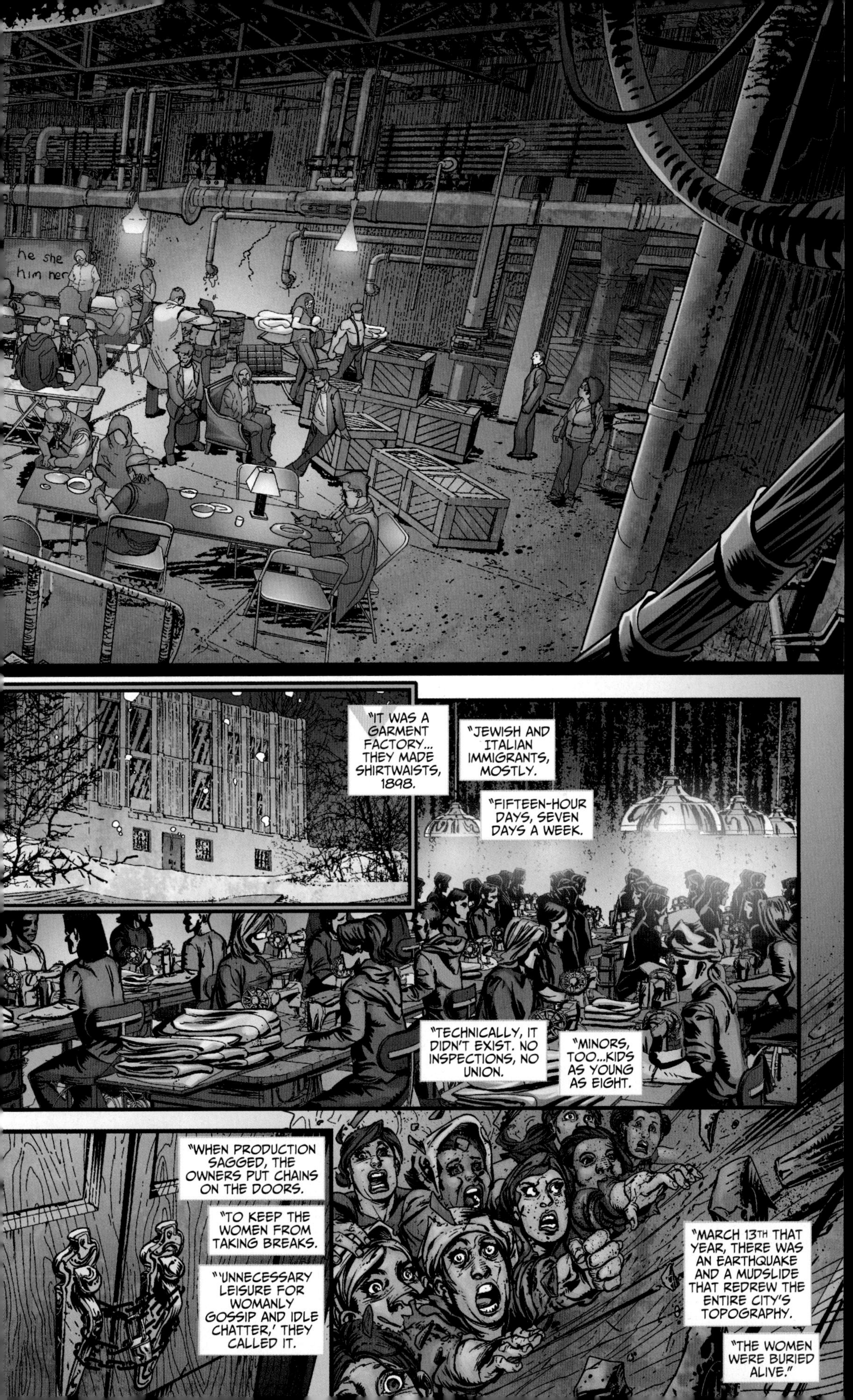
he she
him her
"IT WAS A GARMENT FACTORY... THEY MADE SHIRTWAISTS, 1898.
"JEWISH AND ITALIAN IMMIGRANTS, MOSTLY.
"FIFTEEN-HOUR DAYS, SEVEN DAYS A WEEK.
"TECHNICALLY, IT DIDN'T EXIST. NO INSPECTIONS, NO UNION.
"MINORS, TOO...KIDS AS YOUNG AS EIGHT.
"WHEN PRODUCTION SAGGED, THE OWNERS PUT CHAINS ON THE DOORS.
"TO KEEP THE WOMEN FROM TAKING BREAKS.
"'UNNECESSARY LEISURE FOR WOMANLY GOSSIP AND IDLE CHATTER,' THEY CALLED IT.
"MARCH 13TH THAT YEAR, THERE WAS AN EARTHQUAKE AND A MUDSLIDE THAT REDREW THE ENTIRE CITY'S TOPOGRAPHY.
"THE WOMEN WERE BURIED ALIVE."

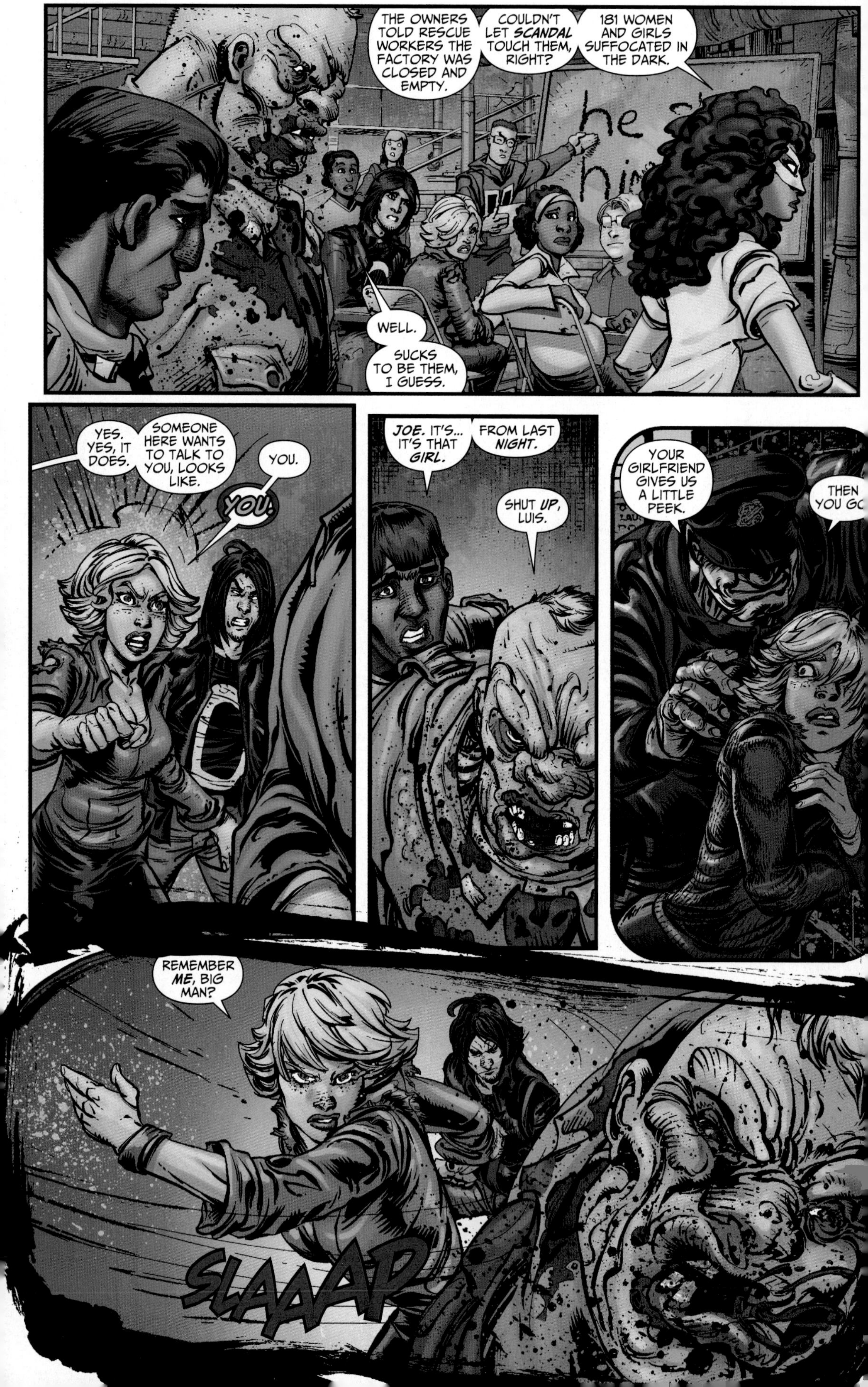
THE OWNERS TOLD RESCUE WORKERS THE FACTORY WAS CLOSED AND EMPTY.
COULDN'T LET *SCANDAL* TOUCH THEM, RIGHT?
181 WOMEN AND GIRLS SUFFOCATED IN THE DARK.
WELL.
SUCKS TO BE THEM, I GUESS.
YES. YES, IT DOES.
SOMEONE HERE WANTS TO TALK TO YOU, LOOKS LIKE.
YOU.
YOU!
JOE. IT'S... IT'S THAT *GIRL.*
FROM LAST *NIGHT.*
SHUT *UP,* LUIS.
YOUR GIRLFRIEND GIVES US A LITTLE PEEK.
THEN YOU GO
REMEMBER *ME,* BIG MAN?
SLAAAP

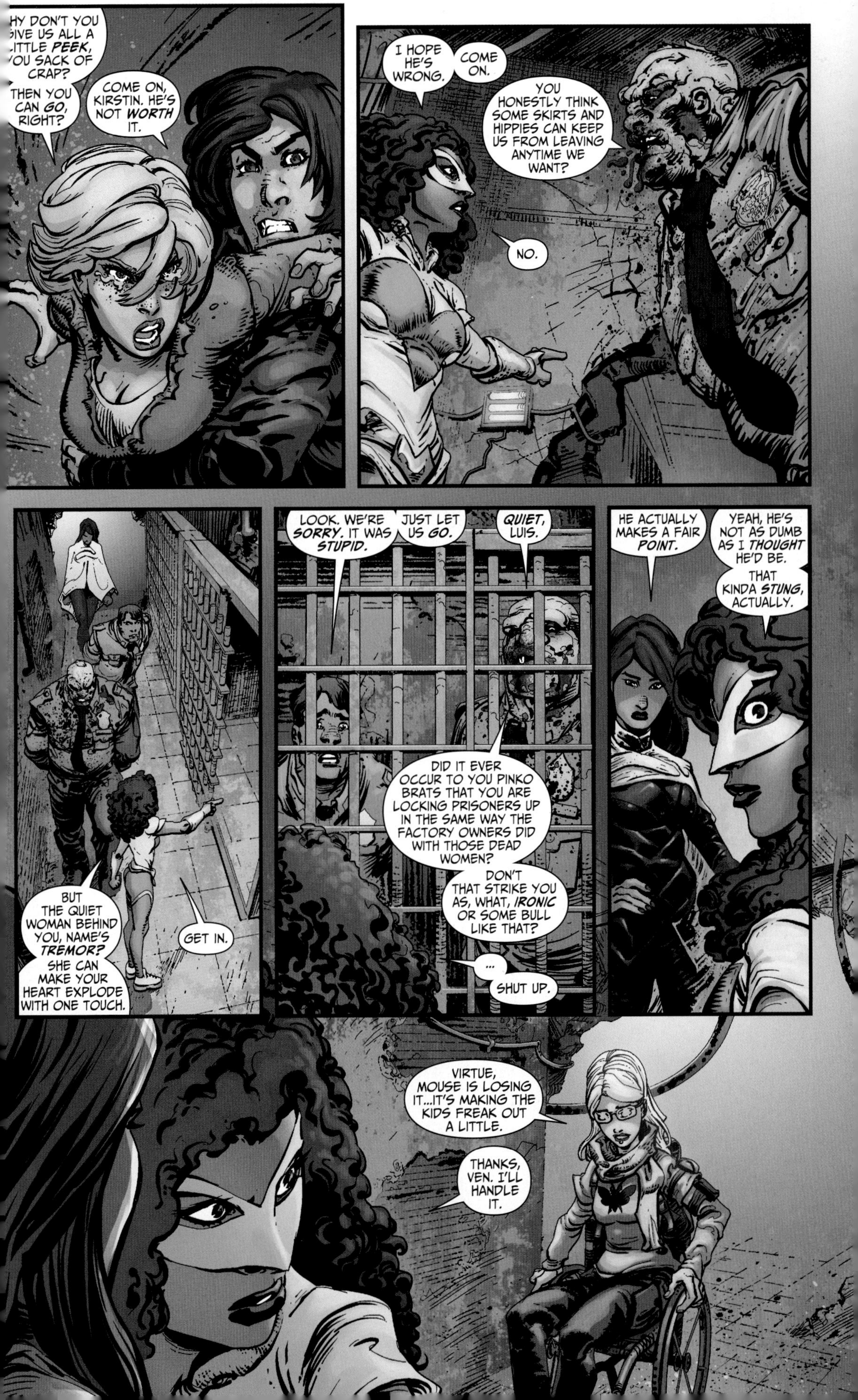
HY DON'T YOU GIVE US ALL A LITTLE PEEK, YOU SACK OF CRAP?
THEN YOU CAN GO, RIGHT?
COME ON, KIRSTIN. HE'S NOT WORTH IT.
I HOPE HE'S WRONG.
COME ON.
YOU HONESTLY THINK SOME SKIRTS AND HIPPIES CAN KEEP US FROM LEAVING ANYTIME WE WANT?
NO.
BUT THE QUIET WOMAN BEHIND YOU, NAME'S TREMOR? SHE CAN MAKE YOUR HEART EXPLODE WITH ONE TOUCH.
GET IN.
LOOK. WE'RE SORRY. IT WAS STUPID.
JUST LET US GO.
QUIET, LUIS.
DID IT EVER OCCUR TO YOU PINKO BRATS THAT YOU ARE LOCKING PRISONERS UP IN THE SAME WAY THE FACTORY OWNERS DID WITH THOSE DEAD WOMEN?
DON'T THAT STRIKE YOU AS, WHAT, IRONIC OR SOME BULL LIKE THAT?
...
SHUT UP.
HE ACTUALLY MAKES A FAIR POINT.
YEAH, HE'S NOT AS DUMB AS I THOUGHT HE'D BE.
THAT KINDA STUNG, ACTUALLY.
VIRTUE, MOUSE IS LOSING IT...IT'S MAKING THE KIDS FREAK OUT A LITTLE.
THANKS, VEN. I'LL HANDLE IT.

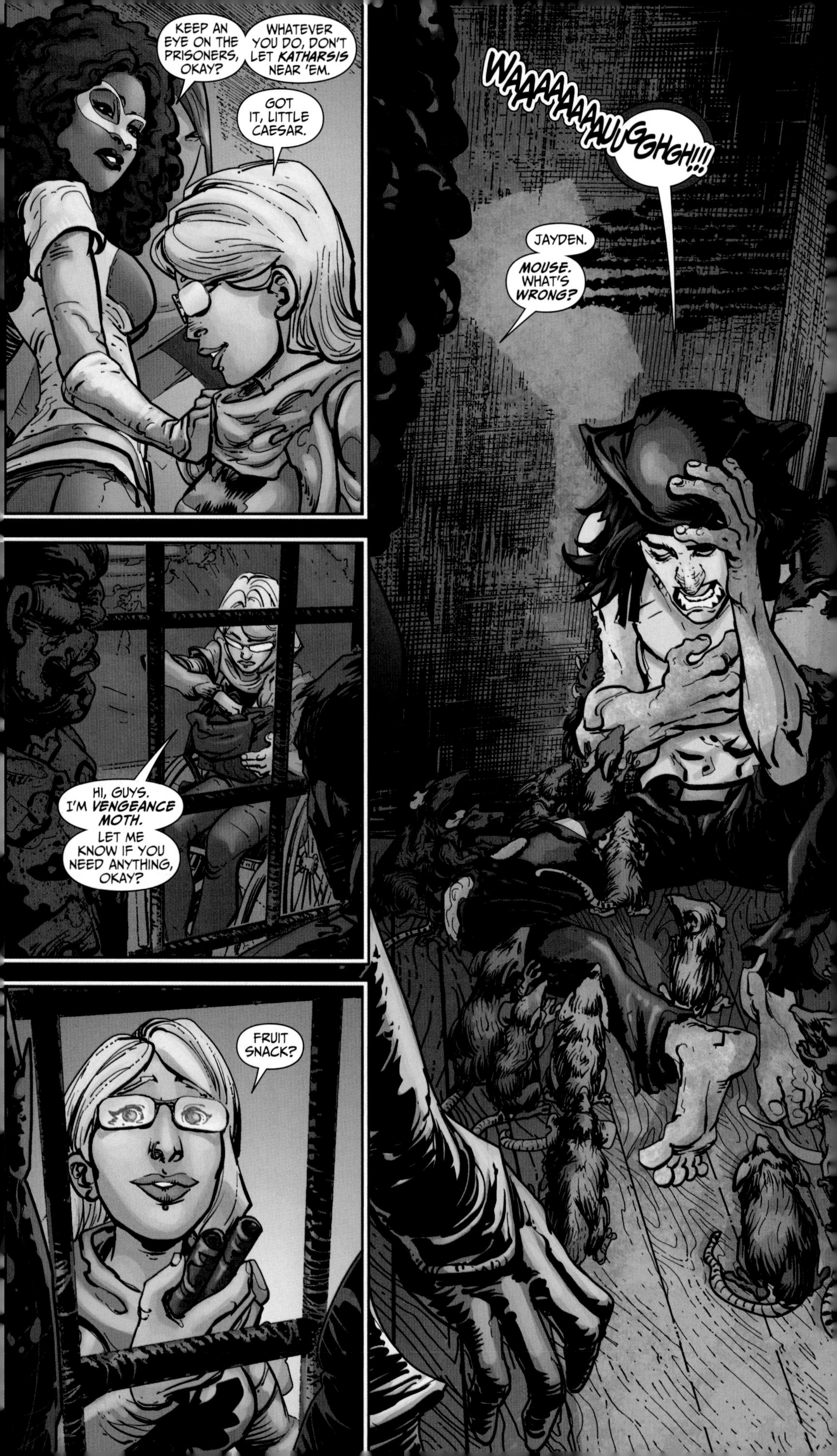
KEEP AN EYE ON THE PRISONERS, OKAY?
WHATEVER YOU DO, DON'T LET KATHARSIS NEAR 'EM.
GOT IT, LITTLE CAESAR.
HI, GUYS. I'M VENGEANCE MOTH. LET ME KNOW IF YOU NEED ANYTHING, OKAY?
FRUIT SNACK?
WAAAAAAAAAUUGGHGH!!!
JAYDEN.
MOUSE. WHAT'S WRONG?

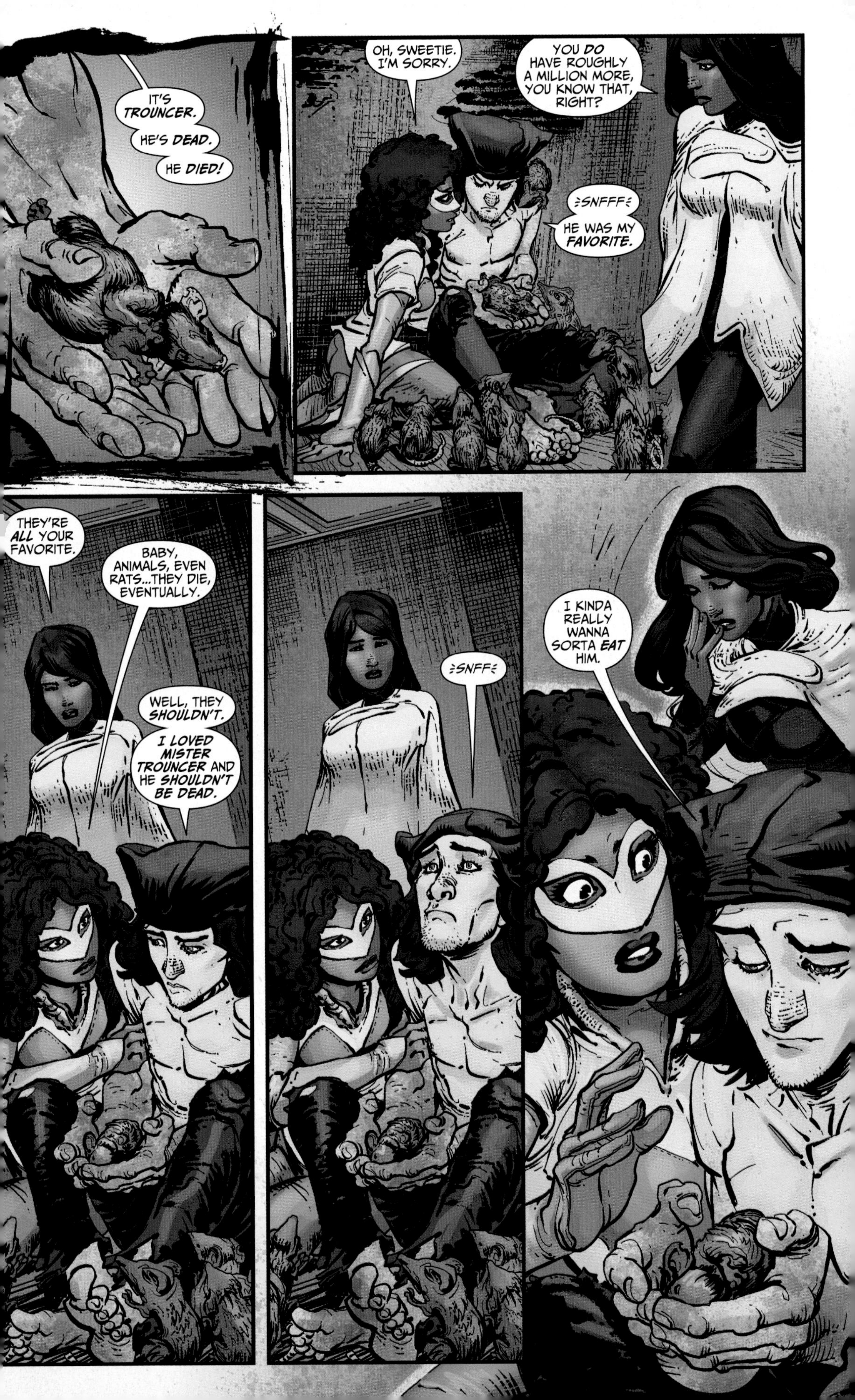

IT'S TROUNCER.
HE'S DEAD.
HE DIED!
OH, SWEETIE. I'M SORRY.
YOU DO HAVE ROUGHLY A MILLION MORE, YOU KNOW THAT, RIGHT?
SNFFF
HE WAS MY FAVORITE.
THEY'RE ALL YOUR FAVORITE.
BABY, ANIMALS, EVEN RATS...THEY DIE, EVENTUALLY.
WELL, THEY SHOULDN'T.
I LOVED MISTER TROUNCER AND HE SHOULDN'T BE DEAD.
SNFF
I KINDA REALLY WANNA SORTA EAT HIM.

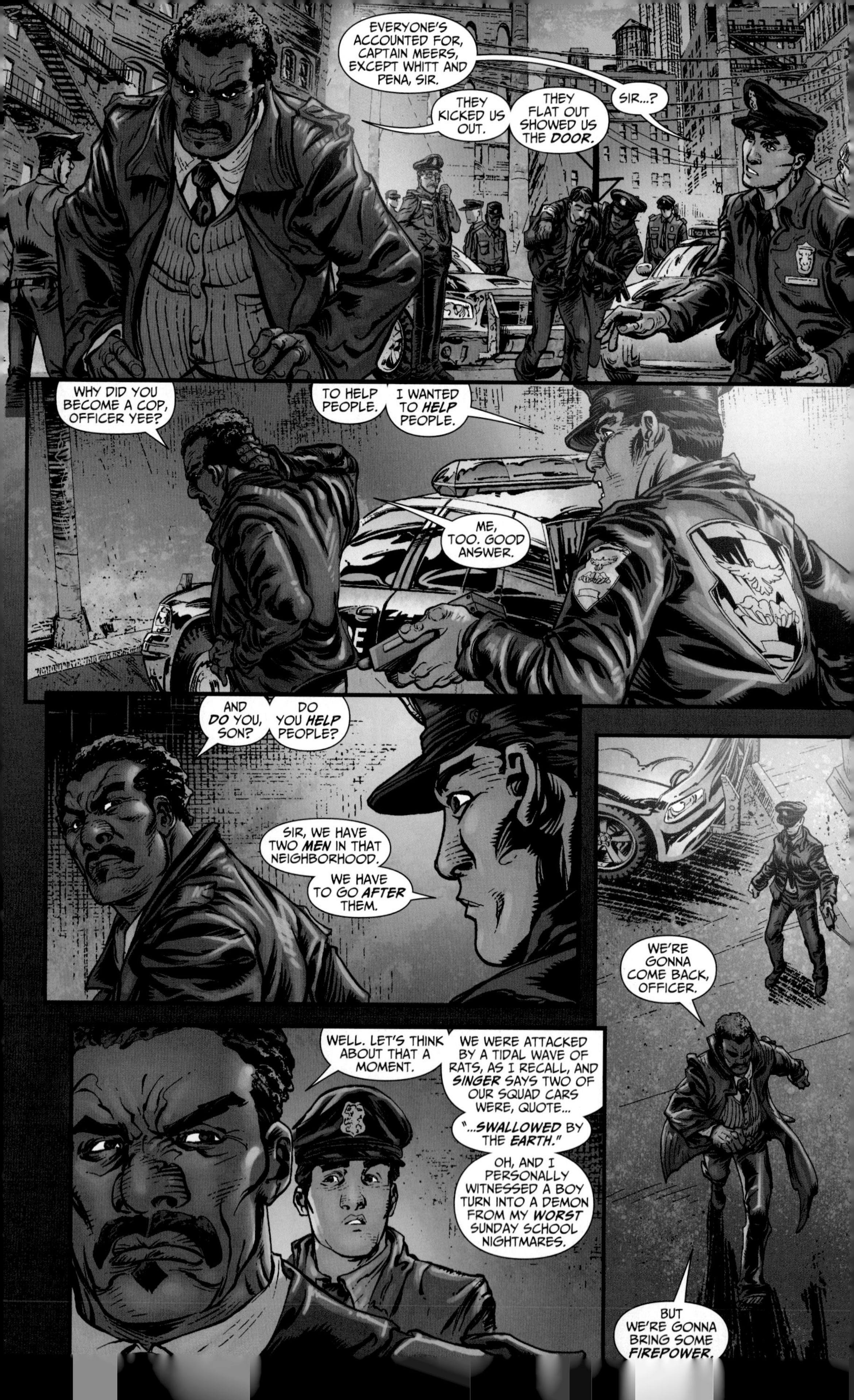
EVERYONE'S ACCOUNTED FOR, CAPTAIN MEERS, EXCEPT WHITT AND PENA, SIR.
SIR...?
THEY KICKED US OUT.
THEY FLAT OUT SHOWED US THE DOOR.
WHY DID YOU BECOME A COP, OFFICER YEE?
TO HELP PEOPLE.
I WANTED TO HELP PEOPLE.
ME, TOO. GOOD ANSWER.
AND DO YOU, SON?
DO YOU HELP PEOPLE?
SIR, WE HAVE TWO MEN IN THAT NEIGHBORHOOD.
WE HAVE TO GO AFTER THEM.
WELL. LET'S THINK ABOUT THAT A MOMENT.
WE WERE ATTACKED BY A TIDAL WAVE OF RATS, AS I RECALL, AND SINGER SAYS TWO OF OUR SQUAD CARS WERE, QUOTE...
"...SWALLOWED BY THE EARTH."
OH, AND I PERSONALLY WITNESSED A BOY TURN INTO A DEMON FROM MY WORST SUNDAY SCHOOL NIGHTMARES.
WE'RE GONNA COME BACK, OFFICER.
BUT WE'RE GONNA BRING SOME FIREPOWER.

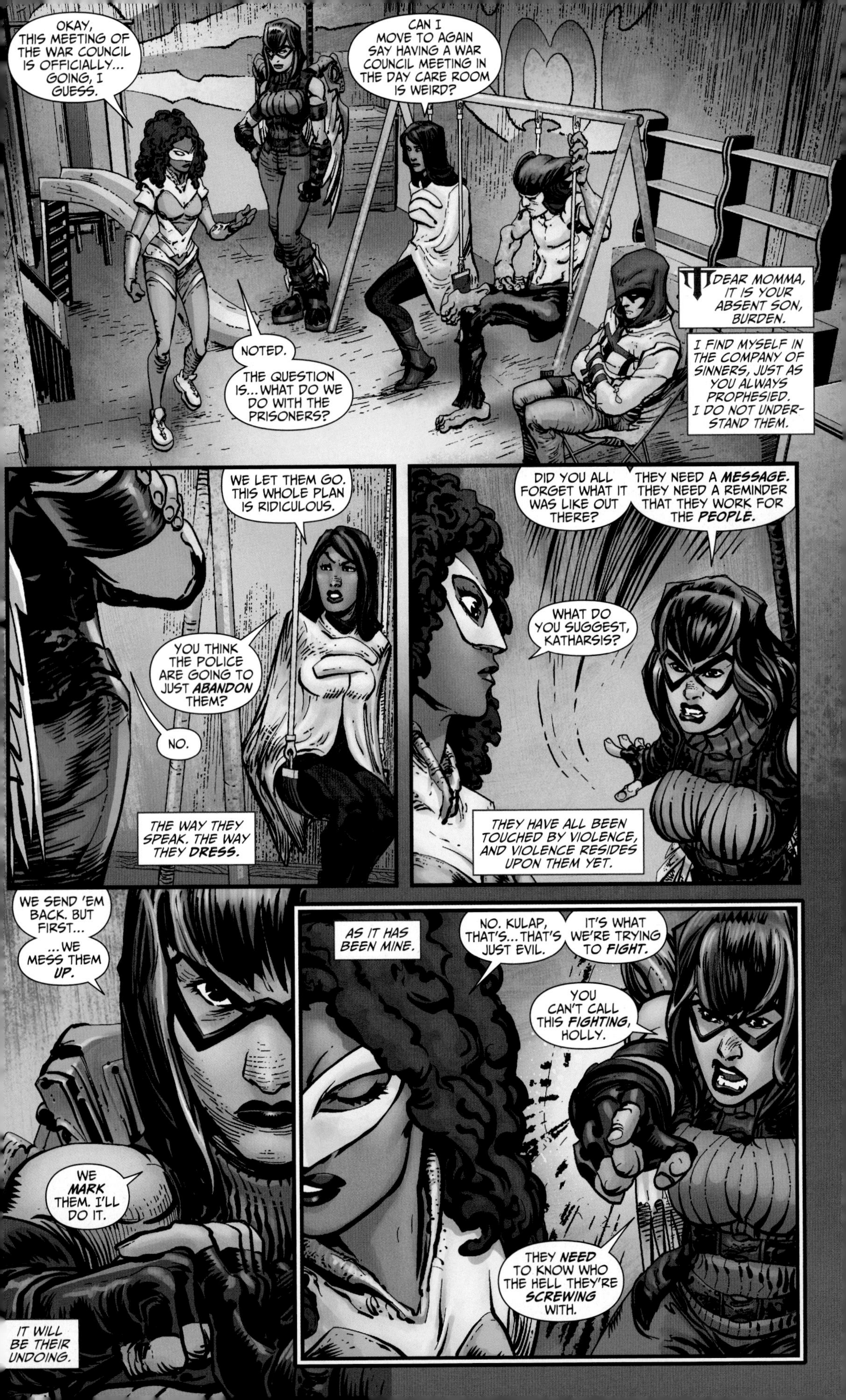
OKAY, THIS MEETING OF THE WAR COUNCIL IS OFFICIALLY... GOING, I GUESS.
CAN I MOVE TO AGAIN SAY HAVING A WAR COUNCIL MEETING IN THE DAY CARE ROOM IS WEIRD?
NOTED.
THE QUESTION IS...WHAT DO WE DO WITH THE PRISONERS?
DEAR MOMMA, IT IS YOUR ABSENT SON, BURDEN.
I FIND MYSELF IN THE COMPANY OF SINNERS, JUST AS YOU ALWAYS PROPHESIED. I DO NOT UNDERSTAND THEM.
WE LET THEM GO. THIS WHOLE PLAN IS RIDICULOUS.
YOU THINK THE POLICE ARE GOING TO JUST ABANDON THEM?
NO.
THE WAY THEY SPEAK. THE WAY THEY DRESS.
DID YOU ALL FORGET WHAT IT WAS LIKE OUT THERE?
THEY NEED A MESSAGE. THEY NEED A REMINDER THAT THEY WORK FOR THE PEOPLE.
WHAT DO YOU SUGGEST, KATHARSIS?
THEY HAVE ALL BEEN TOUCHED BY VIOLENCE, AND VIOLENCE RESIDES UPON THEM YET.
WE SEND 'EM BACK. BUT FIRST...
...WE MESS THEM UP.
WE MARK THEM. I'LL DO IT.
IT WILL BE THEIR UNDOING.
AS IT HAS BEEN MINE.
NO. KULAP, THAT'S...THAT'S JUST EVIL.
IT'S WHAT WE'RE TRYING TO FIGHT.
YOU CAN'T CALL THIS FIGHTING, HOLLY.
THEY NEED TO KNOW WHO THE HELL THEY'RE SCREWING WITH.

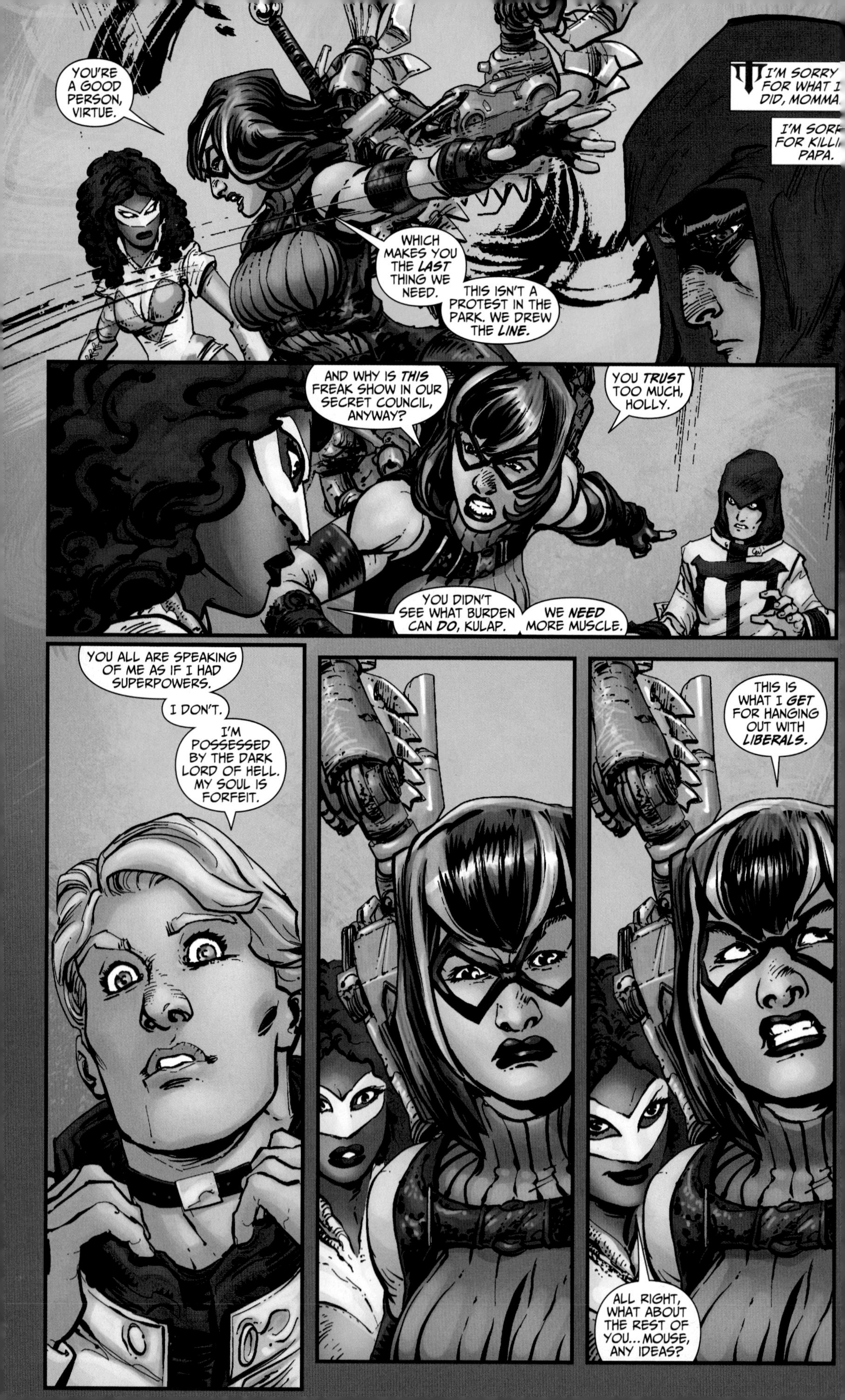
YOU'RE A GOOD PERSON, VIRTUE.
I'M SORRY FOR WHAT I DID, MOMMA.
I'M SORRY FOR KILLING PAPA.
WHICH MAKES YOU THE LAST THING WE NEED.
THIS ISN'T A PROTEST IN THE PARK. WE DREW THE LINE.
AND WHY IS THIS FREAK SHOW IN OUR SECRET COUNCIL, ANYWAY?
YOU TRUST TOO MUCH, HOLLY.
YOU DIDN'T SEE WHAT BURDEN CAN DO, KULAP.
WE NEED MORE MUSCLE.
YOU ALL ARE SPEAKING OF ME AS IF I HAD SUPERPOWERS.
I DON'T.
I'M POSSESSED BY THE DARK LORD OF HELL. MY SOUL IS FORFEIT.
THIS IS WHAT I GET FOR HANGING OUT WITH LIBERALS.
ALL RIGHT, WHAT ABOUT THE REST OF YOU... MOUSE, ANY IDEAS?

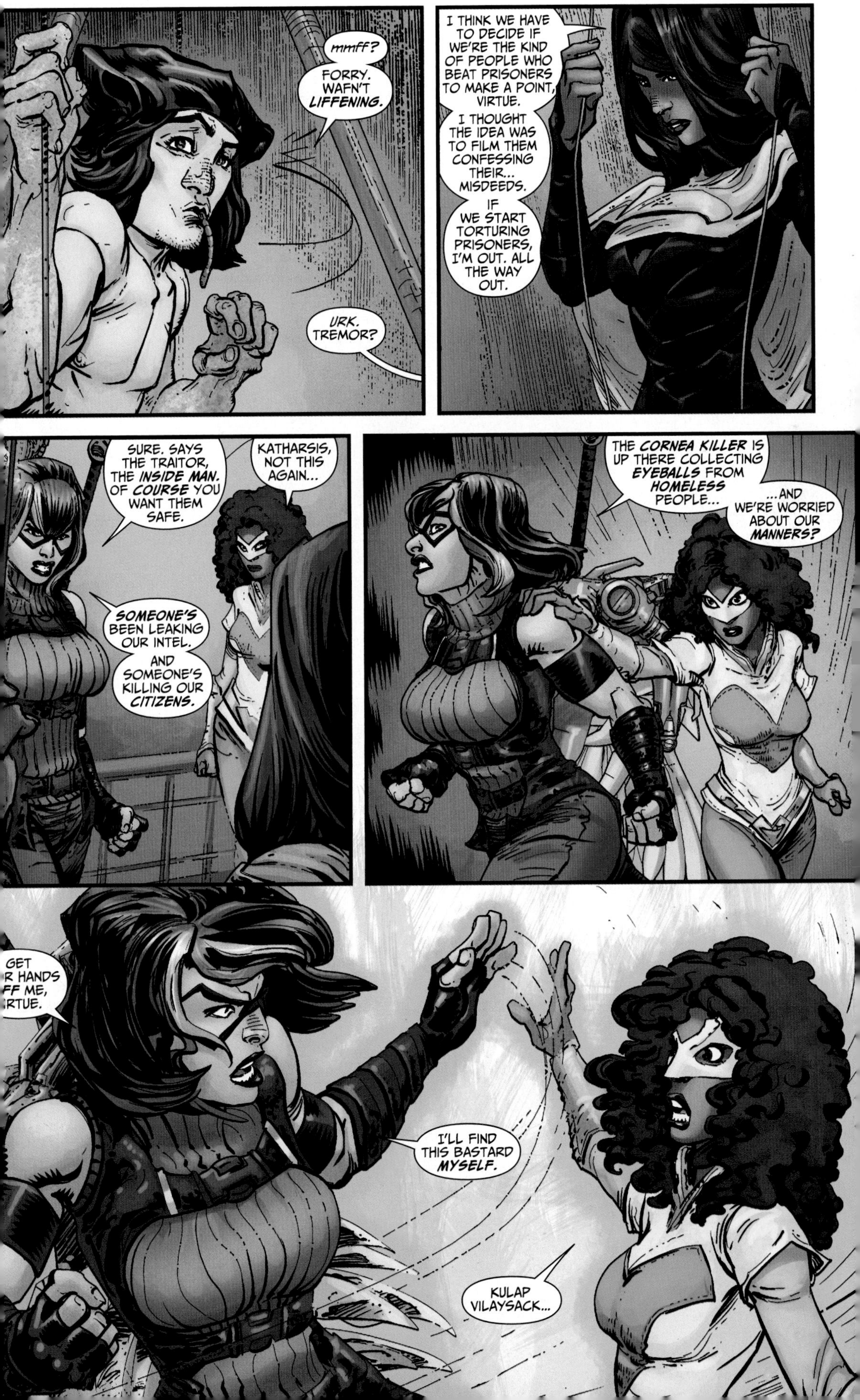
mmff?
FORRY. WAFN'T *LIFFENING.*
URK. TREMOR?
I THINK WE HAVE TO DECIDE IF WE'RE THE KIND OF PEOPLE WHO BEAT PRISONERS TO MAKE A POINT, VIRTUE.
I THOUGHT THE IDEA WAS TO FILM THEM CONFESSING THEIR... MISDEEDS.
IF WE START TORTURING PRISONERS, I'M OUT. ALL THE WAY OUT.
SURE. SAYS THE TRAITOR, THE *INSIDE MAN.* OF *COURSE* YOU WANT THEM SAFE.
KATHARSIS, NOT THIS AGAIN...
SOMEONE'S BEEN LEAKING OUR INTEL.
AND SOMEONE'S KILLING OUR *CITIZENS.*
THE *CORNEA KILLER* IS UP THERE COLLECTING *EYEBALLS* FROM *HOMELESS* PEOPLE...
...AND WE'RE WORRIED ABOUT OUR *MANNERS?*
I'LL FIND THIS BASTARD *MYSELF.*
KULAP VILAYSACK...

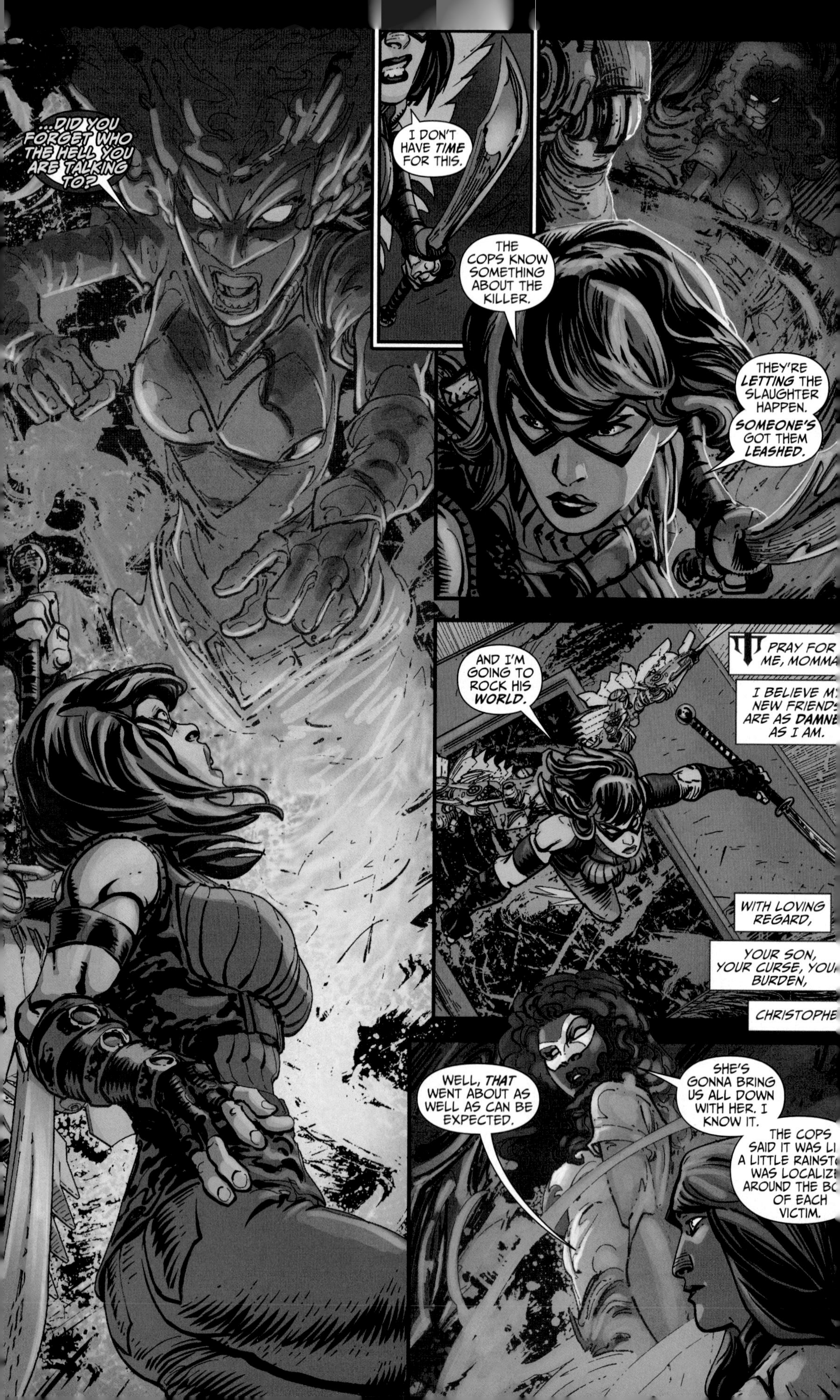
...DID YOU FORGET WHO THE HELL YOU ARE TALKING TO?
I DON'T HAVE TIME FOR THIS.
THE COPS KNOW SOMETHING ABOUT THE KILLER.
THEY'RE LETTING THE SLAUGHTER HAPPEN. SOMEONE'S GOT THEM LEASHED.
AND I'M GOING TO ROCK HIS WORLD.
PRAY FOR ME, MOMMA
I BELIEVE MY NEW FRIENDS ARE AS DAMNE AS I AM.
WITH LOVING REGARD,
YOUR SON, YOUR CURSE, YOU BURDEN,
CHRISTOPHE
WELL, THAT WENT ABOUT AS WELL AS CAN BE EXPECTED.
SHE'S GONNA BRING US ALL DOWN WITH HER. I KNOW IT.
THE COPS SAID IT WAS LI A LITTLE RAINST WAS LOCALIZ AROUND THE BO OF EACH VICTIM.

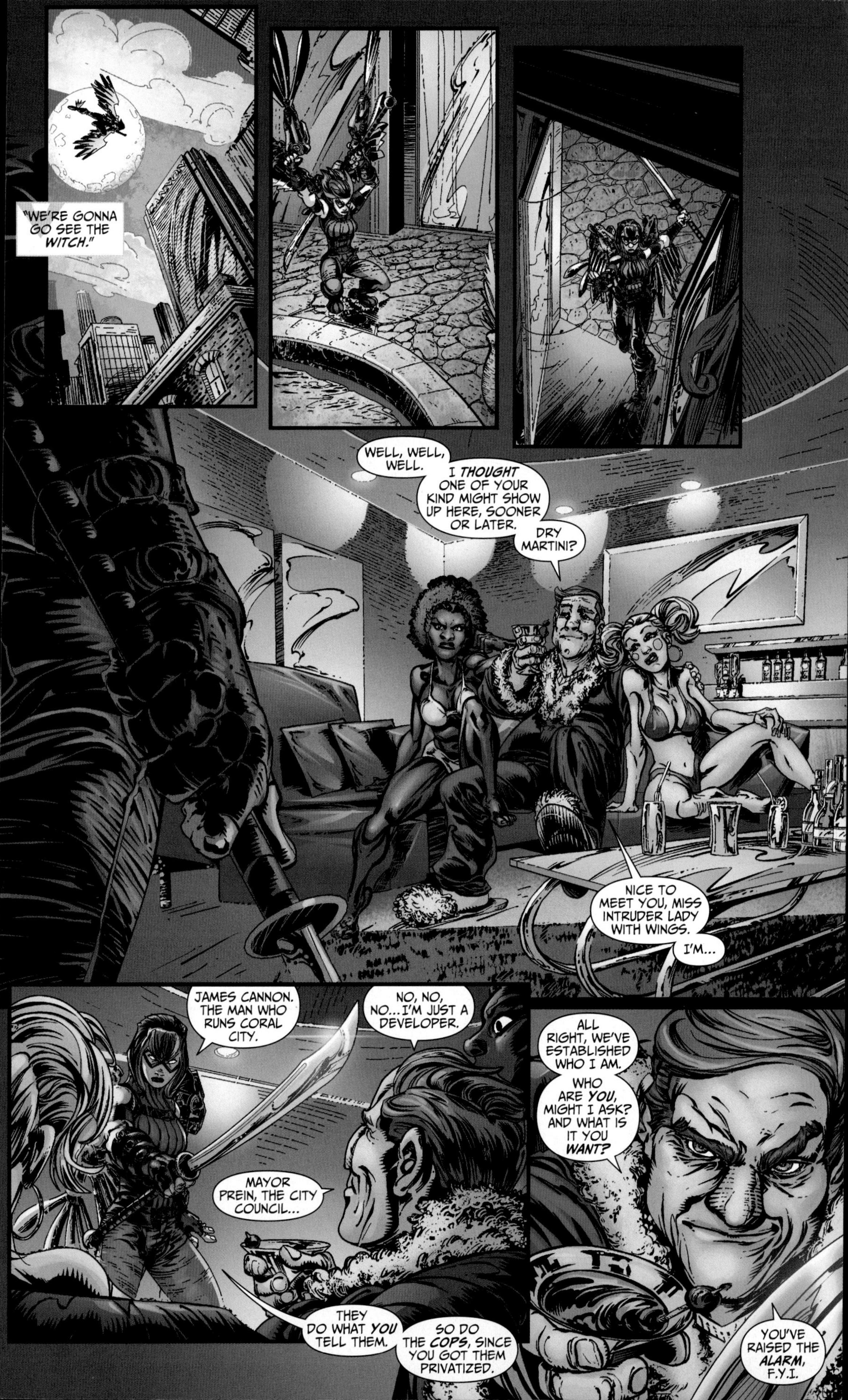
"WE'RE GONNA GO SEE THE *WITCH*."
WELL, WELL, WELL.
I *THOUGHT* ONE OF YOUR KIND MIGHT SHOW UP HERE, SOONER OR LATER.
DRY MARTINI?
NICE TO MEET YOU, MISS INTRUDER LADY WITH WINGS.
I'M...
JAMES CANNON. THE MAN WHO RUNS CORAL CITY.
NO, NO, NO...I'M JUST A DEVELOPER.
MAYOR PREIN, THE CITY COUNCIL...
THEY DO WHAT *YOU* TELL THEM.
SO DO THE *COPS*, SINCE YOU GOT THEM PRIVATIZED.
ALL RIGHT, WE'VE ESTABLISHED WHO I AM.
WHO ARE *YOU*, MIGHT I ASK? AND WHAT IS IT YOU *WANT?*
YOU'VE RAISED THE *ALARM*, F.Y.I.

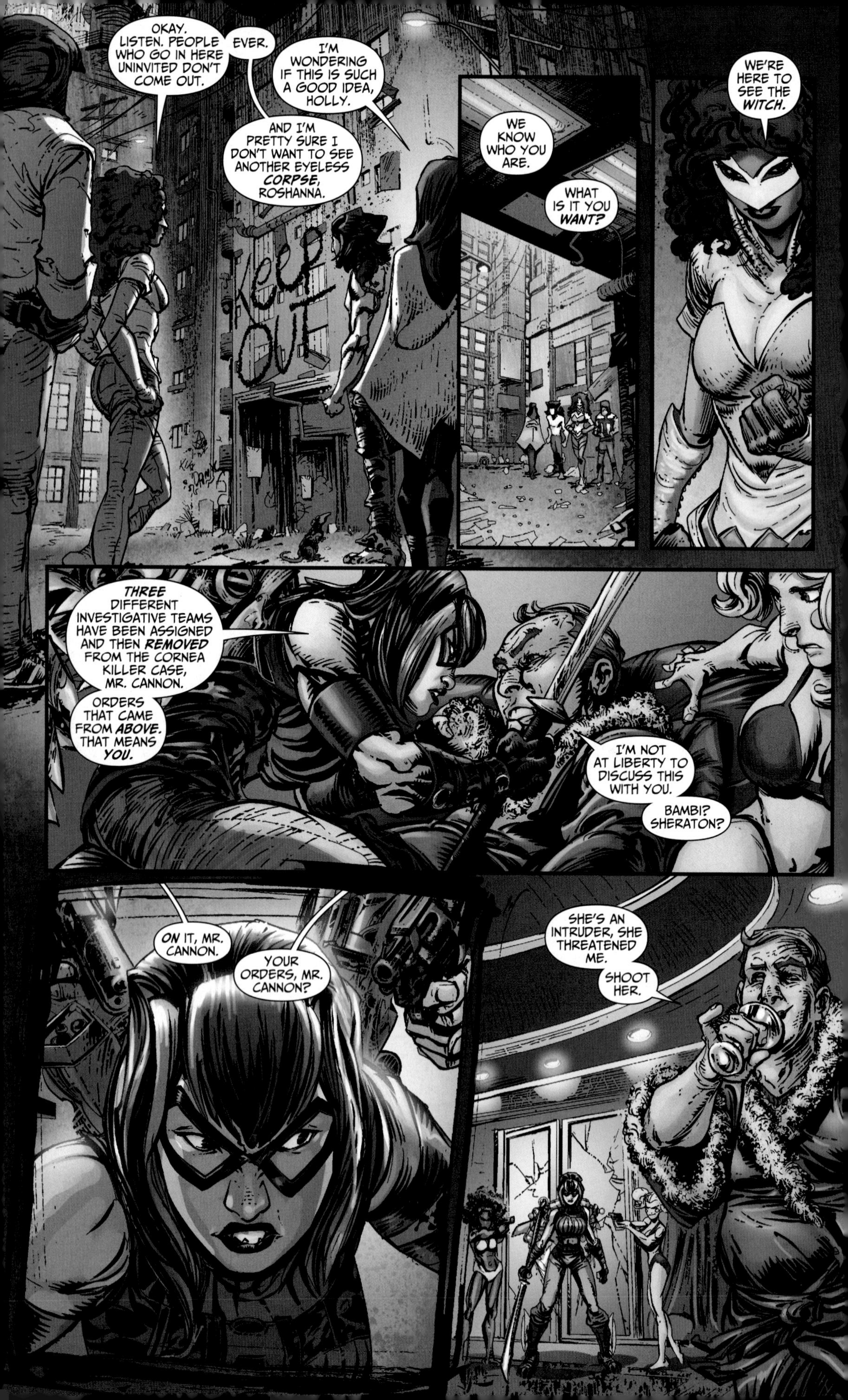
OKAY. LISTEN. PEOPLE WHO GO IN HERE UNINVITED DON'T COME OUT.
EVER.
I'M WONDERING IF THIS IS SUCH A GOOD IDEA, HOLLY.
AND I'M PRETTY SURE I DON'T WANT TO SEE ANOTHER EYELESS CORPSE, ROSHANNA.
KEEP OUT
WE KNOW WHO YOU ARE.
WHAT IS IT YOU WANT?
WE'RE HERE TO SEE THE WITCH.
THREE DIFFERENT INVESTIGATIVE TEAMS HAVE BEEN ASSIGNED AND THEN REMOVED FROM THE CORNEA KILLER CASE, MR. CANNON.
ORDERS THAT CAME FROM ABOVE. THAT MEANS YOU.
I'M NOT AT LIBERTY TO DISCUSS THIS WITH YOU.
BAMBI? SHERATON?
ON IT, MR. CANNON.
YOUR ORDERS, MR. CANNON?
SHE'S AN INTRUDER, SHE THREATENED ME.
SHOOT HER.

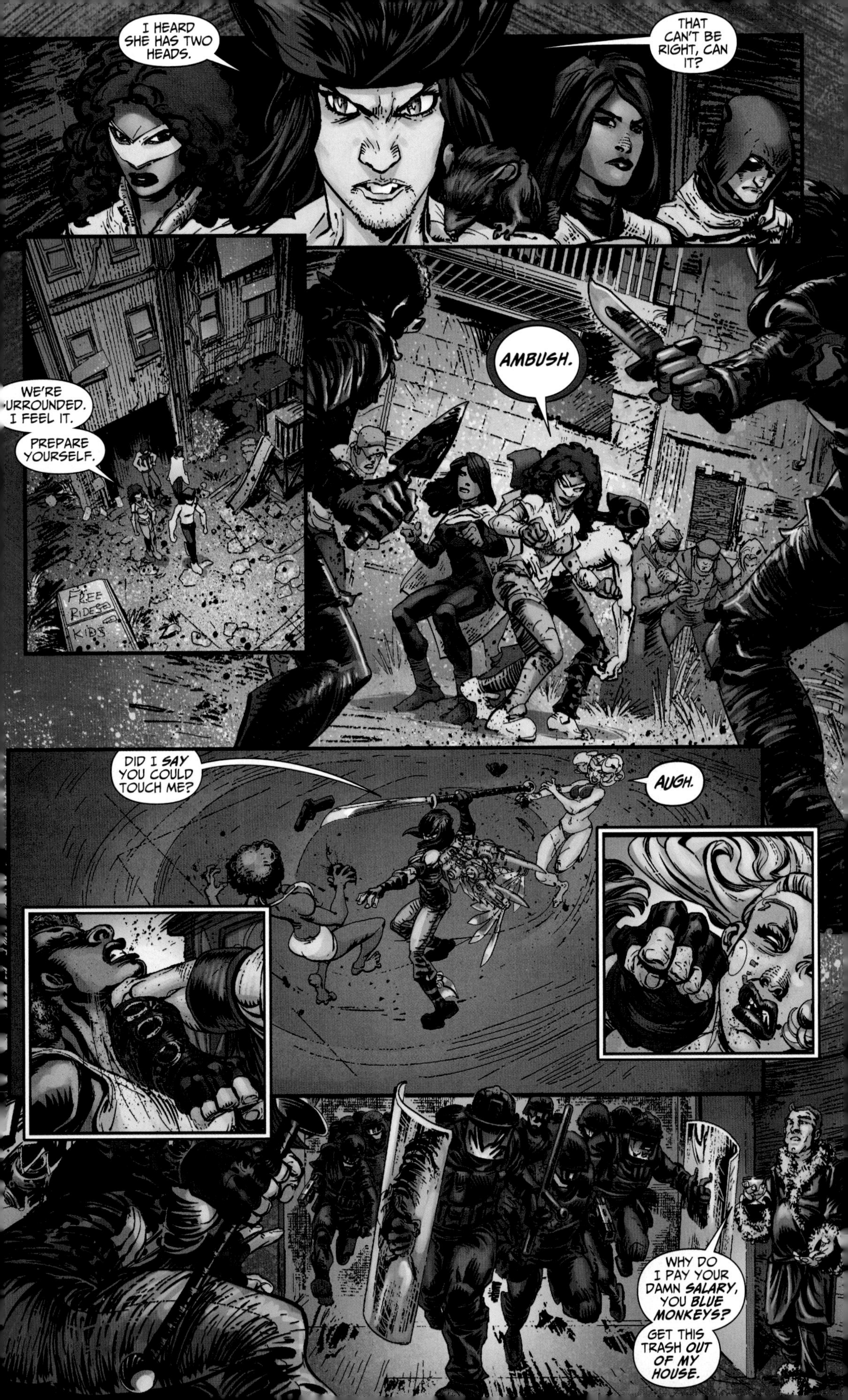
I HEARD SHE HAS TWO HEADS.
THAT CAN'T BE RIGHT, CAN IT?
WE'RE URROUNDED. I FEEL IT.
PREPARE YOURSELF.
FREE RIDES TO KIDS
AMBUSH.
DID I SAY YOU COULD TOUCH ME?
AUGH.
WHY DO I PAY YOUR DAMN SALARY, YOU BLUE MONKEYS?
GET THIS TRASH OUT OF MY HOUSE.

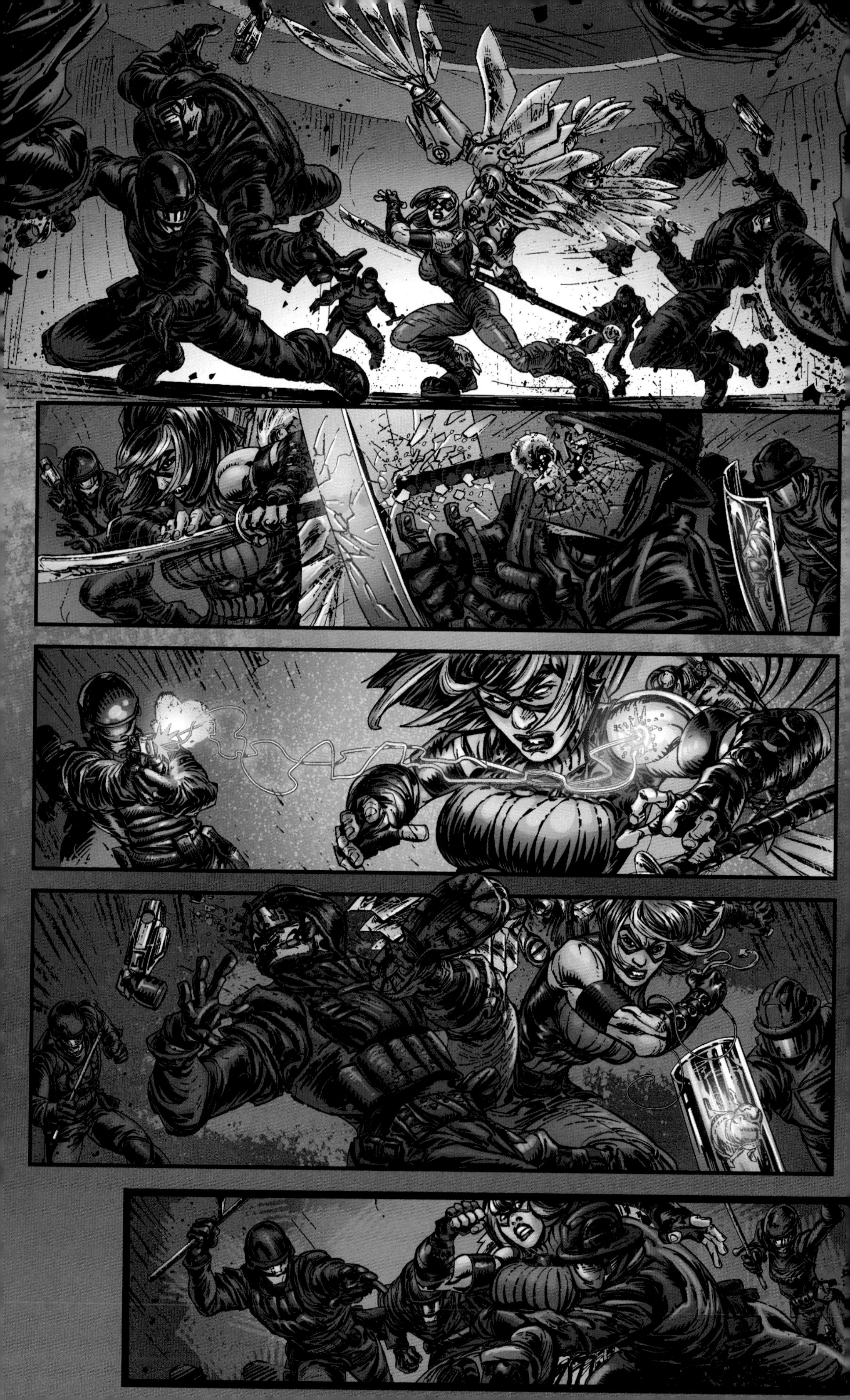

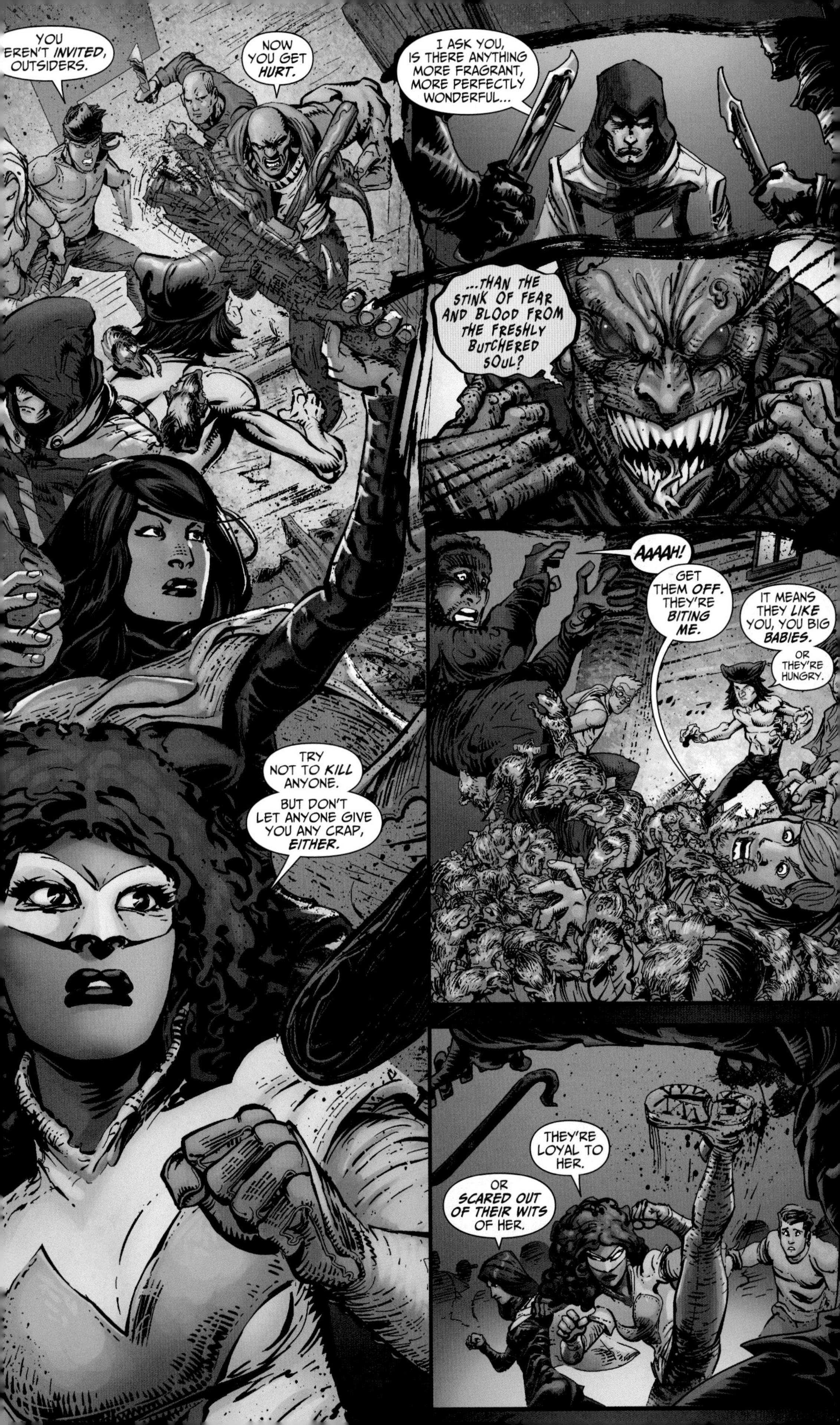
YOU EREN'T INVITED, OUTSIDERS.
NOW YOU GET HURT.
I ASK YOU, IS THERE ANYTHING MORE FRAGRANT, MORE PERFECTLY WONDERFUL...
...THAN THE STINK OF FEAR AND BLOOD FROM THE FRESHLY BUTCHERED SOUL?
AAAAH!
GET THEM OFF. THEY'RE BITING ME.
IT MEANS THEY LIKE YOU, YOU BIG BABIES.
OR THEY'RE HUNGRY.
TRY NOT TO KILL ANYONE.
BUT DON'T LET ANYONE GIVE YOU ANY CRAP, EITHER.
THEY'RE LOYAL TO HER.
OR SCARED OUT OF THEIR WITS OF HER.

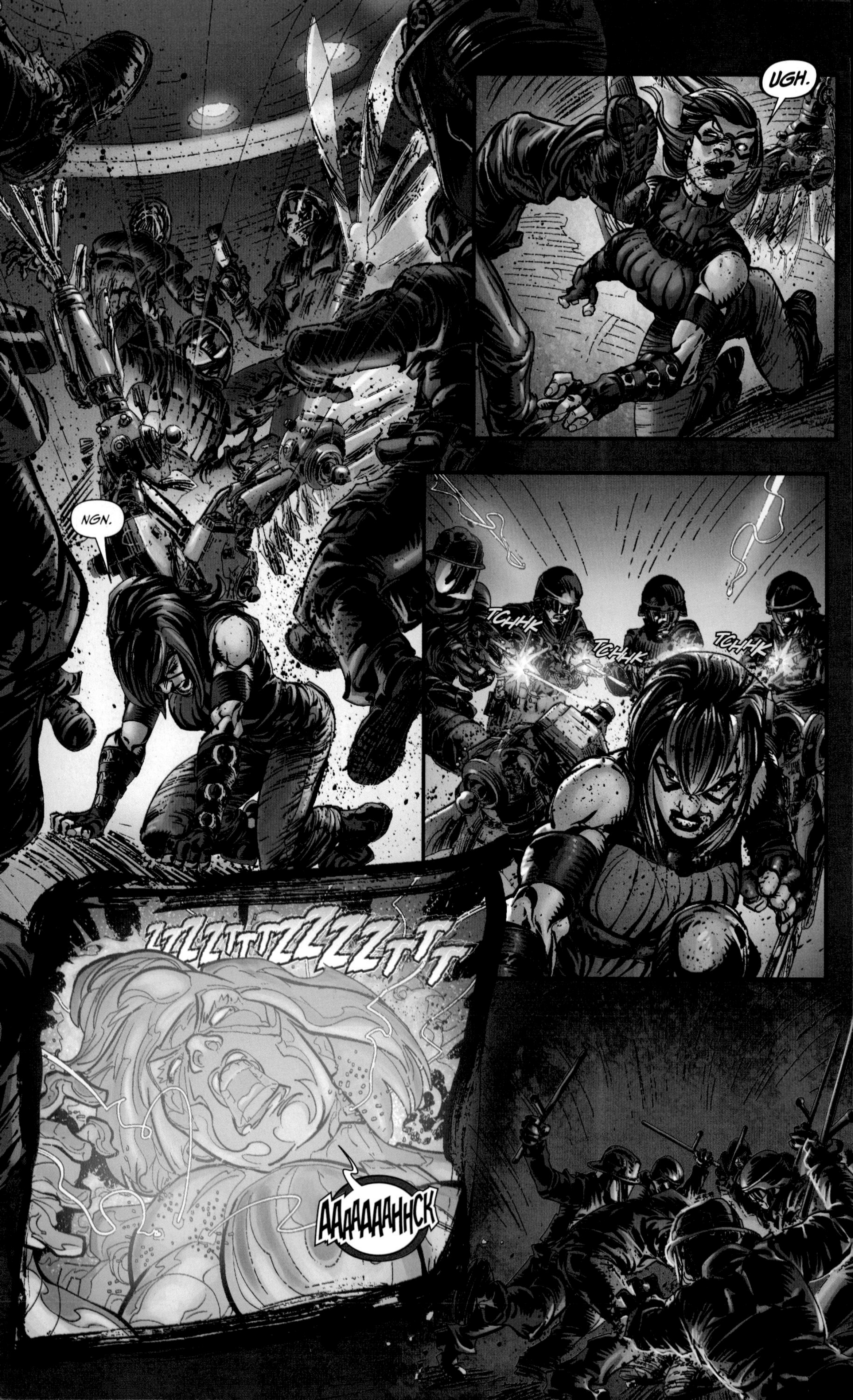
UGH.
NGN.
TCHHK
TCHHK
TCHHK
ZZZZTTTZZZZZTTT
AAAAAAAHHCK

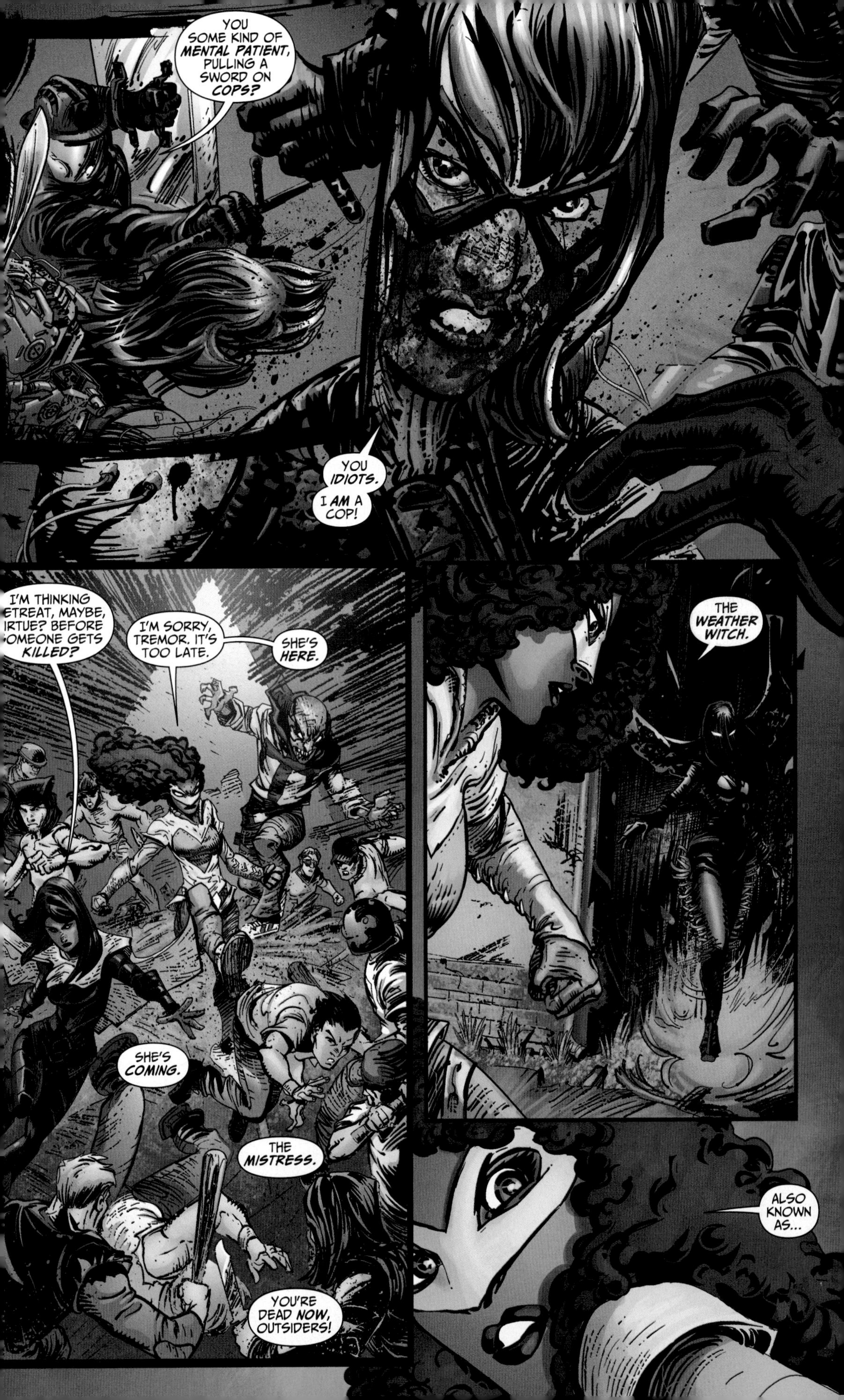

YOU SOME KIND OF MENTAL PATIENT, PULLING A SWORD ON COPS?
YOU IDIOTS.
I AM A COP!
I'M THINKING ETREAT, MAYBE, IRTUE? BEFORE OMEONE GETS KILLED?
I'M SORRY, TREMOR. IT'S TOO LATE.
SHE'S HERE.
THE WEATHER WITCH.
SHE'S COMING.
THE MISTRESS.
YOU'RE DEAD NOW, OUTSIDERS!
ALSO KNOWN AS...

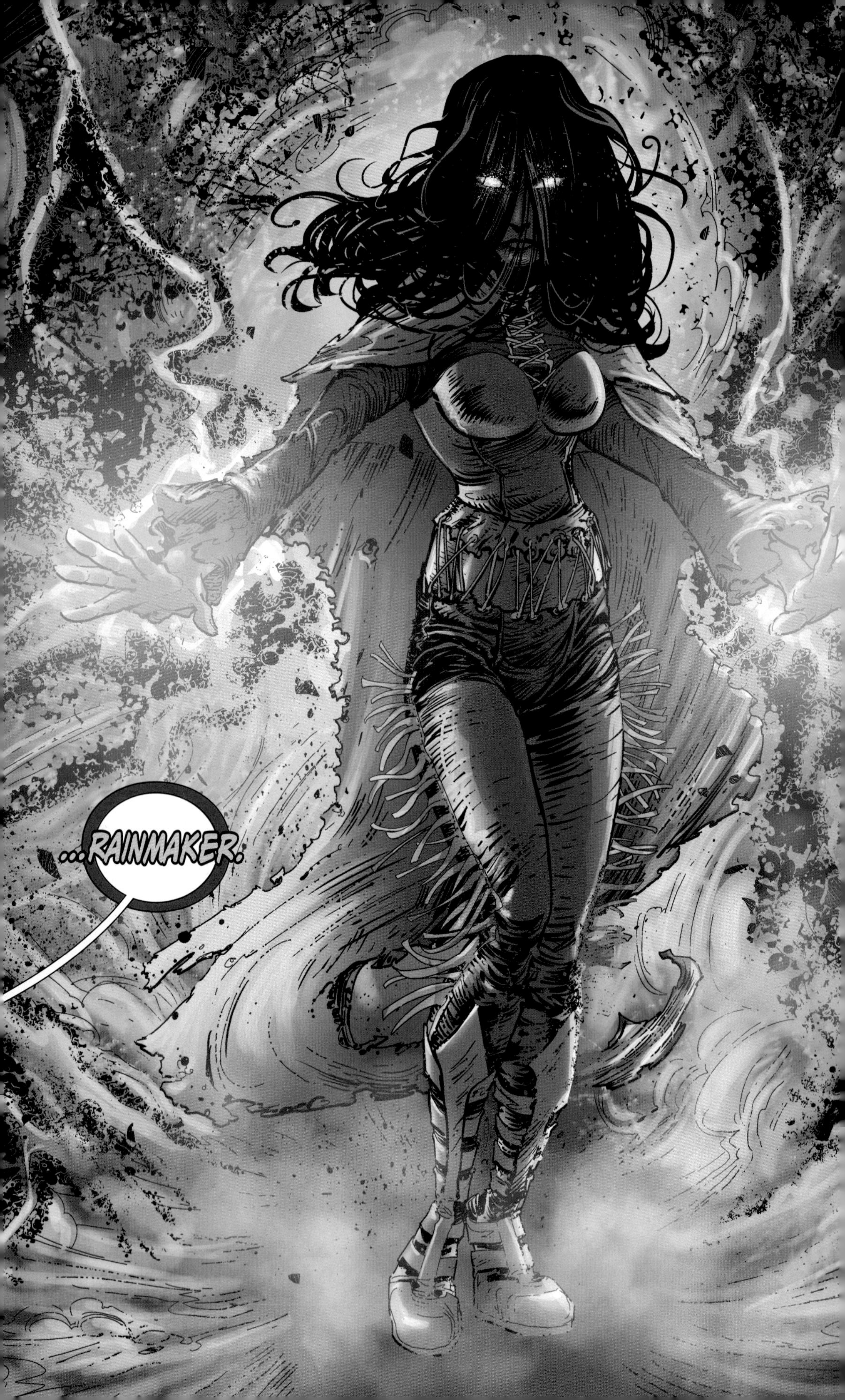
...RAINMAKER.

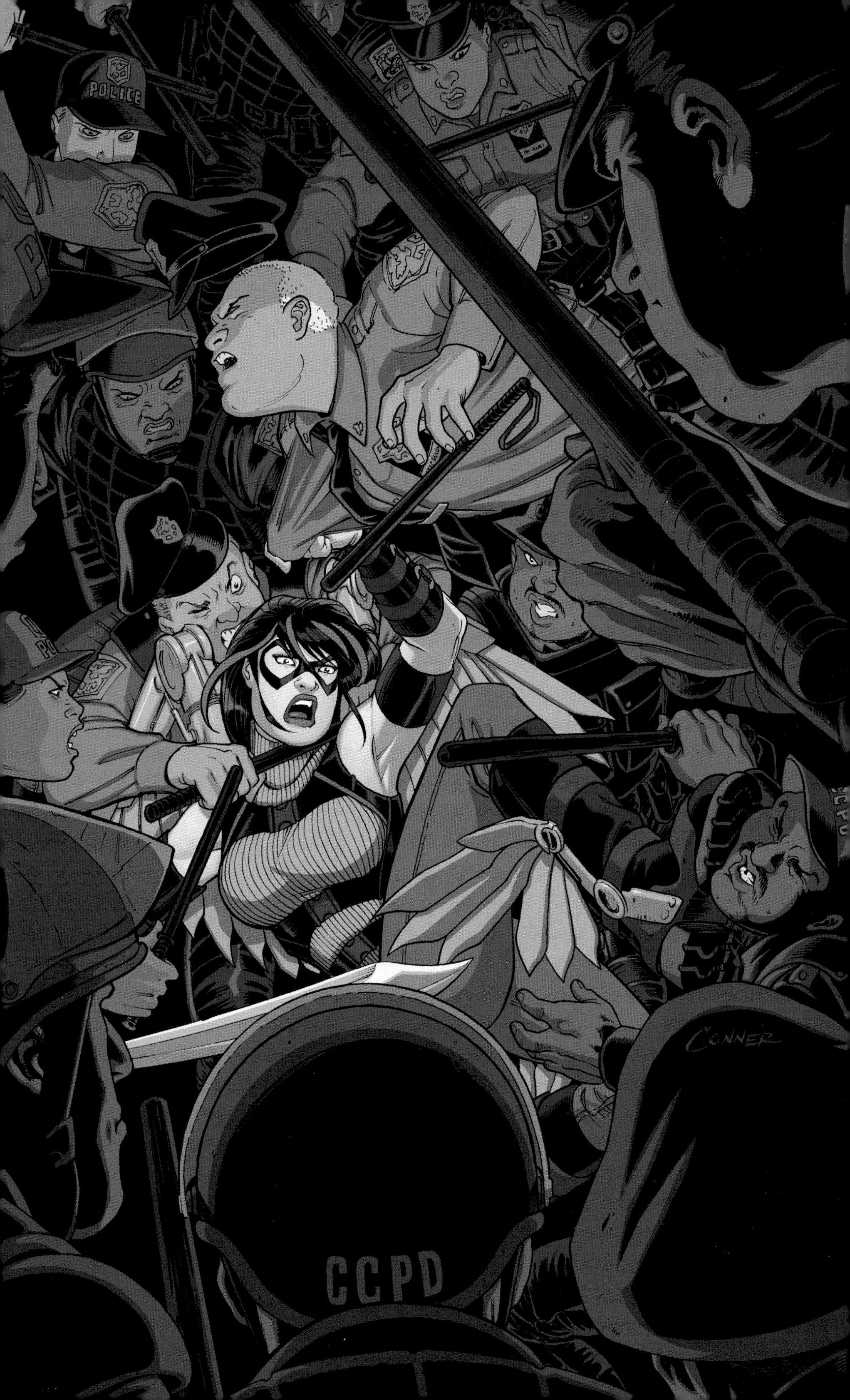
POLICE
CONNER
CCPD

The Movement #3 cover by Amanda Conner & Dave McCaig

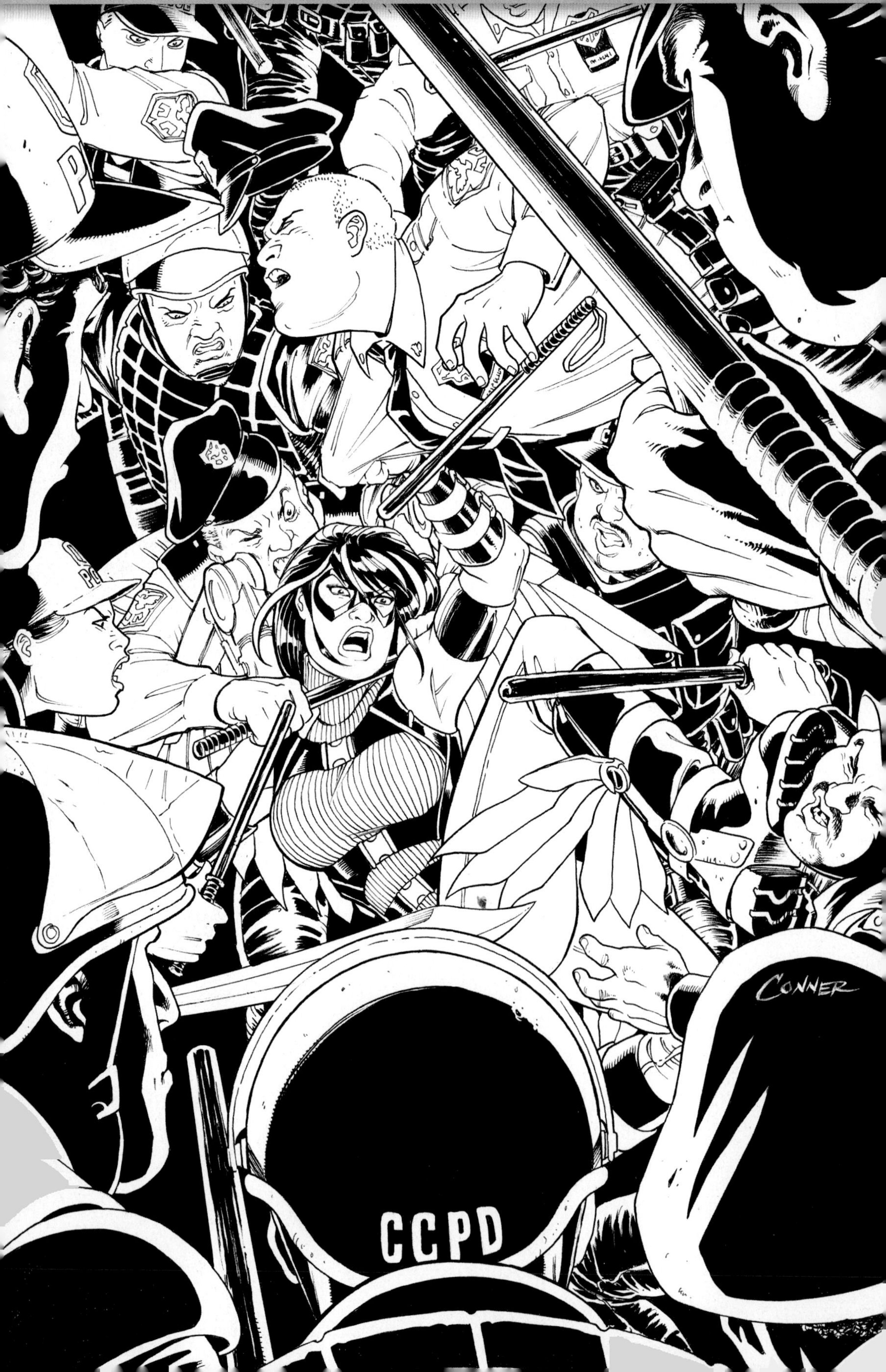
CONNER
CCPD

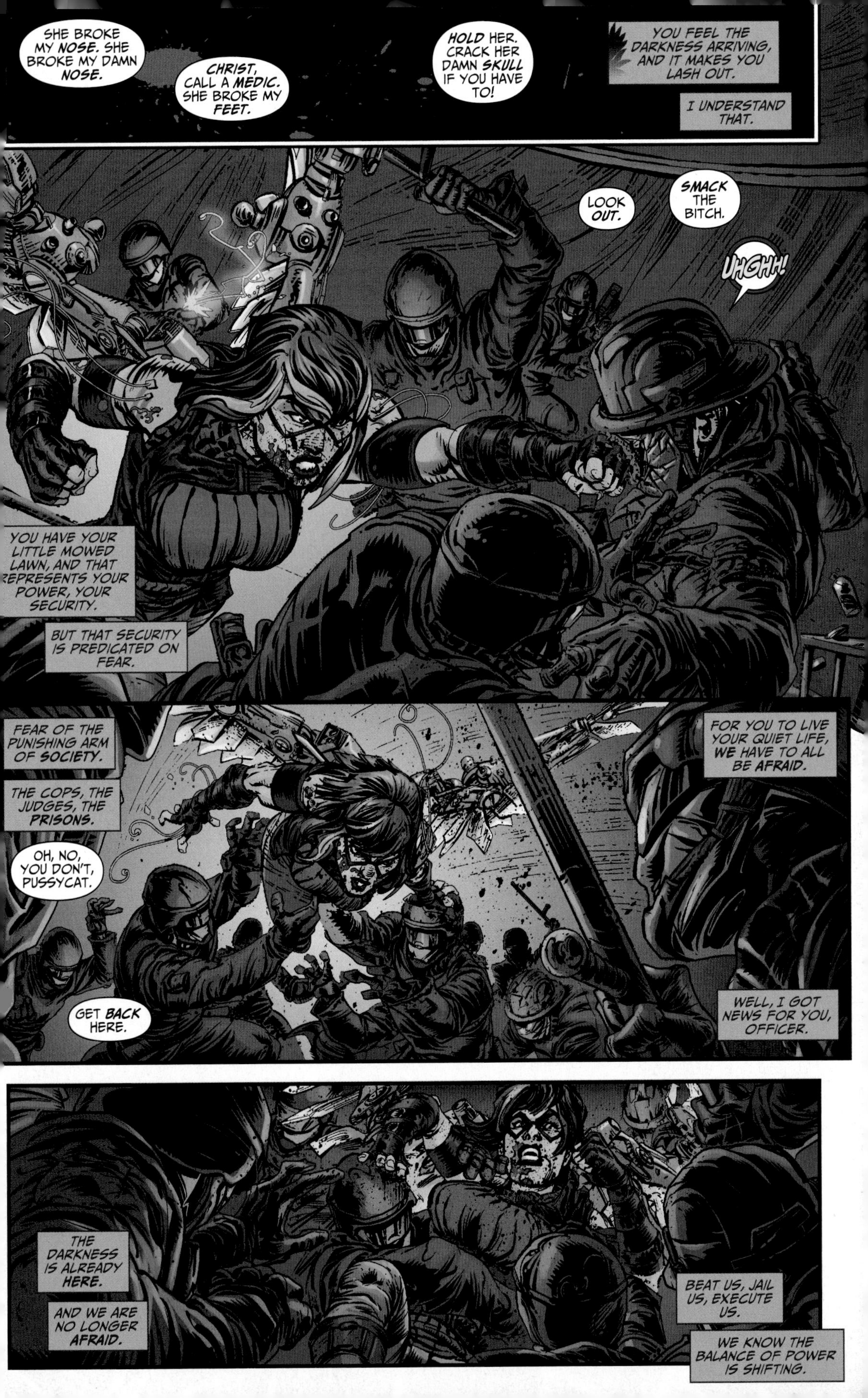
SHE BROKE MY NOSE. SHE BROKE MY DAMN NOSE.
CHRIST, CALL A MEDIC. SHE BROKE MY FEET.
HOLD HER. CRACK HER DAMN SKULL IF YOU HAVE TO!
YOU FEEL THE DARKNESS ARRIVING, AND IT MAKES YOU LASH OUT.
I UNDERSTAND THAT.
LOOK OUT.
SMACK THE BITCH.
UHGHH!
YOU HAVE YOUR LITTLE MOWED LAWN, AND THAT REPRESENTS YOUR POWER, YOUR SECURITY.
BUT THAT SECURITY IS PREDICATED ON FEAR.
FEAR OF THE PUNISHING ARM OF SOCIETY.
THE COPS, THE JUDGES, THE PRISONS.
OH, NO, YOU DON'T, PUSSYCAT.
GET BACK HERE.
FOR YOU TO LIVE YOUR QUIET LIFE, WE HAVE TO ALL BE AFRAID.
WELL, I GOT NEWS FOR YOU, OFFICER.
THE DARKNESS IS ALREADY HERE.
AND WE ARE NO LONGER AFRAID.
BEAT US, JAIL US, EXECUTE US.
WE KNOW THE BALANCE OF POWER IS SHIFTING.

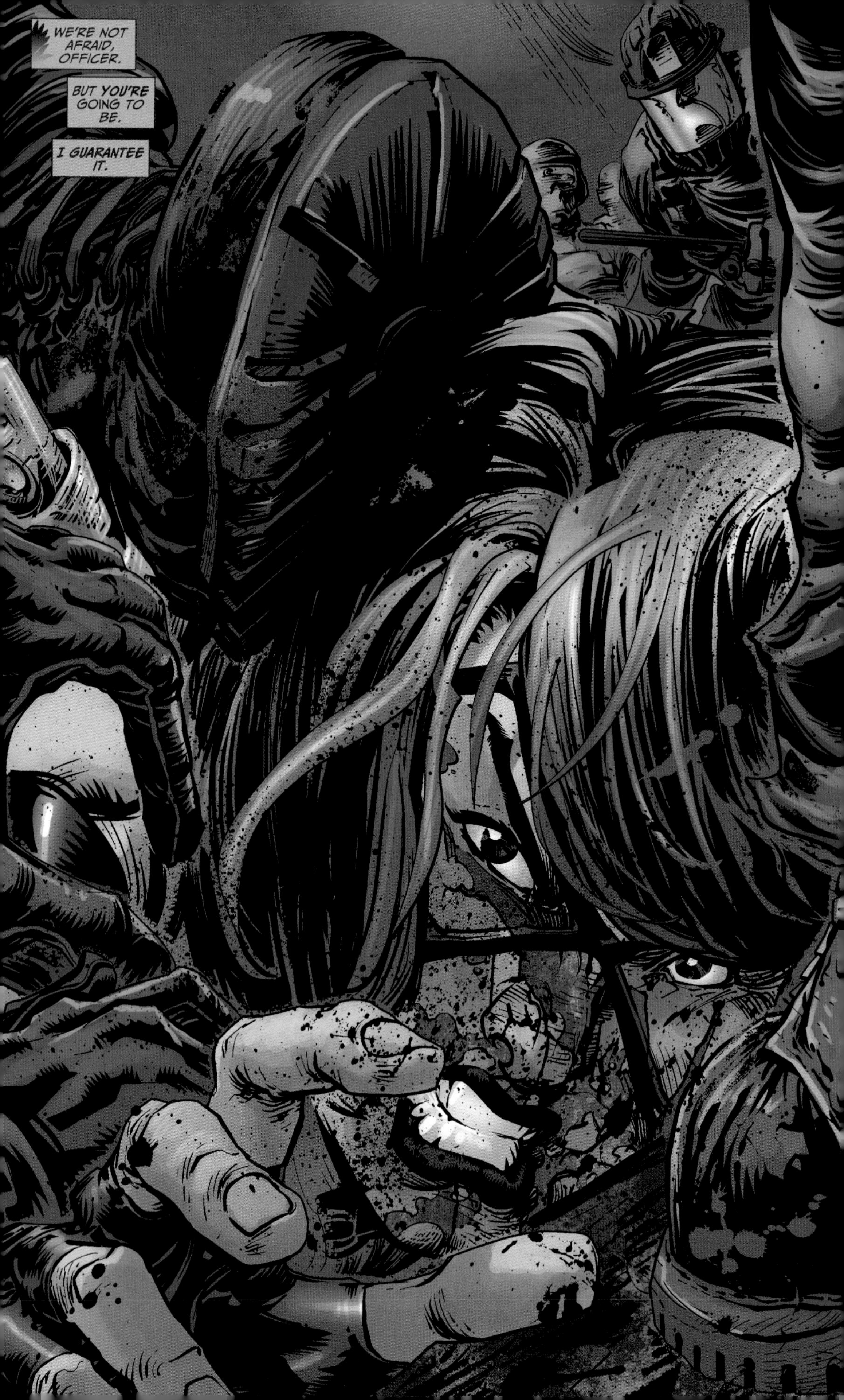
WE'RE NOT AFRAID, OFFICER.
BUT YOU'RE GOING TO BE.
I GUARANTEE IT.

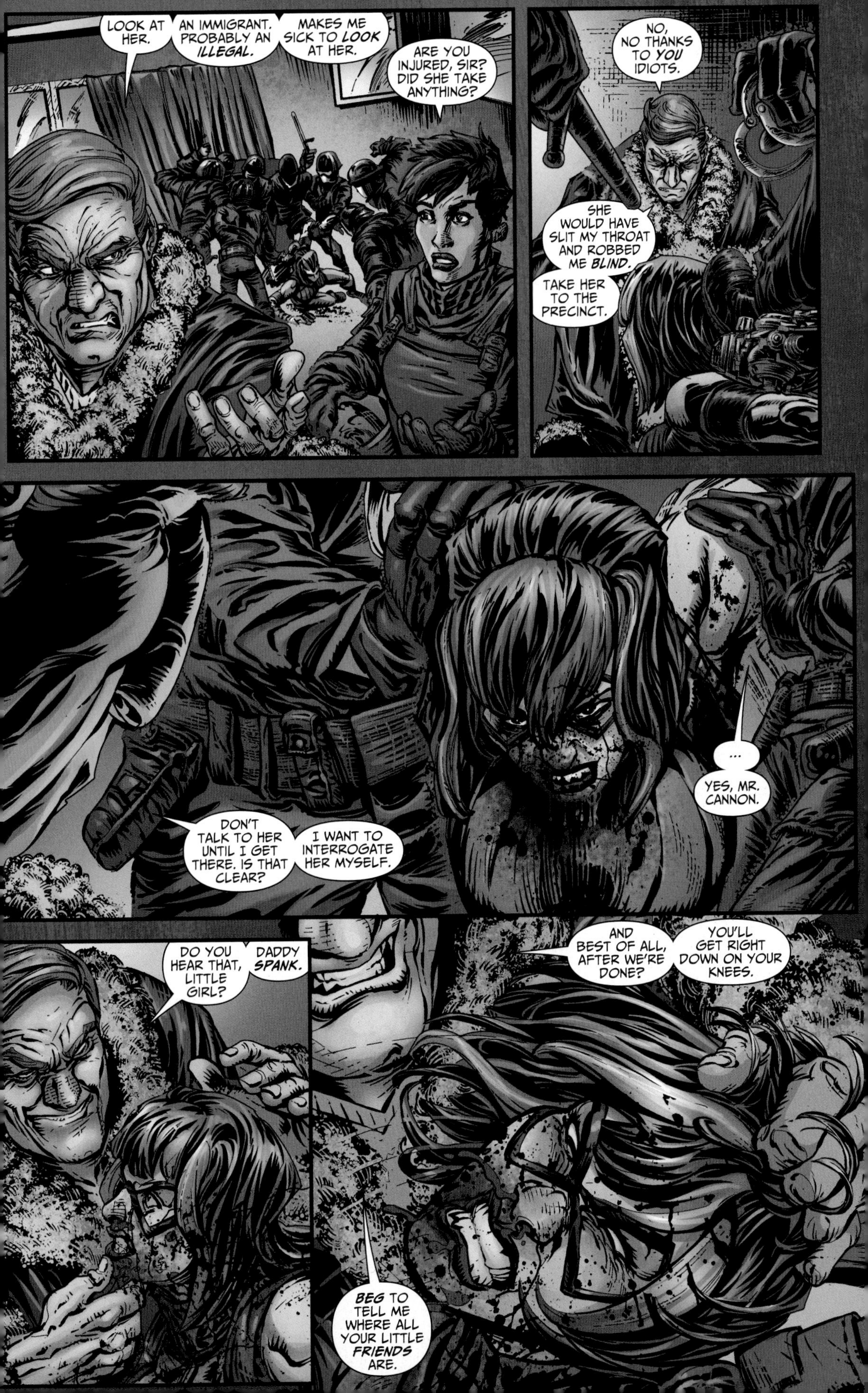
LOOK AT HER.
AN IMMIGRANT. PROBABLY AN ILLEGAL.
MAKES ME SICK TO LOOK AT HER.
ARE YOU INJURED, SIR? DID SHE TAKE ANYTHING?
NO, NO THANKS TO YOU IDIOTS.
SHE WOULD HAVE SLIT MY THROAT AND ROBBED ME BLIND.
TAKE HER TO THE PRECINCT.
DON'T TALK TO HER UNTIL I GET THERE. IS THAT CLEAR?
I WANT TO INTERROGATE HER MYSELF.
...
YES, MR. CANNON.
DO YOU HEAR THAT, LITTLE GIRL?
DADDY SPANK.
AND BEST OF ALL, AFTER WE'RE DONE?
YOU'LL GET RIGHT DOWN ON YOUR KNEES.
BEG TO TELL ME WHERE ALL YOUR LITTLE FRIENDS ARE.

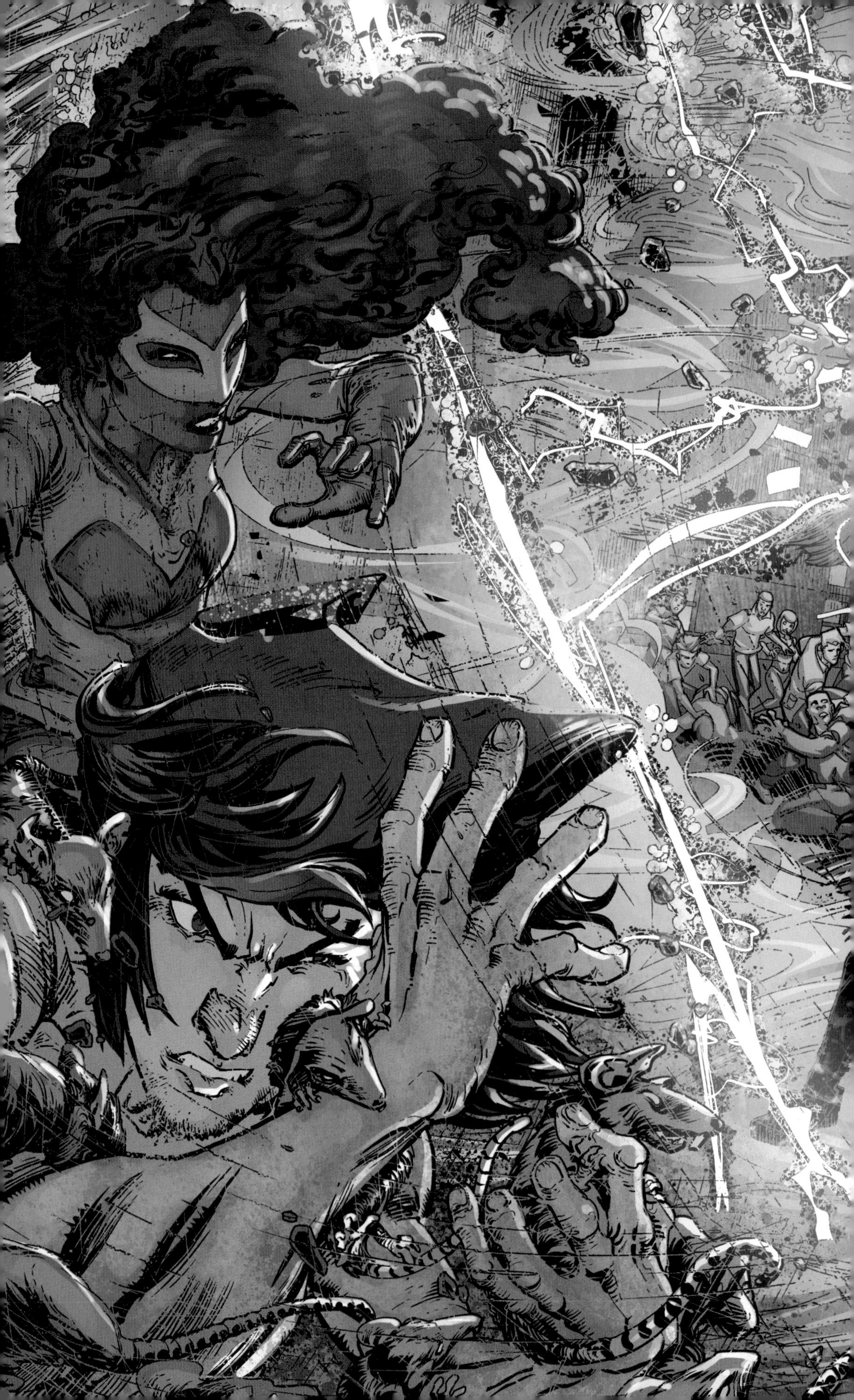

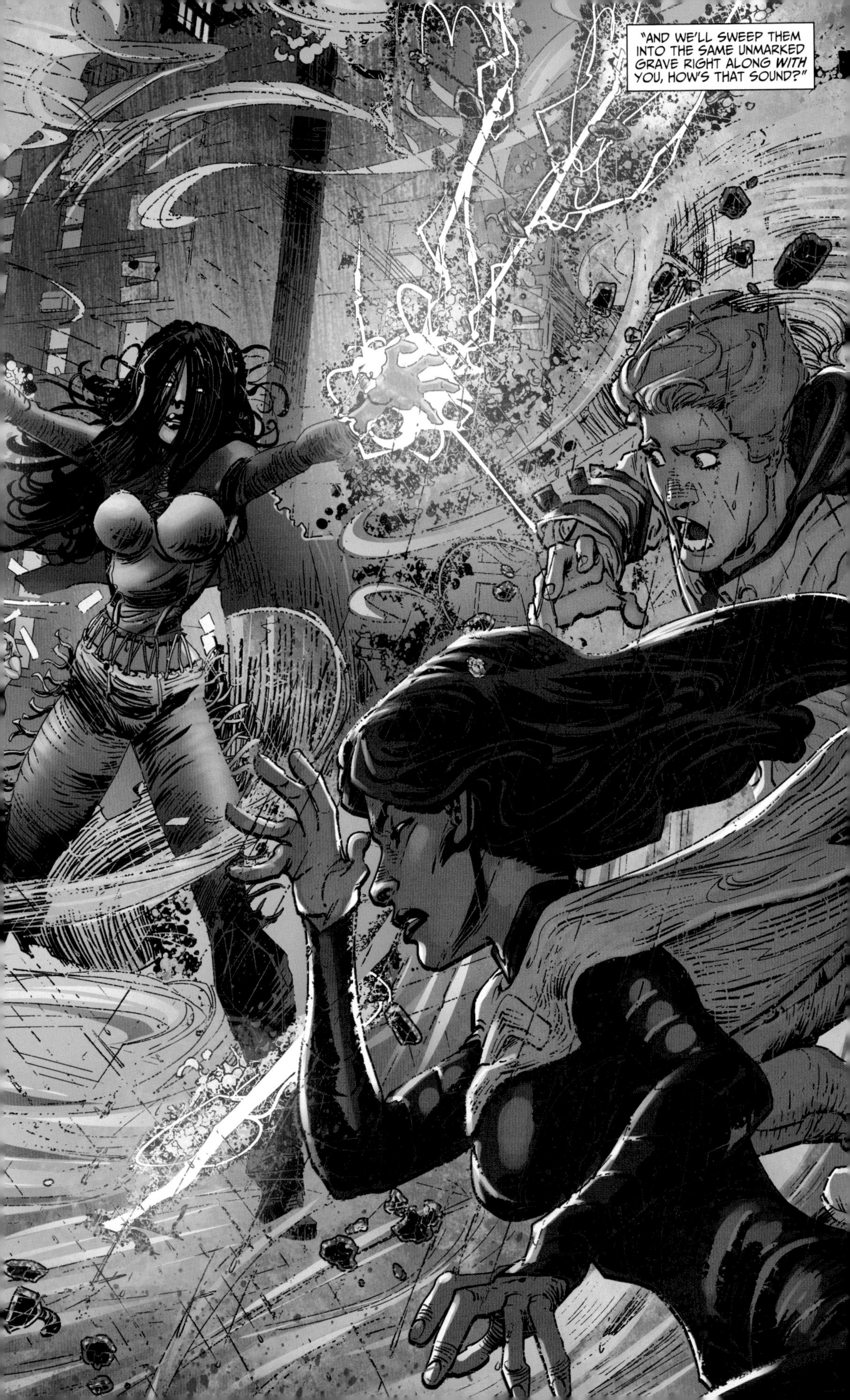
"AND WE'LL SWEEP THEM INTO THE SAME UNMARKED GRAVE RIGHT ALONG WITH YOU, HOW'S THAT SOUND?"

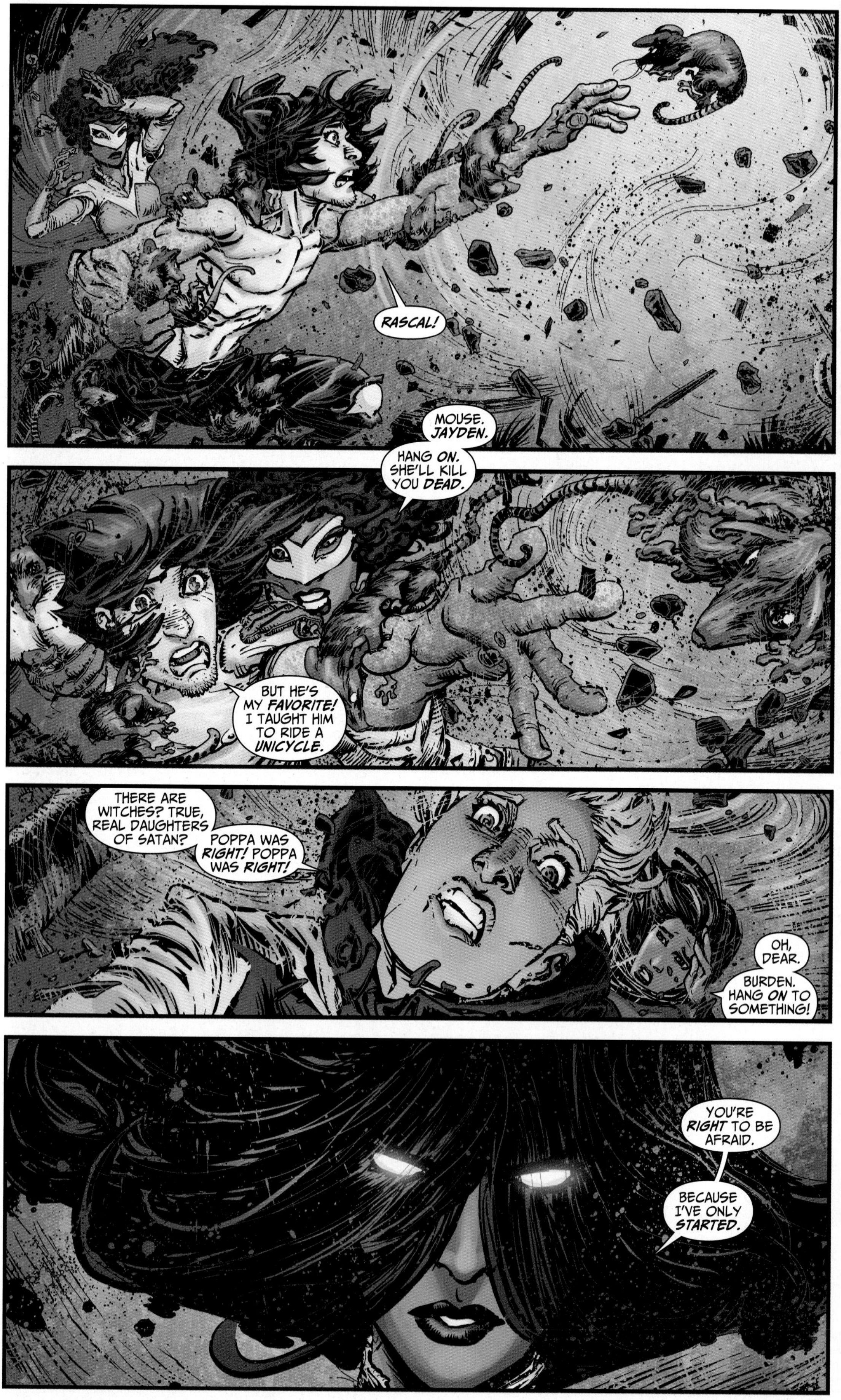
RASCAL!
MOUSE. JAYDEN.
HANG ON. SHE'LL KILL YOU DEAD.
BUT HE'S MY FAVORITE! I TAUGHT HIM TO RIDE A UNICYCLE.
THERE ARE WITCHES? TRUE, REAL DAUGHTERS OF SATAN?
POPPA WAS RIGHT! POPPA WAS RIGHT!
OH, DEAR.
BURDEN. HANG ON TO SOMETHING!
YOU'RE RIGHT TO BE AFRAID.
BECAUSE I'VE ONLY STARTED.

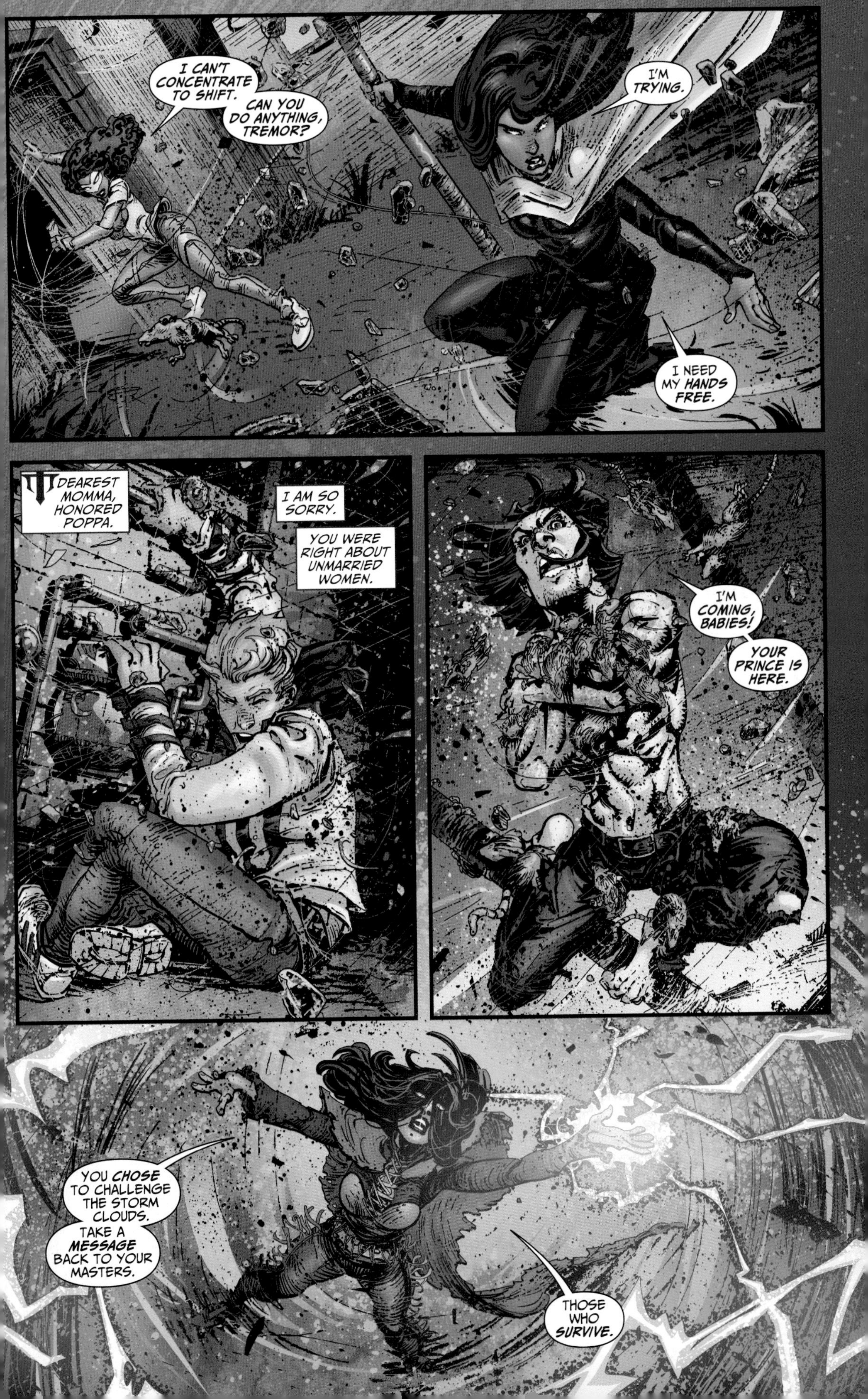
I CAN'T CONCENTRATE TO SHIFT.
CAN YOU DO ANYTHING, TREMOR?
I'M TRYING.
I NEED MY HANDS FREE.
DEAREST MOMMA, HONORED POPPA.
I AM SO SORRY.
YOU WERE RIGHT ABOUT UNMARRIED WOMEN.
I'M COMING, BABIES!
YOUR PRINCE IS HERE.
YOU CHOSE TO CHALLENGE THE STORM CLOUDS.
TAKE A MESSAGE BACK TO YOUR MASTERS.
THOSE WHO SURVIVE.

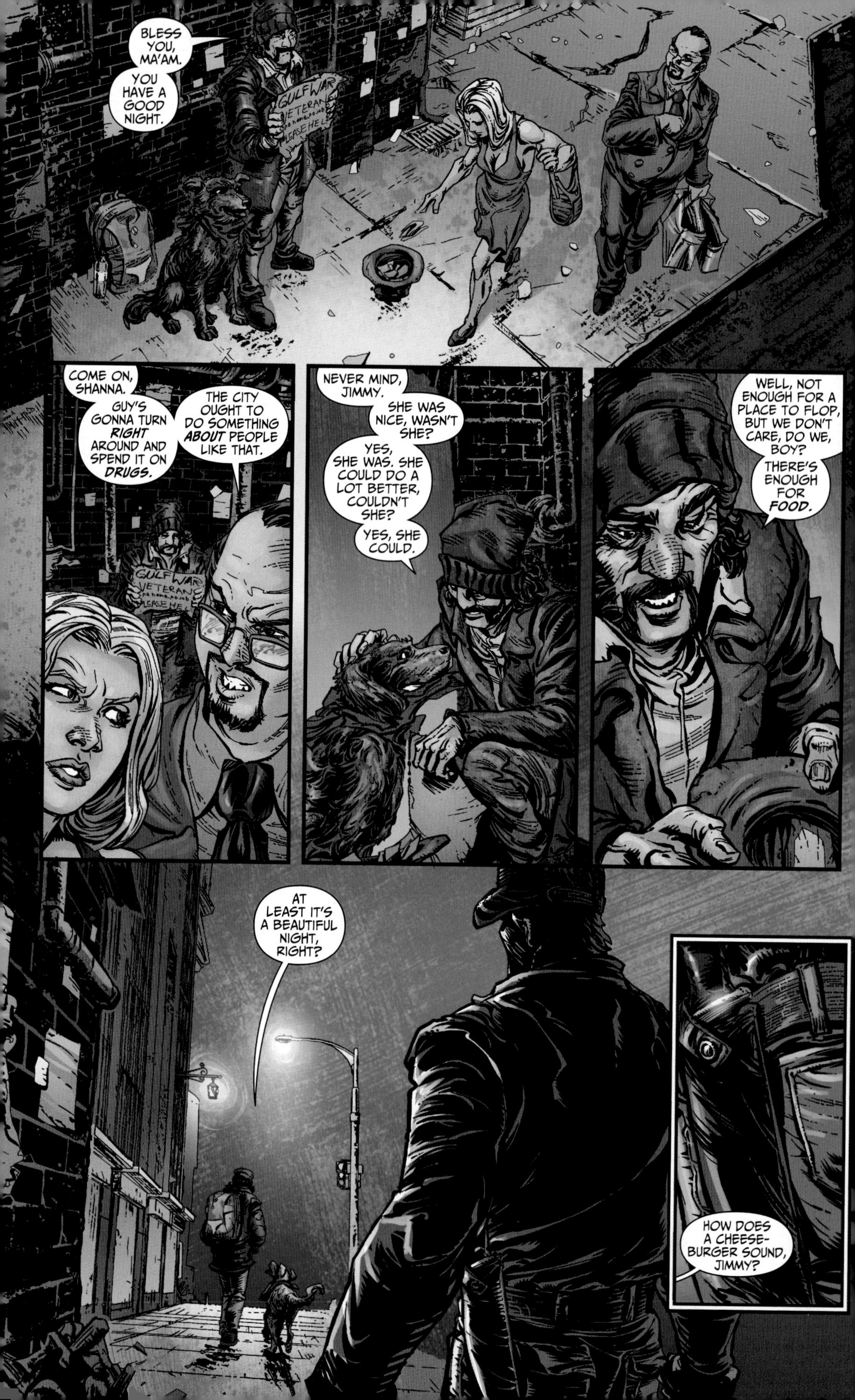

BLESS YOU, MA'AM.
YOU HAVE A GOOD NIGHT.
GULF WAR VETERAN
COME ON, SHANNA.
GUY'S GONNA TURN *RIGHT* AROUND AND SPEND IT ON *DRUGS.*
THE CITY OUGHT TO DO SOMETHING *ABOUT* PEOPLE LIKE THAT.
NEVER MIND, JIMMY.
SHE WAS NICE, WASN'T SHE?
YES, SHE WAS. SHE COULD DO A LOT BETTER, COULDN'T SHE?
YES, SHE COULD.
WELL, NOT ENOUGH FOR A PLACE TO FLOP, BUT WE DON'T CARE, DO WE, BOY?
THERE'S ENOUGH FOR *FOOD.*
AT LEAST IT'S A BEAUTIFUL NIGHT, RIGHT?
HOW DOES A CHEESE-BURGER SOUND, JIMMY?

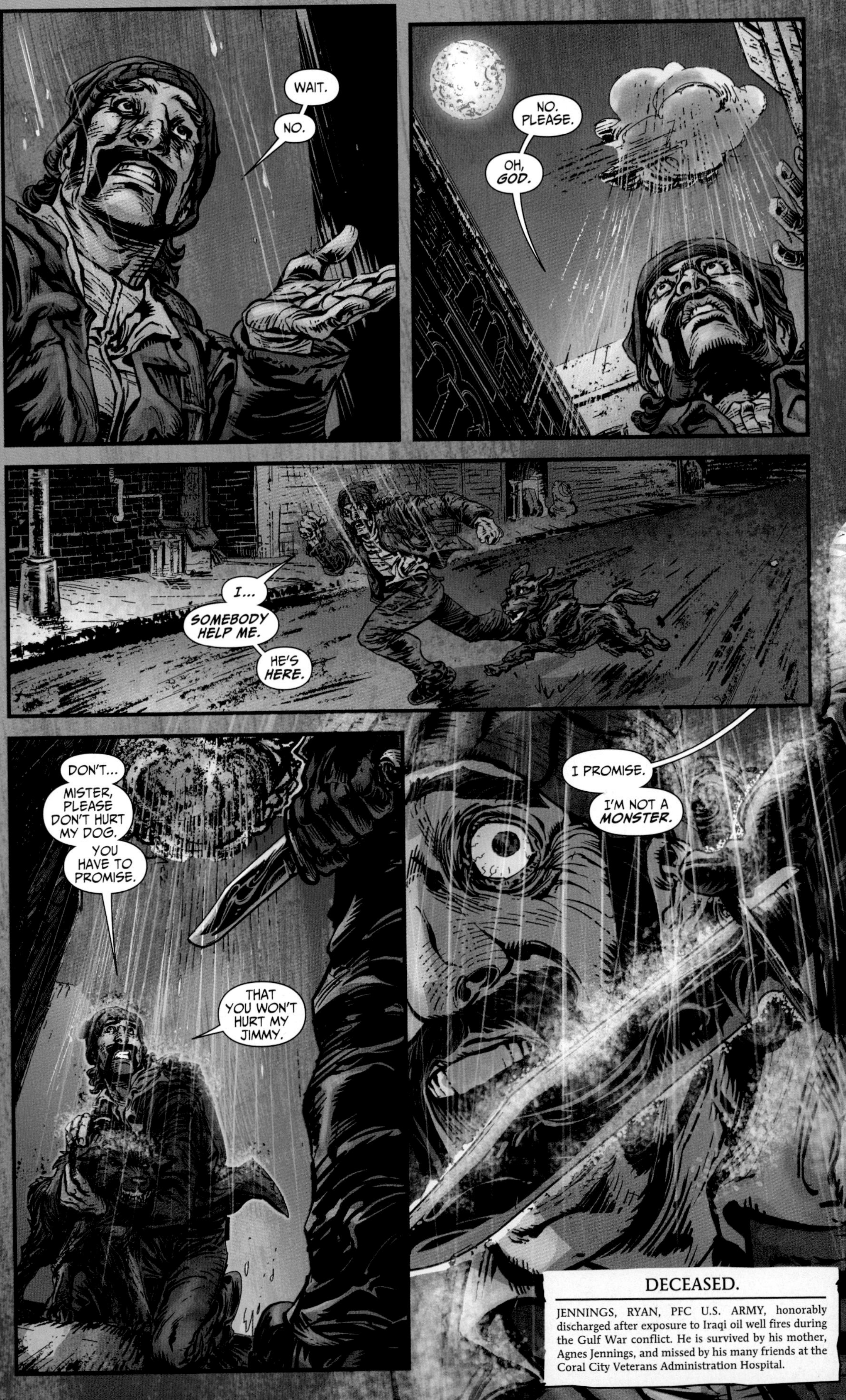
WAIT.
NO.
NO. PLEASE.
OH, GOD.
I...
SOMEBODY HELP ME.
HE'S HERE.
DON'T...
MISTER, PLEASE DON'T HURT MY DOG.
YOU HAVE TO PROMISE.
THAT YOU WON'T HURT MY JIMMY.
I PROMISE.
I'M NOT A MONSTER.
DECEASED.
JENNINGS, RYAN, PFC U.S. ARMY, honorably discharged after exposure to Iraqi oil well fires during the Gulf War conflict. He is survived by his mother, Agnes Jennings, and missed by his many friends at the Coral City Veterans Administration Hospital.

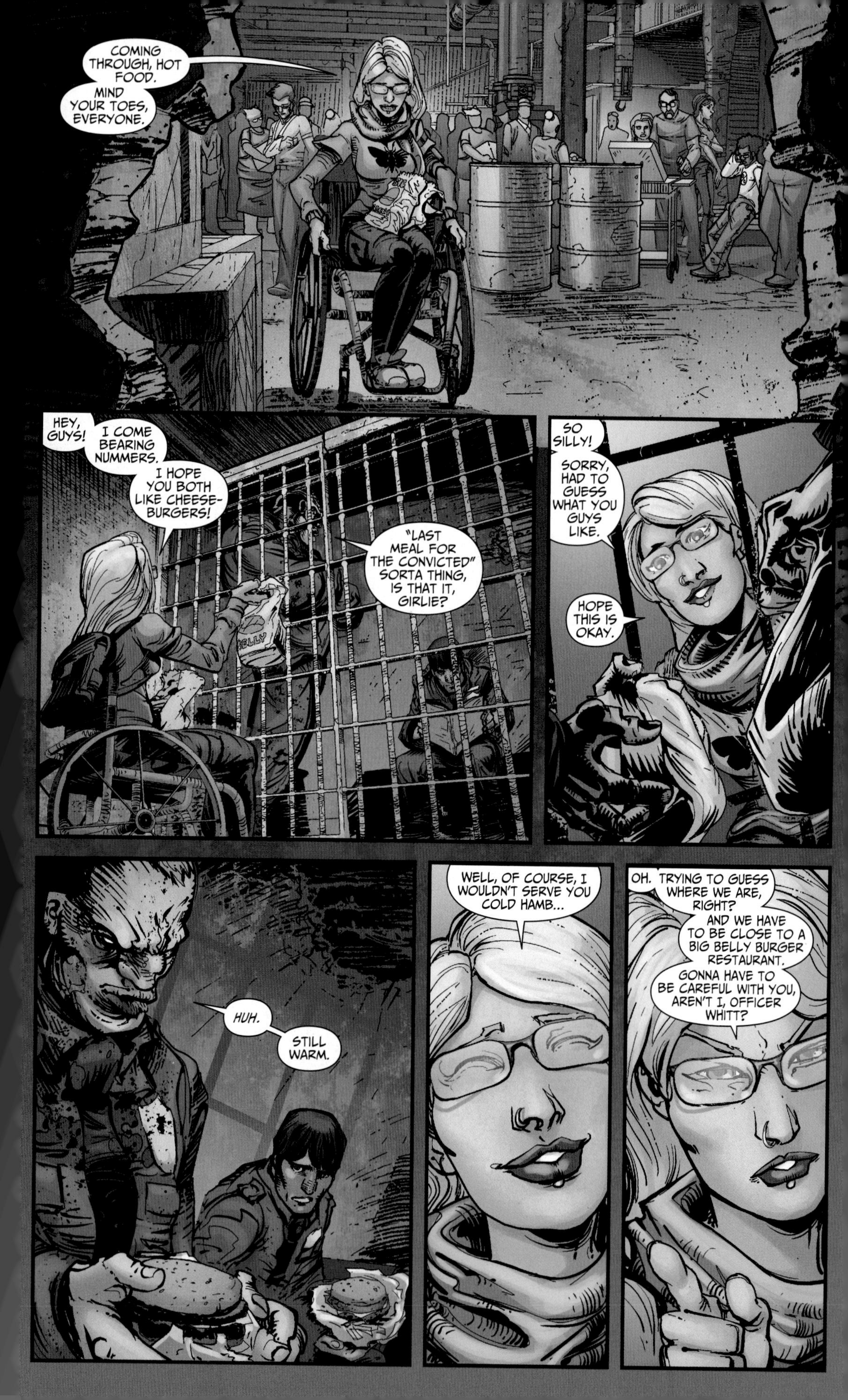
COMING THROUGH, HOT FOOD.
MIND YOUR TOES, EVERYONE.
HEY, GUYS!
I COME BEARING NUMMERS.
I HOPE YOU BOTH LIKE CHEESE-BURGERS!
"LAST MEAL FOR THE CONVICTED" SORTA THING, IS THAT IT, GIRLIE?
SO SILLY!
SORRY, HAD TO GUESS WHAT YOU GUYS LIKE.
HOPE THIS IS OKAY.
HUH.
STILL WARM.
WELL, OF COURSE, I WOULDN'T SERVE YOU COLD HAMB...
OH.
TRYING TO GUESS WHERE WE ARE, RIGHT?
AND WE HAVE TO BE CLOSE TO A BIG BELLY BURGER RESTAURANT.
GONNA HAVE TO BE CAREFUL WITH YOU, AREN'T I, OFFICER WHITT?

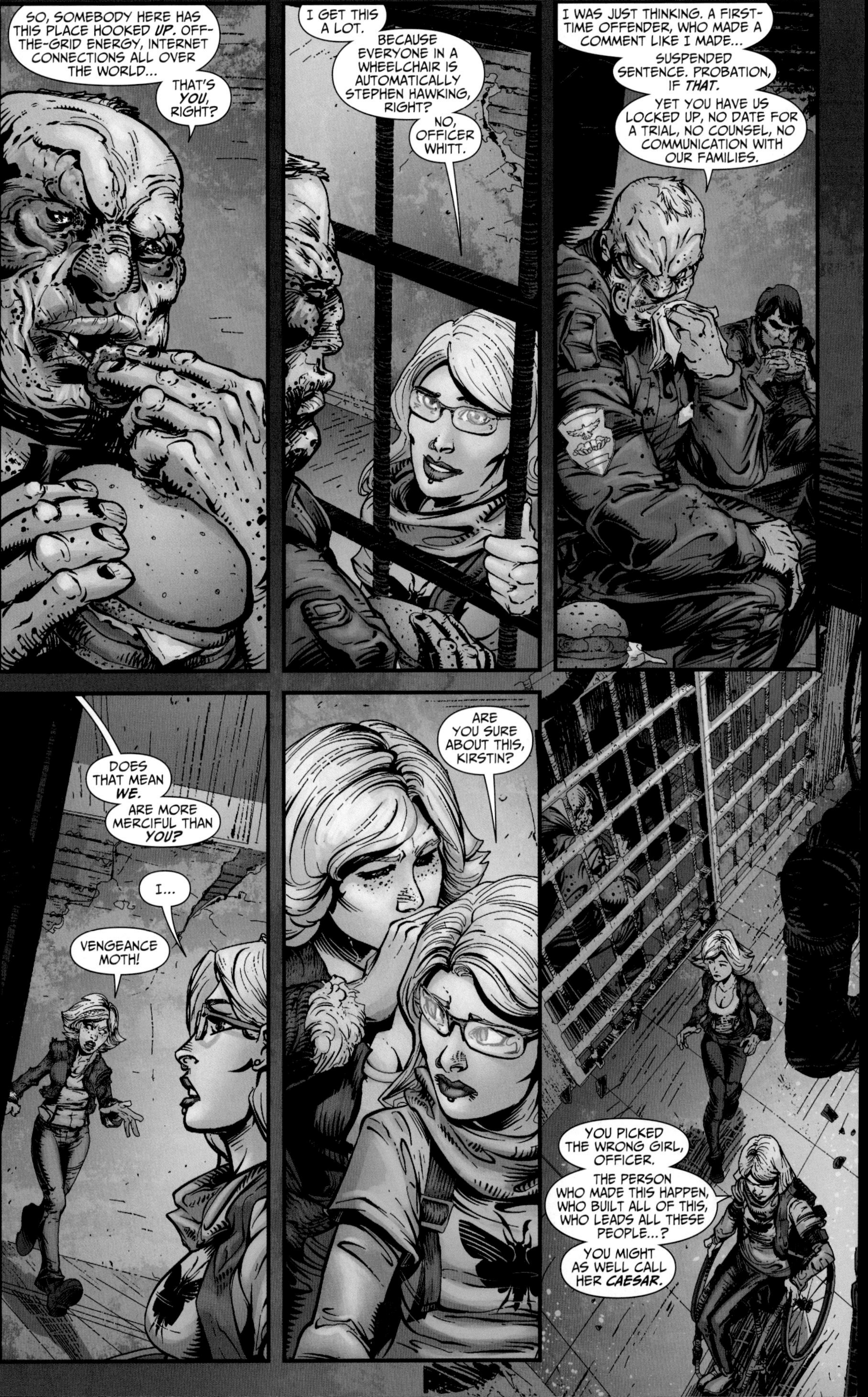

SO, SOMEBODY HERE HAS THIS PLACE HOOKED *UP*. OFF-THE-GRID ENERGY, INTERNET CONNECTIONS ALL OVER THE WORLD...
THAT'S *YOU*, RIGHT?
I GET THIS A LOT.
BECAUSE EVERYONE IN A WHEELCHAIR IS AUTOMATICALLY STEPHEN HAWKING, RIGHT?
NO, OFFICER WHITT.
I WAS JUST THINKING. A FIRST-TIME OFFENDER, WHO MADE A COMMENT LIKE I MADE...
SUSPENDED SENTENCE. PROBATION, IF *THAT.*
YET YOU HAVE US LOCKED UP, NO DATE FOR A TRIAL, NO COUNSEL, NO COMMUNICATION WITH OUR FAMILIES.
DOES THAT MEAN *WE*...
ARE MORE MERCIFUL THAN *YOU?*
I...
VENGEANCE MOTH!
ARE YOU SURE ABOUT THIS, KIRSTIN?
YOU PICKED THE WRONG GIRL, OFFICER.
THE PERSON WHO MADE THIS HAPPEN, WHO BUILT ALL OF THIS, WHO LEADS ALL THESE PEOPLE...?
YOU MIGHT AS WELL CALL HER *CAESAR.*

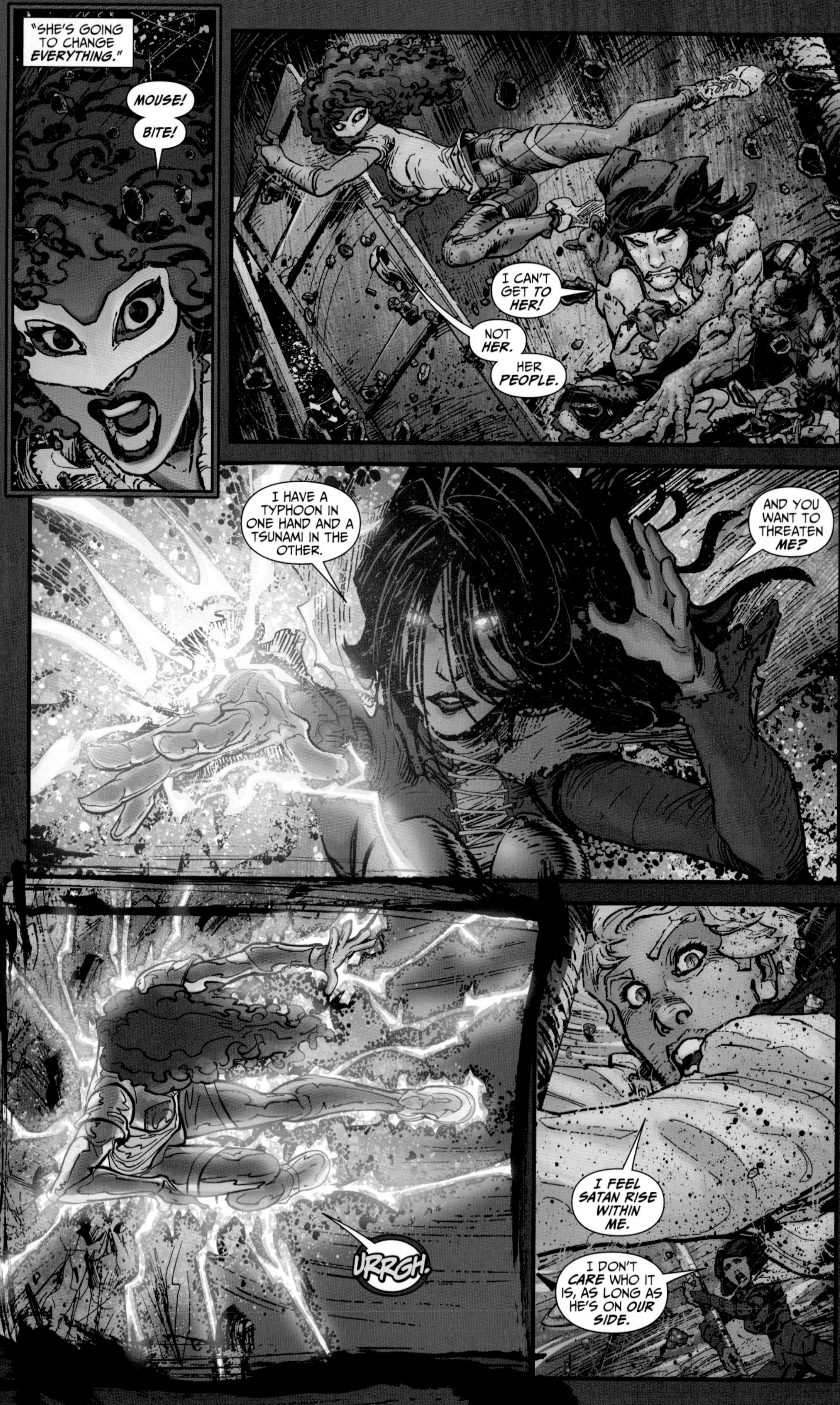
"SHE'S GOING TO CHANGE EVERYTHING."
MOUSE!
BITE!
I CAN'T GET TO HER!
NOT HER.
HER PEOPLE.
I HAVE A TYPHOON IN ONE HAND AND A TSUNAMI IN THE OTHER.
AND YOU WANT TO THREATEN ME?
URRGH.
I FEEL SATAN RISE WITHIN ME.
I DON'T CARE WHO IT IS, AS LONG AS HE'S ON OUR SIDE.

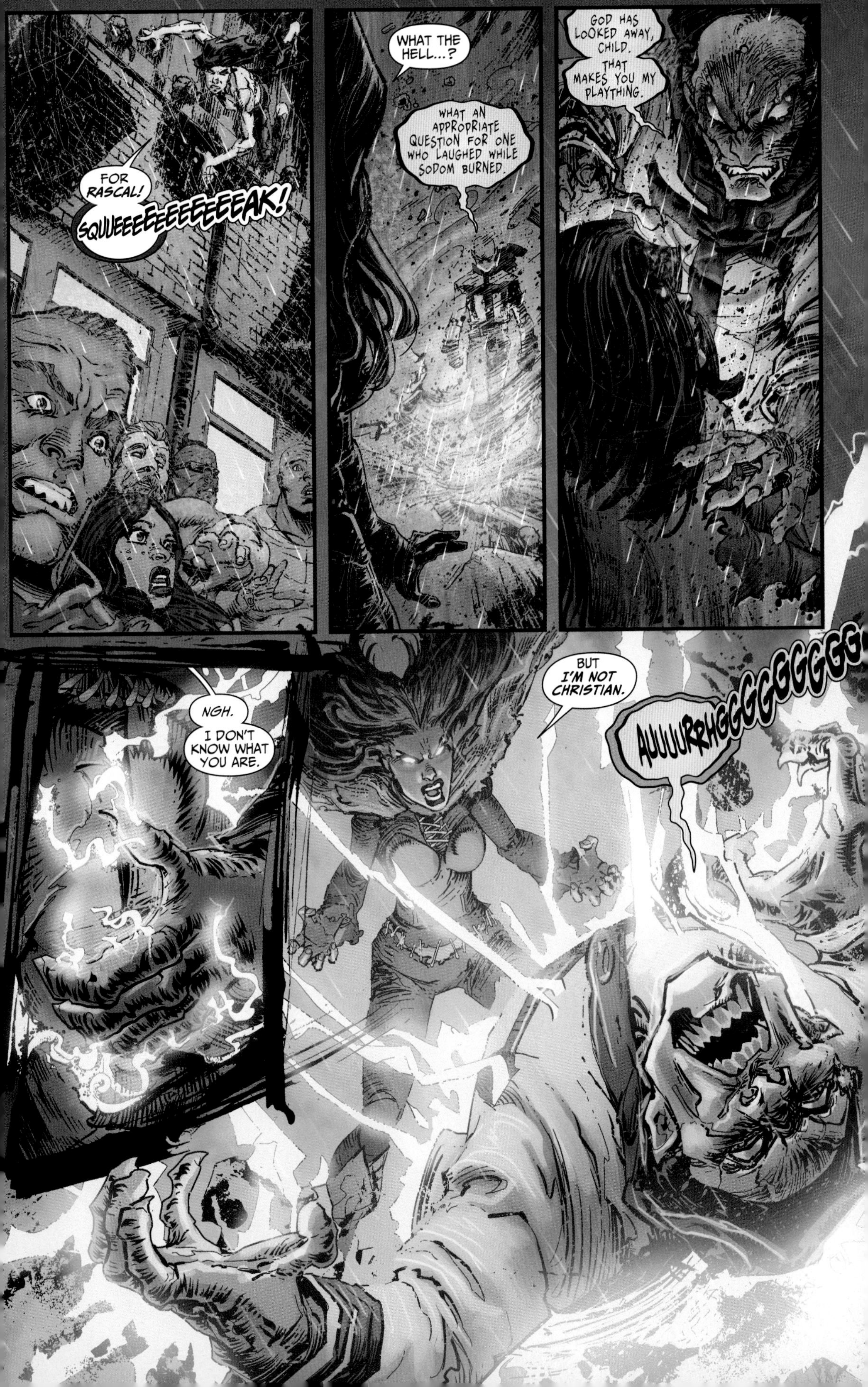
FOR RASCAL!
SQUEEEEEEEEEEEEAK!
WHAT THE HELL...?
WHAT AN APPROPRIATE QUESTION FOR ONE WHO LAUGHED WHILE SODOM BURNED.
GOD HAS LOOKED AWAY, CHILD.
THAT MAKES YOU MY PLAYTHING.
NGH.
I DON'T KNOW WHAT YOU ARE.
BUT I'M NOT CHRISTIAN.
AUUUURRHGGGGGGGGG

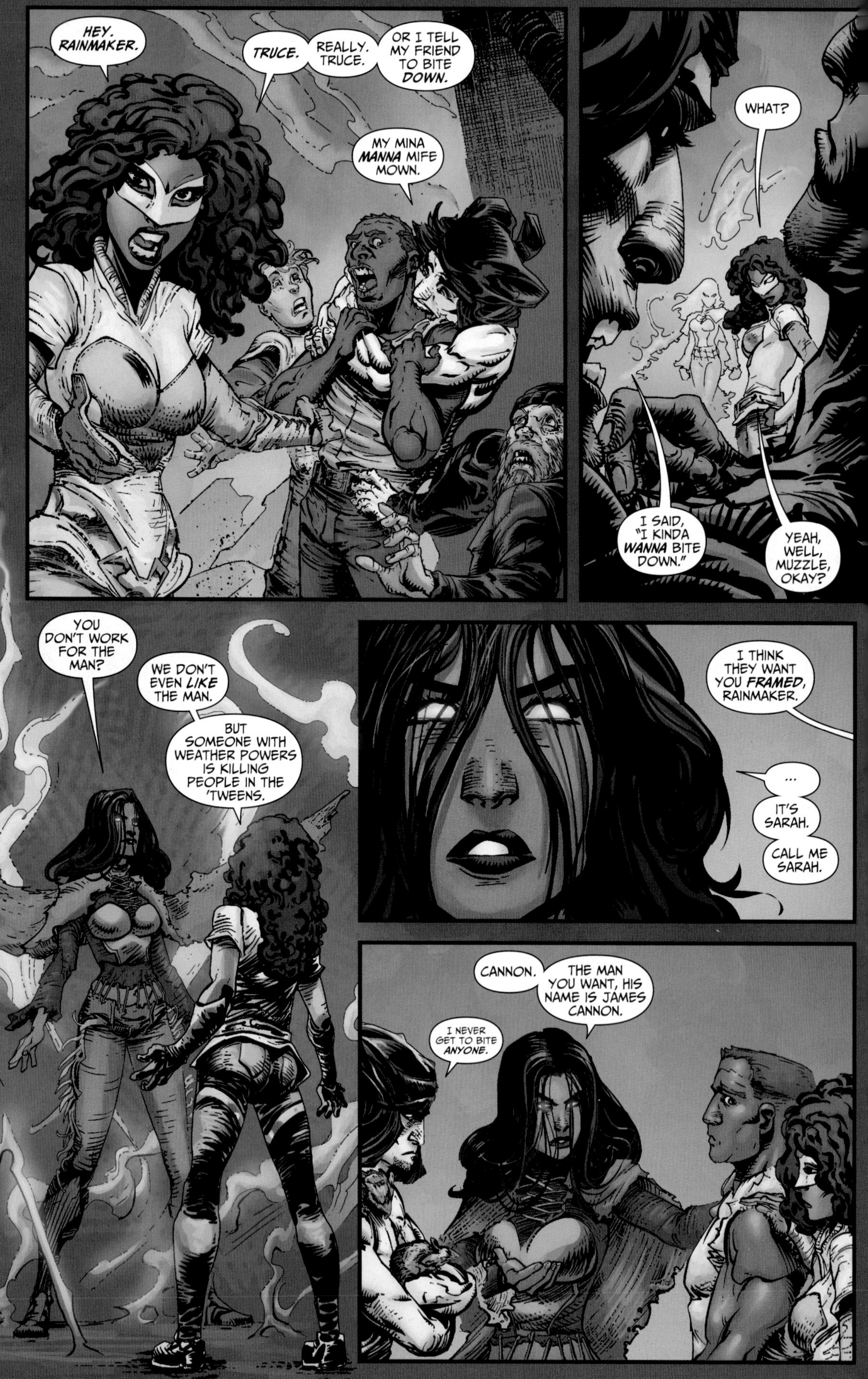

HEY. RAINMAKER.
TRUCE.
REALLY. TRUCE.
OR I TELL MY FRIEND TO BITE DOWN.
MY MINA MANNA MIFE MOWN.
WHAT?
I SAID, "I KINDA WANNA BITE DOWN."
YEAH, WELL, MUZZLE, OKAY?
YOU DON'T WORK FOR THE MAN?
WE DON'T EVEN LIKE THE MAN.
BUT SOMEONE WITH WEATHER POWERS IS KILLING PEOPLE IN THE 'TWEENS.
I THINK THEY WANT YOU FRAMED, RAINMAKER.
...
IT'S SARAH.
CALL ME SARAH.
CANNON.
THE MAN YOU WANT, HIS NAME IS JAMES CANNON.
I NEVER GET TO BITE ANYONE.

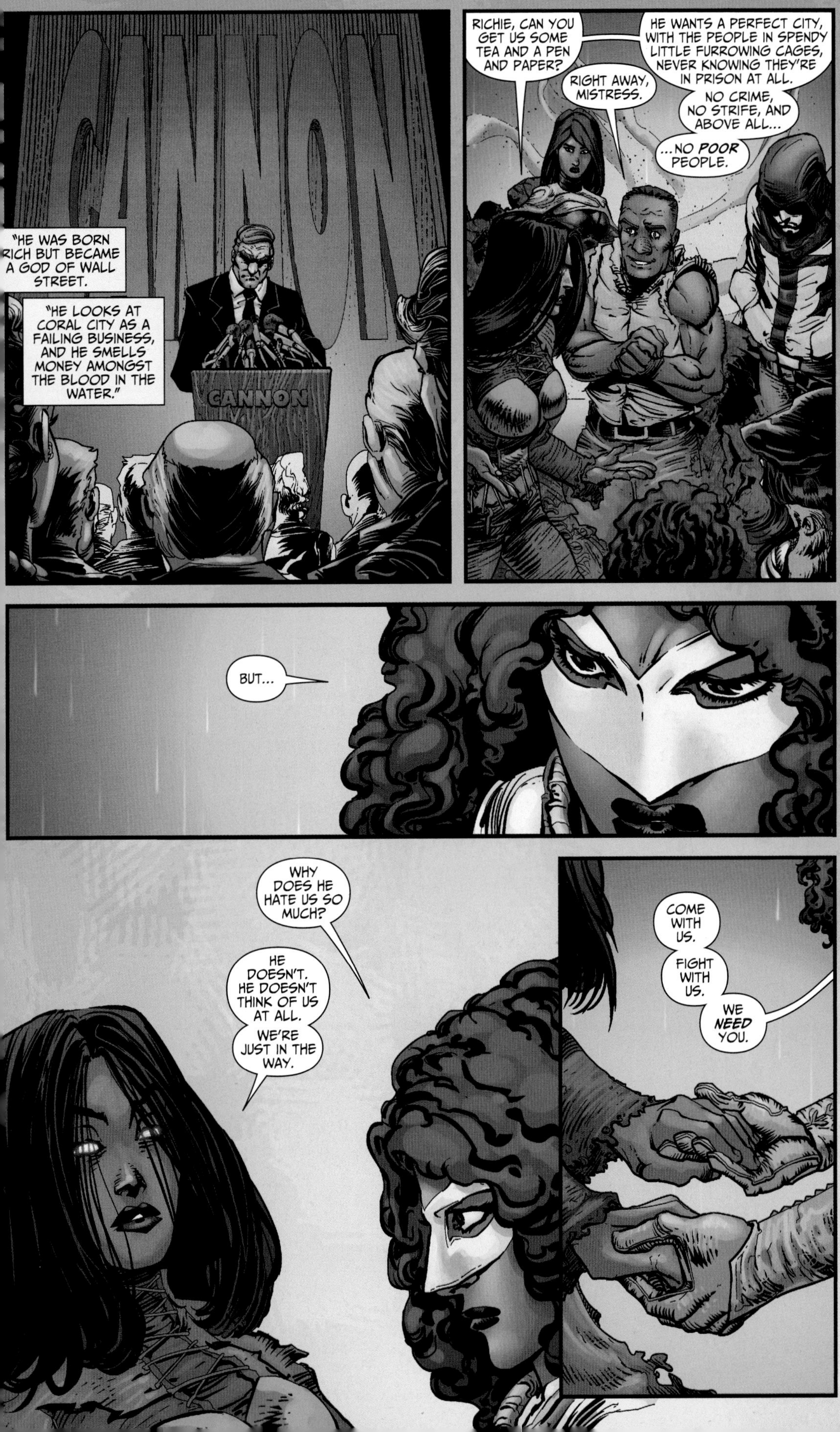
CANNON
"HE WAS BORN RICH BUT BECAME A GOD OF WALL STREET.
"HE LOOKS AT CORAL CITY AS A FAILING BUSINESS, AND HE SMELLS MONEY AMONGST THE BLOOD IN THE WATER."
CANNON
RICHIE, CAN YOU GET US SOME TEA AND A PEN AND PAPER?
HE WANTS A PERFECT CITY, WITH THE PEOPLE IN SPENDY LITTLE FURROWING CAGES, NEVER KNOWING THEY'RE IN PRISON AT ALL.
RIGHT AWAY, MISTRESS.
NO CRIME, NO STRIFE, AND ABOVE ALL...
...NO POOR PEOPLE.
BUT...
WHY DOES HE HATE US SO MUCH?
HE DOESN'T. HE DOESN'T THINK OF US AT ALL.
WE'RE JUST IN THE WAY.
COME WITH US.
FIGHT WITH US.
WE NEED YOU.

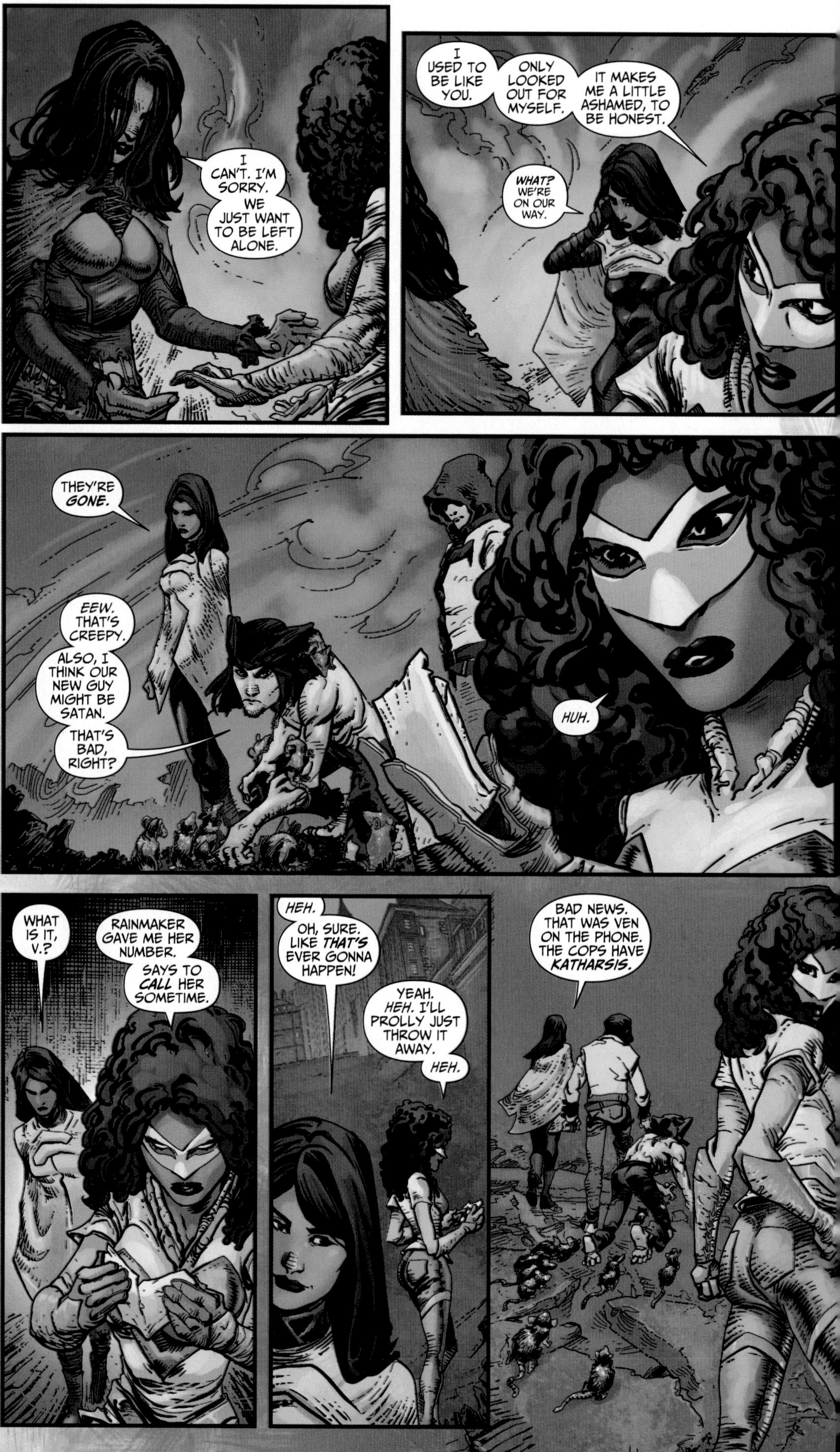
I CAN'T. I'M SORRY.
WE JUST WANT TO BE LEFT ALONE.
I USED TO BE LIKE YOU.
ONLY LOOKED OUT FOR MYSELF.
IT MAKES ME A LITTLE ASHAMED, TO BE HONEST.
WHAT? WE'RE ON OUR WAY.
THEY'RE GONE.
EEW. THAT'S CREEPY.
ALSO, I THINK OUR NEW GUY MIGHT BE SATAN.
THAT'S BAD, RIGHT?
HUH.
WHAT IS IT, V.?
RAINMAKER GAVE ME HER NUMBER.
SAYS TO CALL HER SOMETIME.
HEH.
OH, SURE. LIKE THAT'S EVER GONNA HAPPEN!
YEAH. HEH. I'LL PROLLY JUST THROW IT AWAY.
HEH.
BAD NEWS. THAT WAS VEN ON THE PHONE. THE COPS HAVE KATHARSIS.

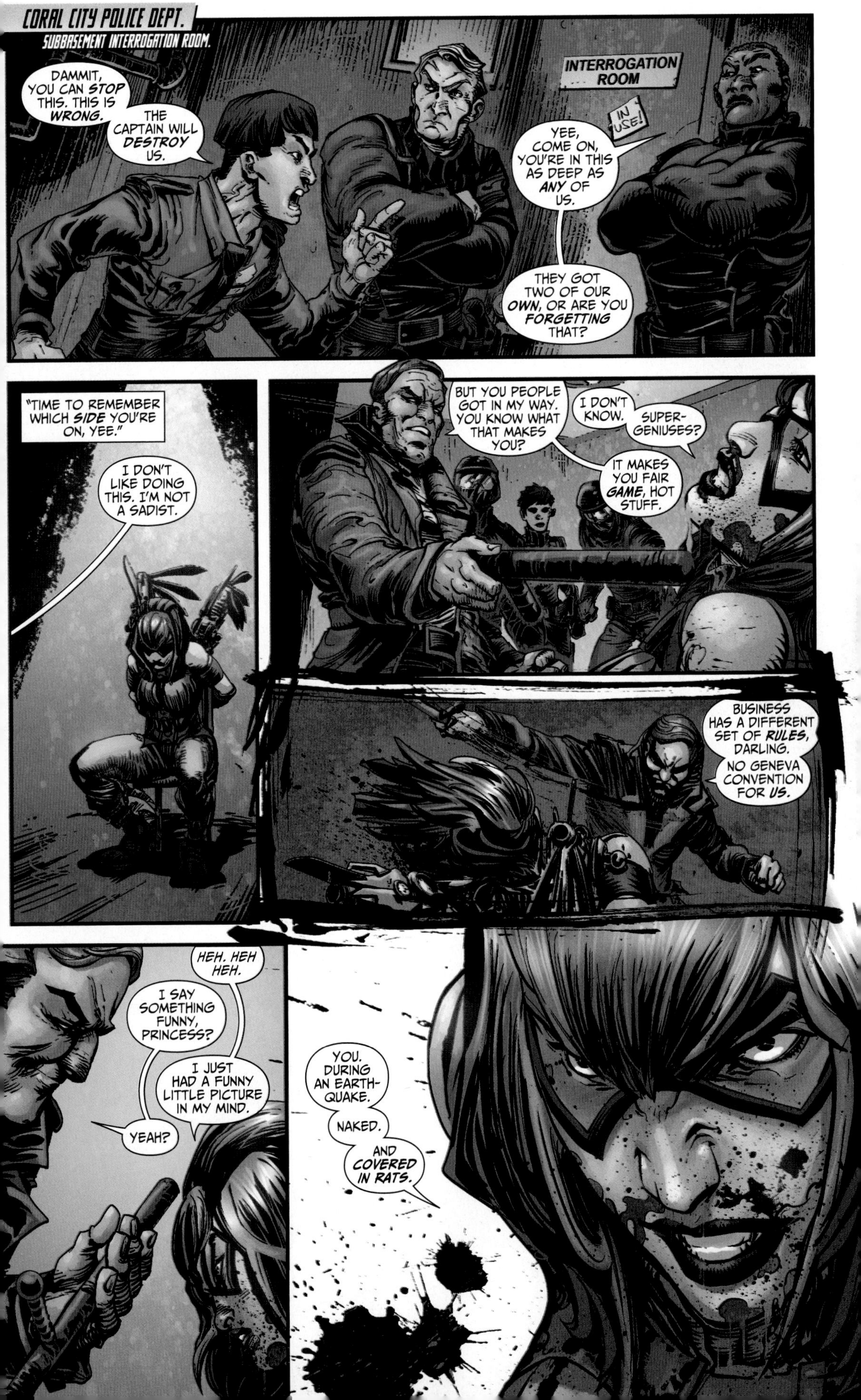
CORAL CITY POLICE DEPT.
SUBBASEMENT INTERROGATION ROOM.
DAMMIT, YOU CAN STOP THIS. THIS IS WRONG.
THE CAPTAIN WILL DESTROY US.
INTERROGATION ROOM
IN USE!
YEE, COME ON, YOU'RE IN THIS AS DEEP AS ANY OF US.
THEY GOT TWO OF OUR OWN, OR ARE YOU FORGETTING THAT?
"TIME TO REMEMBER WHICH SIDE YOU'RE ON, YEE."
I DON'T LIKE DOING THIS. I'M NOT A SADIST.
BUT YOU PEOPLE GOT IN MY WAY. YOU KNOW WHAT THAT MAKES YOU?
I DON'T KNOW.
SUPER-GENIUSES?
IT MAKES YOU FAIR GAME, HOT STUFF.
BUSINESS HAS A DIFFERENT SET OF RULES, DARLING.
NO GENEVA CONVENTION FOR US.
HEH. HEH HEH.
I SAY SOMETHING FUNNY, PRINCESS?
I JUST HAD A FUNNY LITTLE PICTURE IN MY MIND.
YEAH?
YOU. DURING AN EARTH-QUAKE.
NAKED.
AND COVERED IN RATS.

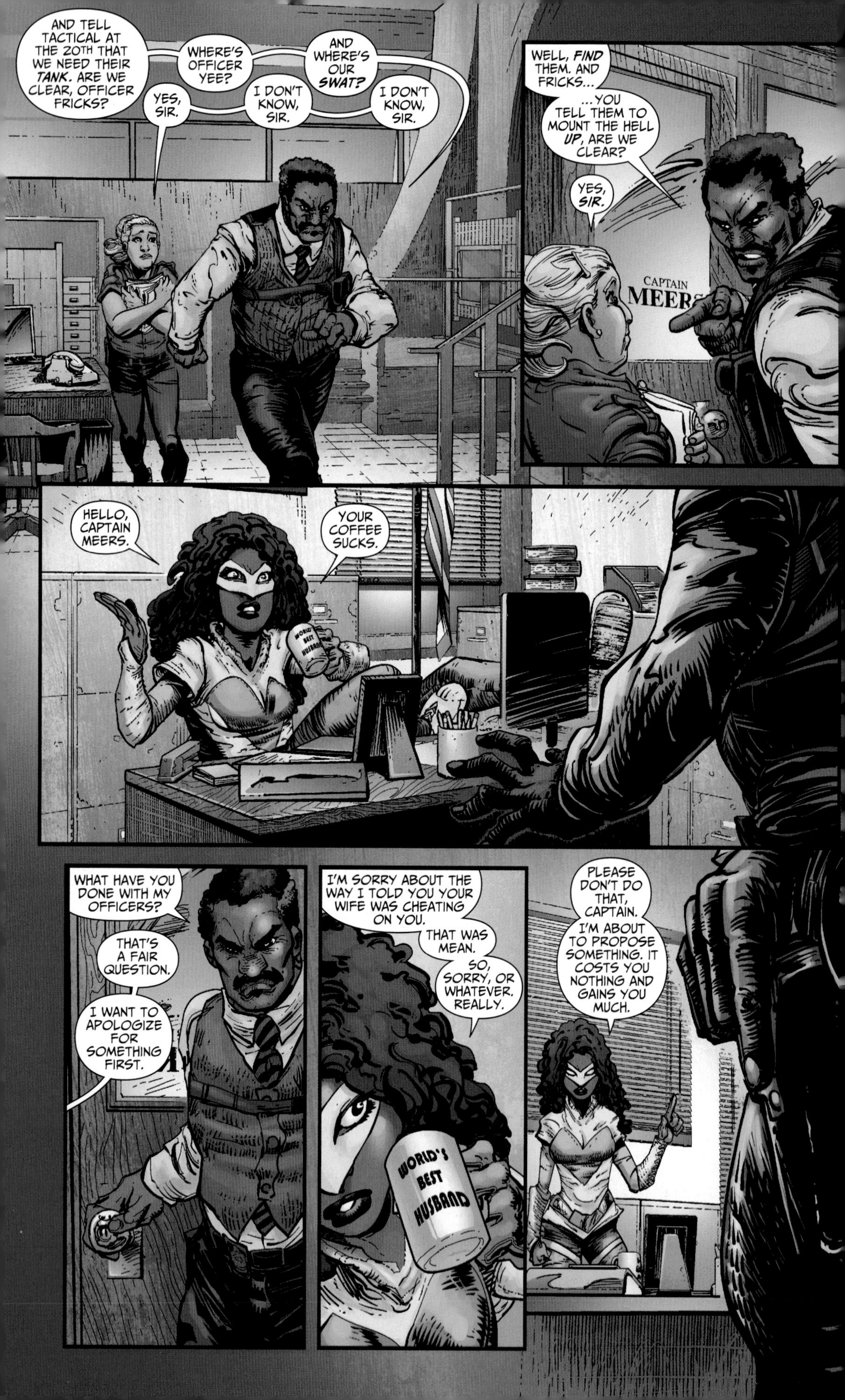
AND TELL TACTICAL AT THE 20TH THAT WE NEED THEIR *TANK*. ARE WE CLEAR, OFFICER FRICKS?
YES, SIR.
WHERE'S OFFICER YEE?
I DON'T KNOW, SIR.
AND WHERE'S OUR *SWAT?*
I DON'T KNOW, SIR.
WELL, *FIND* THEM. AND FRICKS...
...YOU TELL THEM TO MOUNT THE HELL *UP*, ARE WE CLEAR?
YES, *SIR.*
CAPTAIN MEERS
HELLO, CAPTAIN MEERS.
YOUR COFFEE SUCKS.
WORLD'S BEST HUSBAND
WHAT HAVE YOU DONE WITH MY OFFICERS?
THAT'S A FAIR QUESTION.
I WANT TO APOLOGIZE FOR SOMETHING FIRST.
I'M SORRY ABOUT THE WAY I TOLD YOU YOUR WIFE WAS CHEATING ON YOU.
THAT WAS MEAN.
SO, SORRY, OR WHATEVER. REALLY.
WORLD'S BEST HUSBAND
PLEASE DON'T DO THAT, CAPTAIN.
I'M ABOUT TO PROPOSE SOMETHING. IT COSTS YOU NOTHING AND GAINS YOU MUCH.

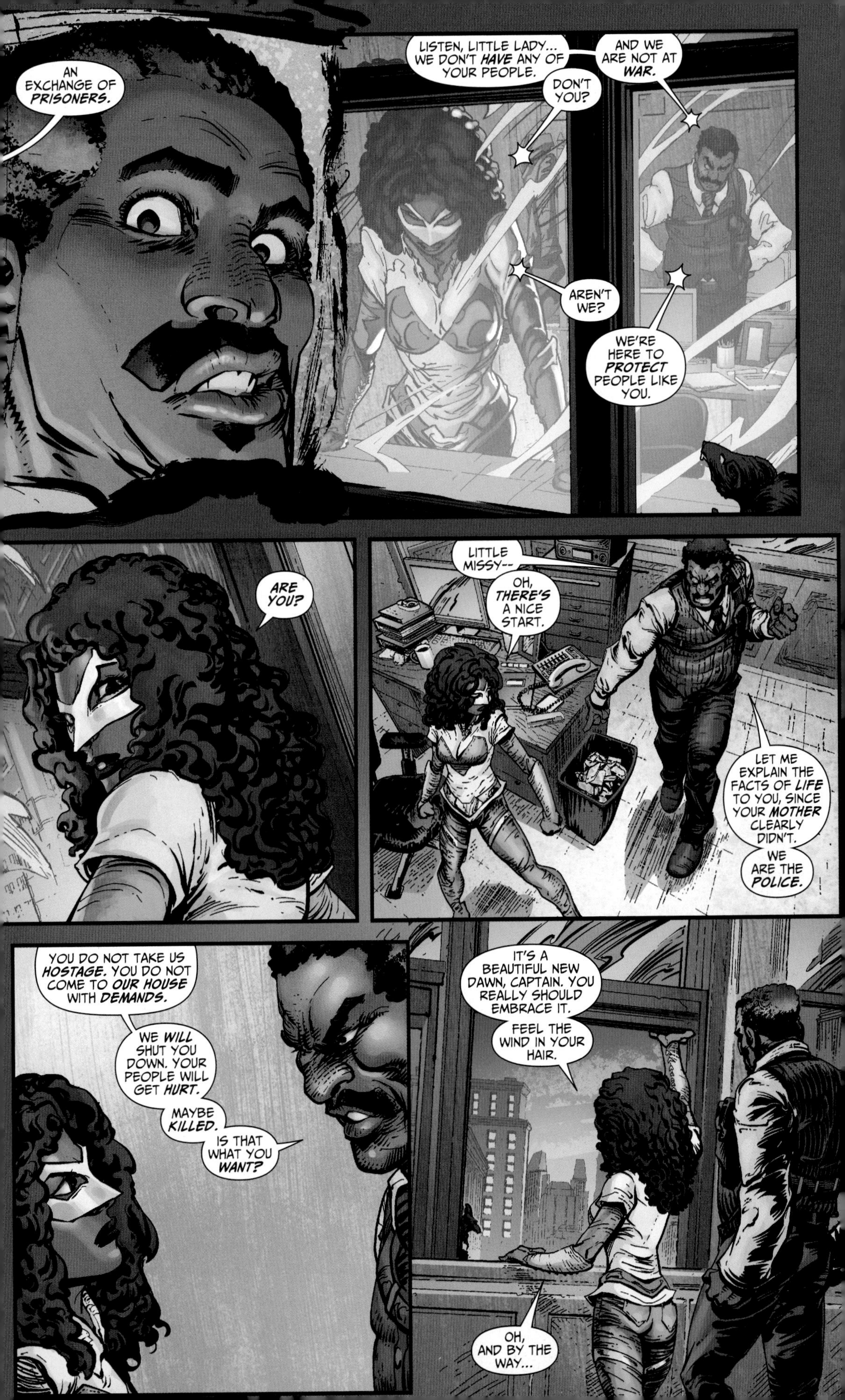
AN EXCHANGE OF PRISONERS.
LISTEN, LITTLE LADY... WE DON'T HAVE ANY OF YOUR PEOPLE.
AND WE ARE NOT AT WAR.
DON'T YOU?
AREN'T WE?
WE'RE HERE TO PROTECT PEOPLE LIKE YOU.
ARE YOU?
LITTLE MISSY--
OH, THERE'S A NICE START.
LET ME EXPLAIN THE FACTS OF LIFE TO YOU, SINCE YOUR MOTHER CLEARLY DIDN'T.
WE ARE THE POLICE.
YOU DO NOT TAKE US HOSTAGE. YOU DO NOT COME TO OUR HOUSE WITH DEMANDS.
WE WILL SHUT YOU DOWN. YOUR PEOPLE WILL GET HURT.
MAYBE KILLED.
IS THAT WHAT YOU WANT?
IT'S A BEAUTIFUL NEW DAWN, CAPTAIN. YOU REALLY SHOULD EMBRACE IT.
FEEL THE WIND IN YOUR HAIR.
OH, AND BY THE WAY...

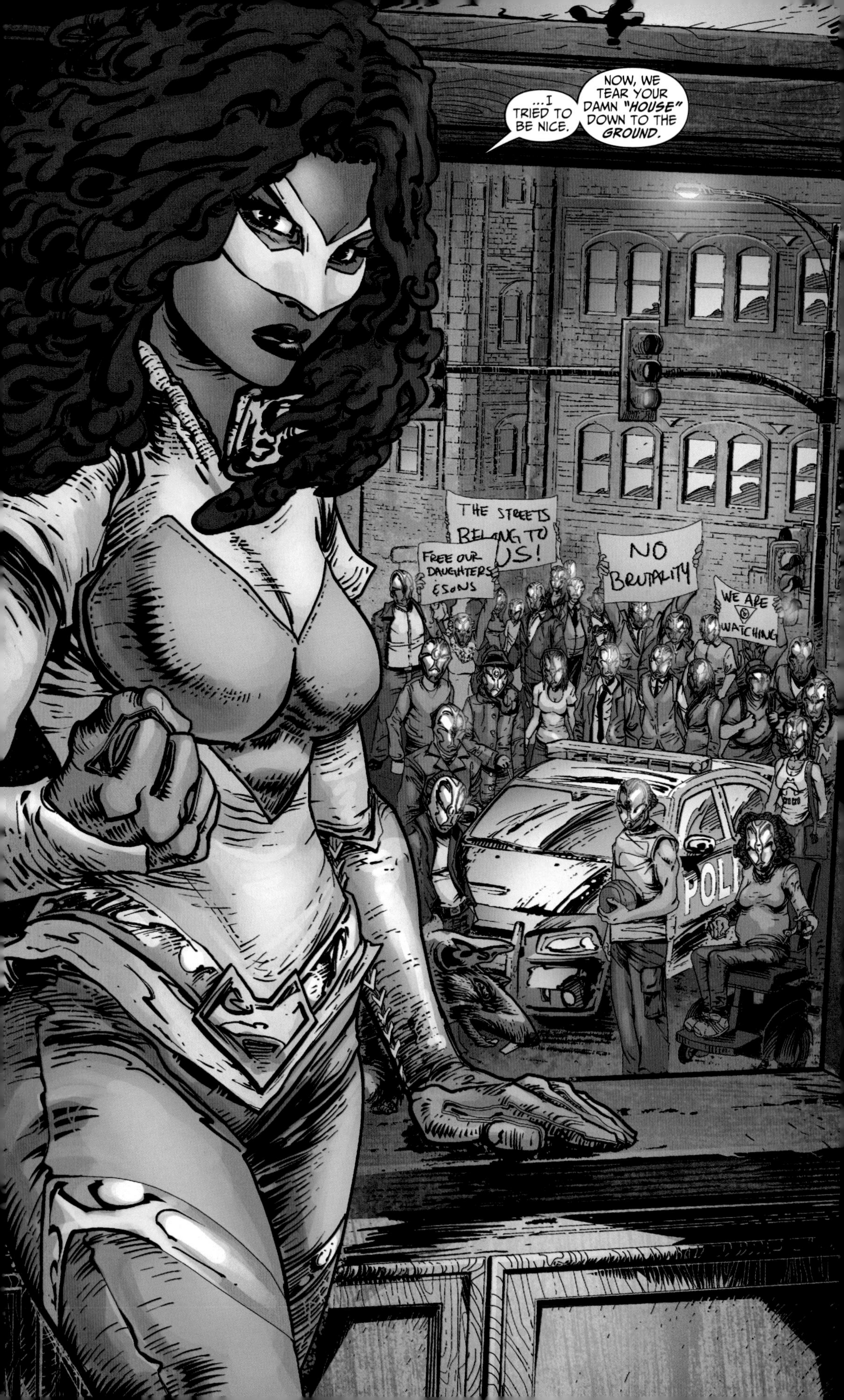
...I TRIED TO BE NICE.
NOW, WE TEAR YOUR DAMN "HOUSE" DOWN TO THE GROUND.
THE STREETS BELONG TO US!
FREE OUR DAUGHTERS &SONS
NO BRUTALITY
WE ARE WATCHING
POLI

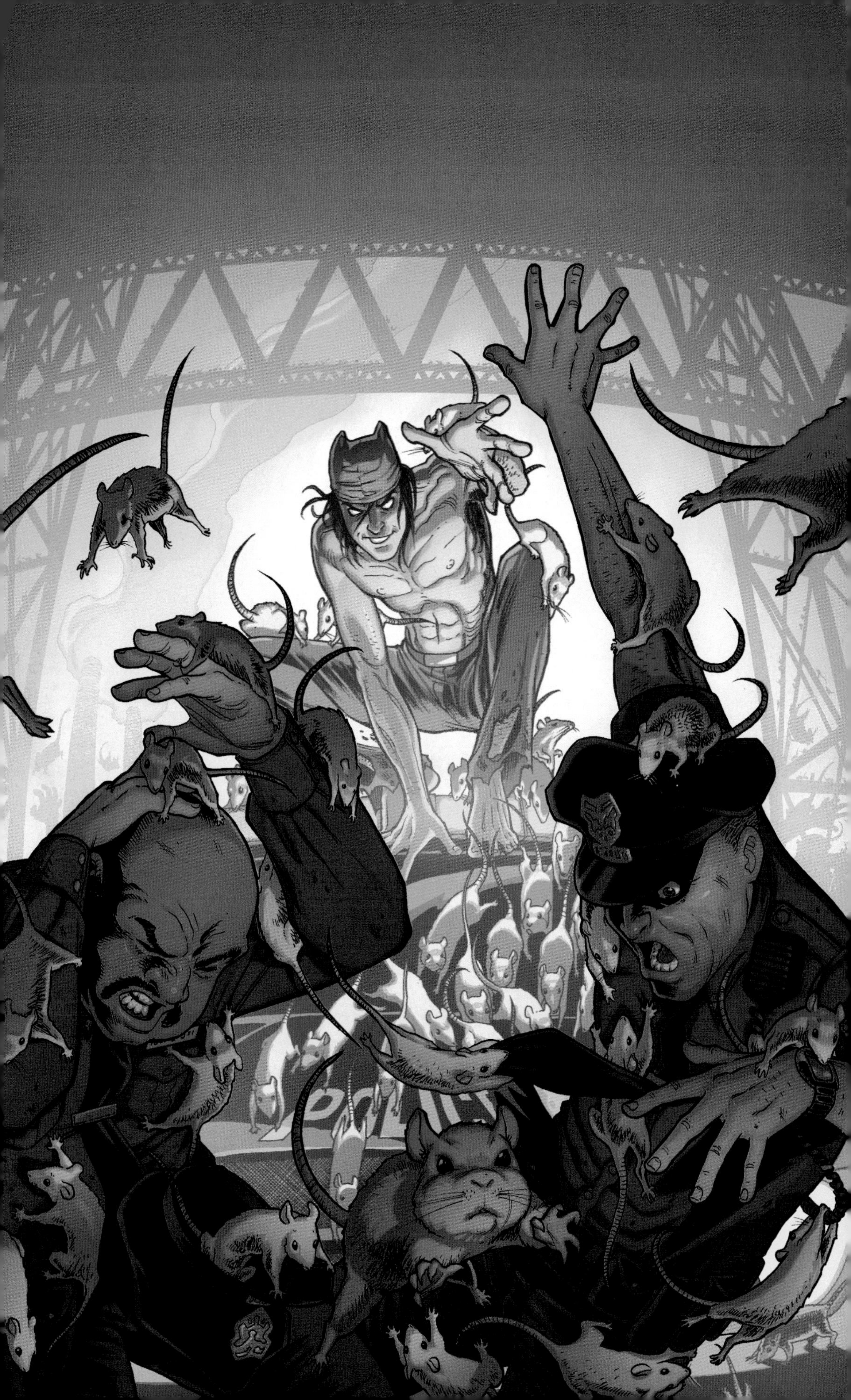

The Movement #4 cover by Amanda Conner & Dave McCaig

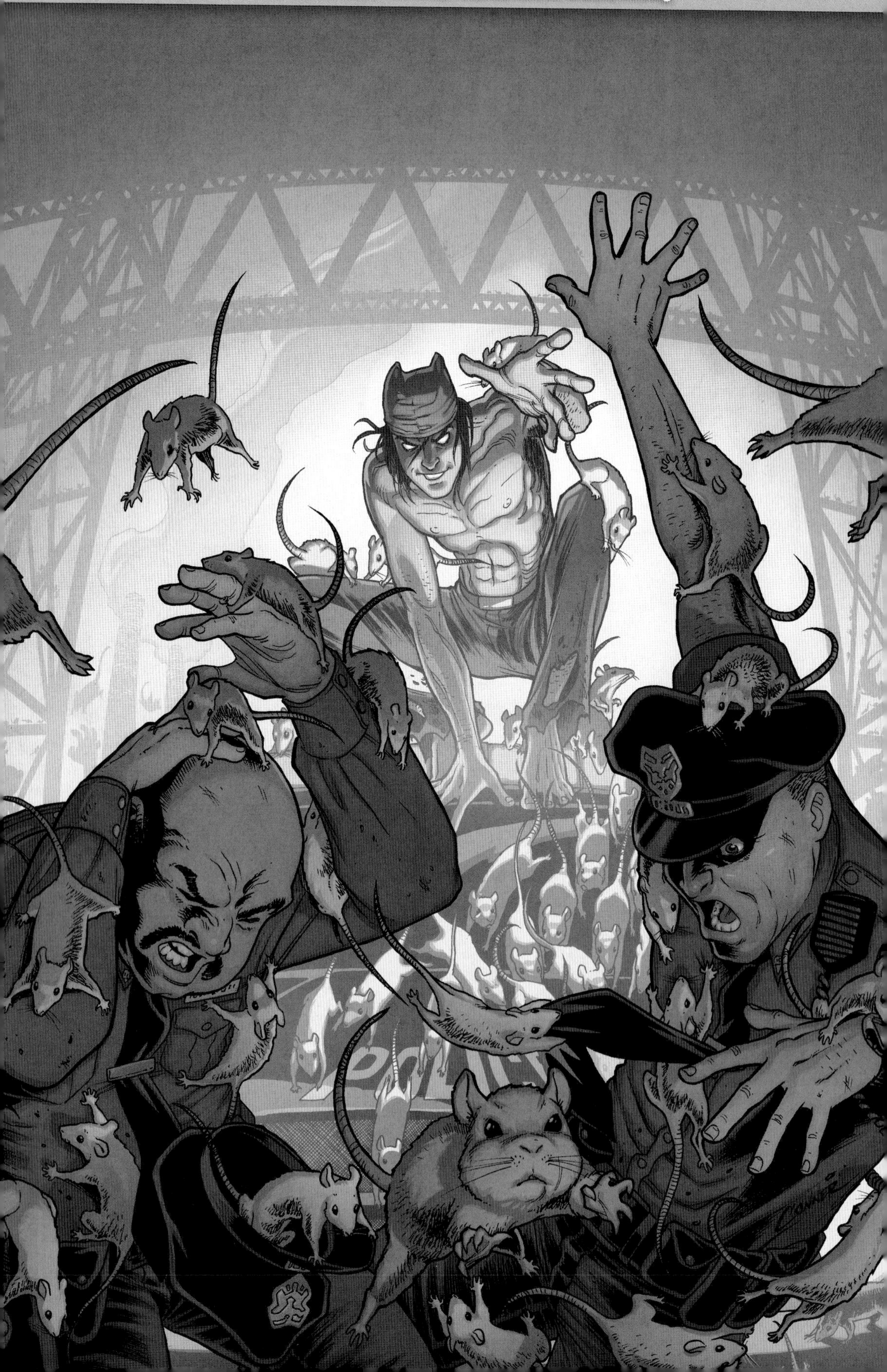

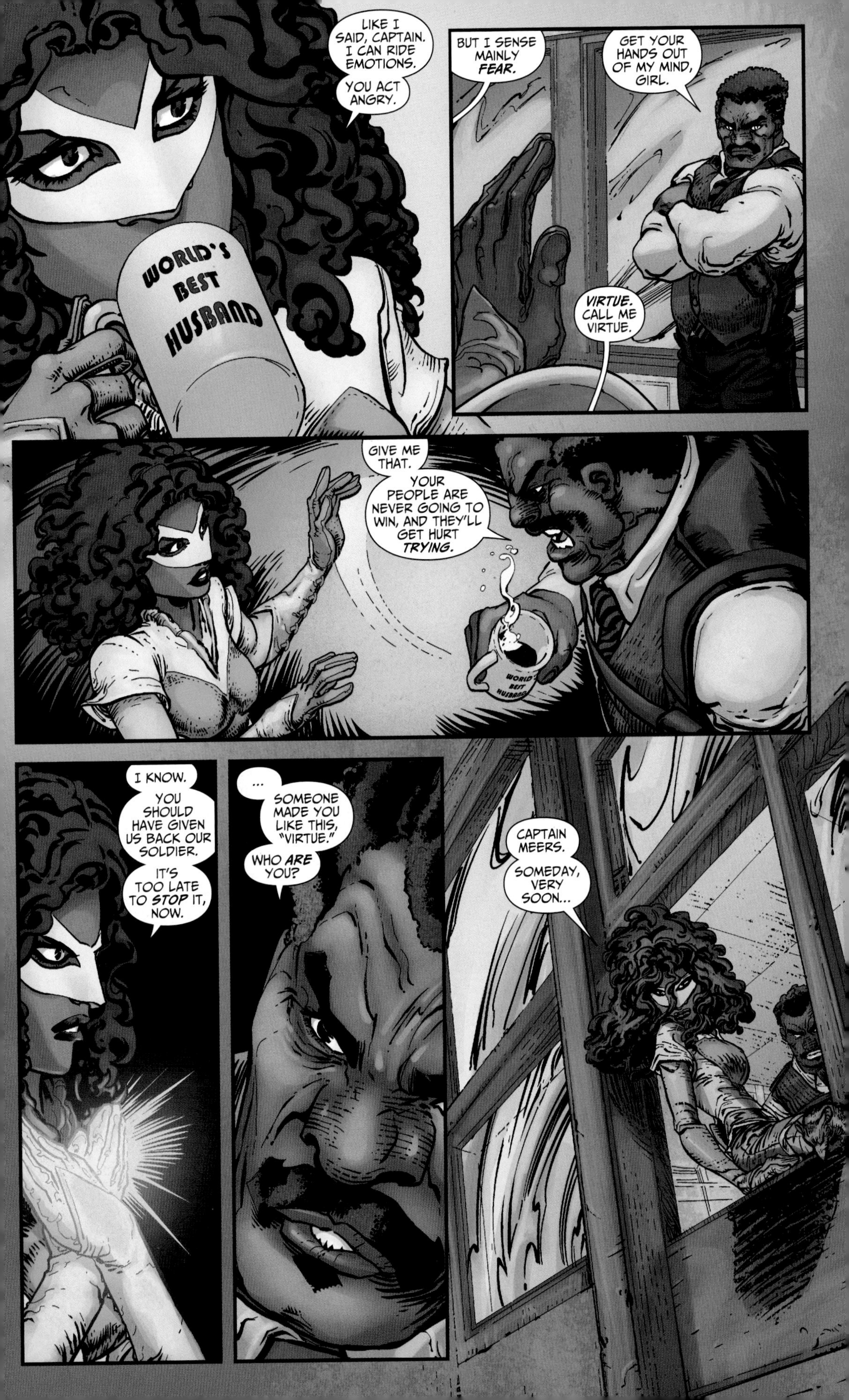
LIKE I SAID, CAPTAIN. I CAN RIDE EMOTIONS.
YOU ACT ANGRY.
WORLD'S BEST HUSBAND
BUT I SENSE MAINLY *FEAR.*
GET YOUR HANDS OUT OF MY MIND, GIRL.
VIRTUE. CALL ME VIRTUE.
GIVE ME THAT.
YOUR PEOPLE ARE NEVER GOING TO WIN, AND THEY'LL GET HURT *TRYING.*
WORLD'S BEST HUSBAND
I KNOW.
YOU SHOULD HAVE GIVEN US BACK OUR SOLDIER.
IT'S TOO LATE TO *STOP* IT, NOW.
...
SOMEONE MADE YOU LIKE THIS, "VIRTUE."
WHO *ARE* YOU?
CAPTAIN MEERS.
SOMEDAY, VERY SOON...

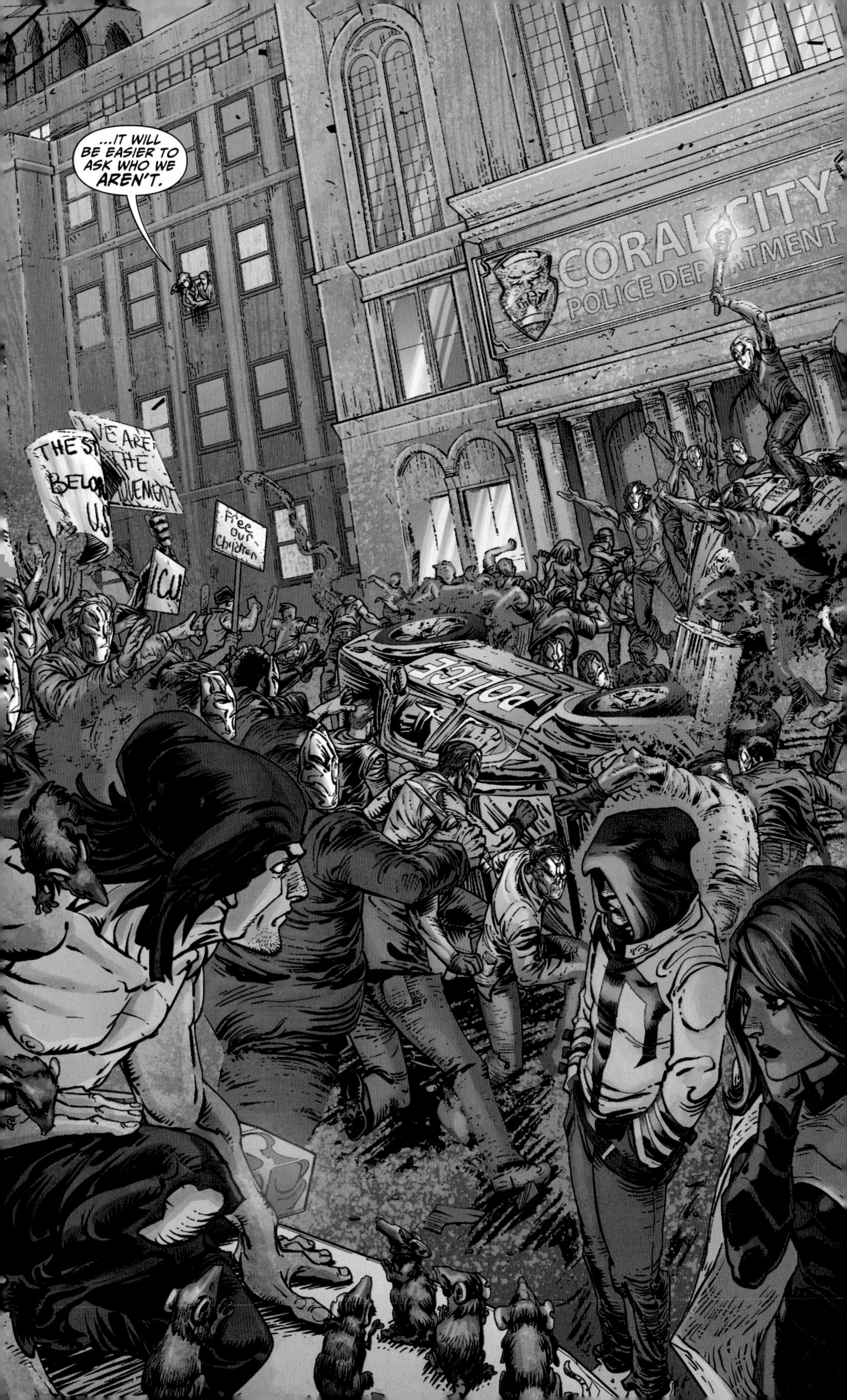
...IT WILL BE EASIER TO ASK WHO WE AREN'T.
CORAL CITY
Free our Children
POLICE

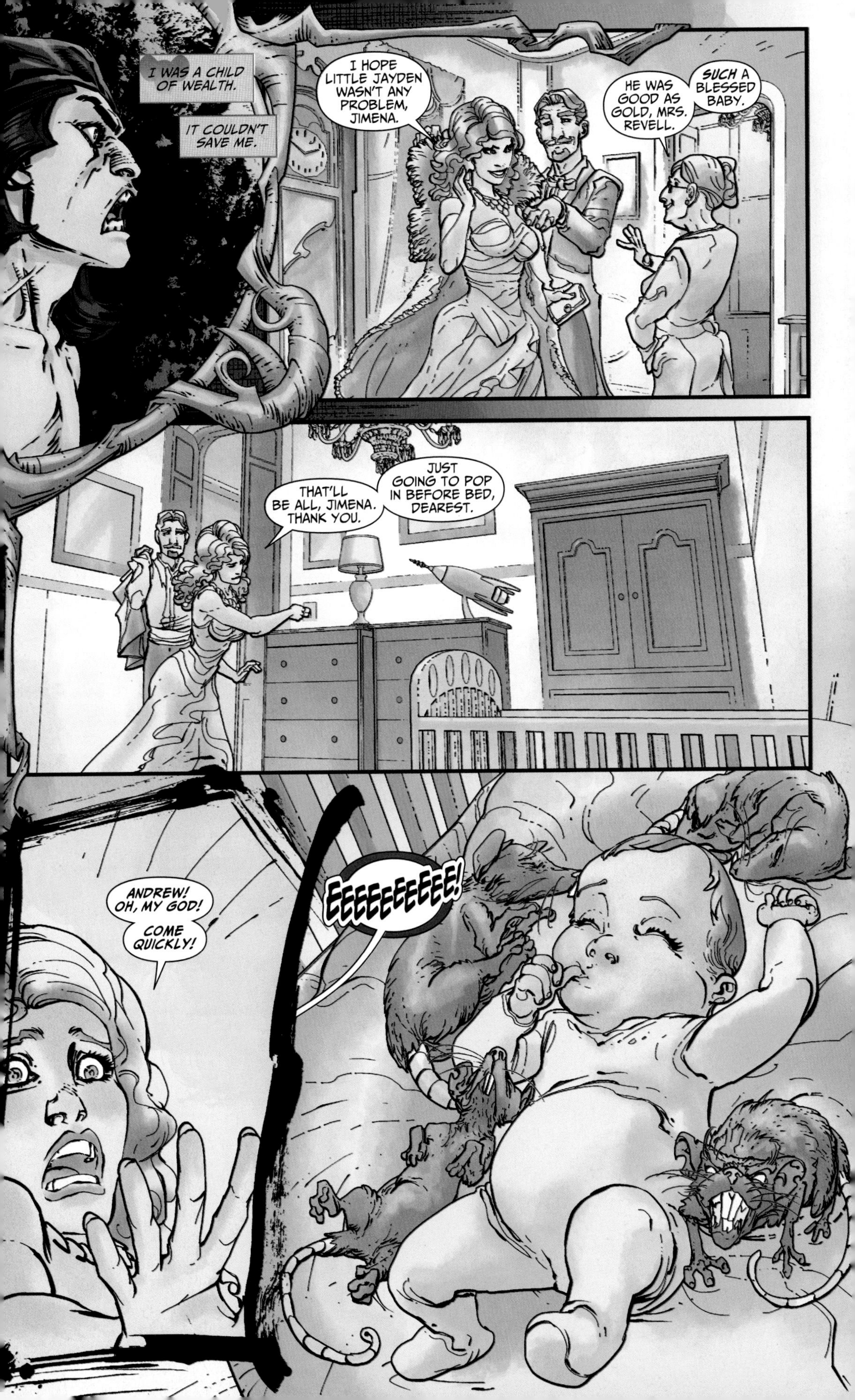
I WAS A CHILD OF WEALTH.
IT COULDN'T SAVE ME.
I HOPE LITTLE JAYDEN WASN'T ANY PROBLEM, JIMENA.
HE WAS GOOD AS GOLD, MRS. REVELL.
SUCH A BLESSED BABY.
THAT'LL BE ALL, JIMENA. THANK YOU.
JUST GOING TO POP IN BEFORE BED, DEAREST.
ANDREW! OH, MY GOD!
COME QUICKLY!
EEEEEEEEEE!

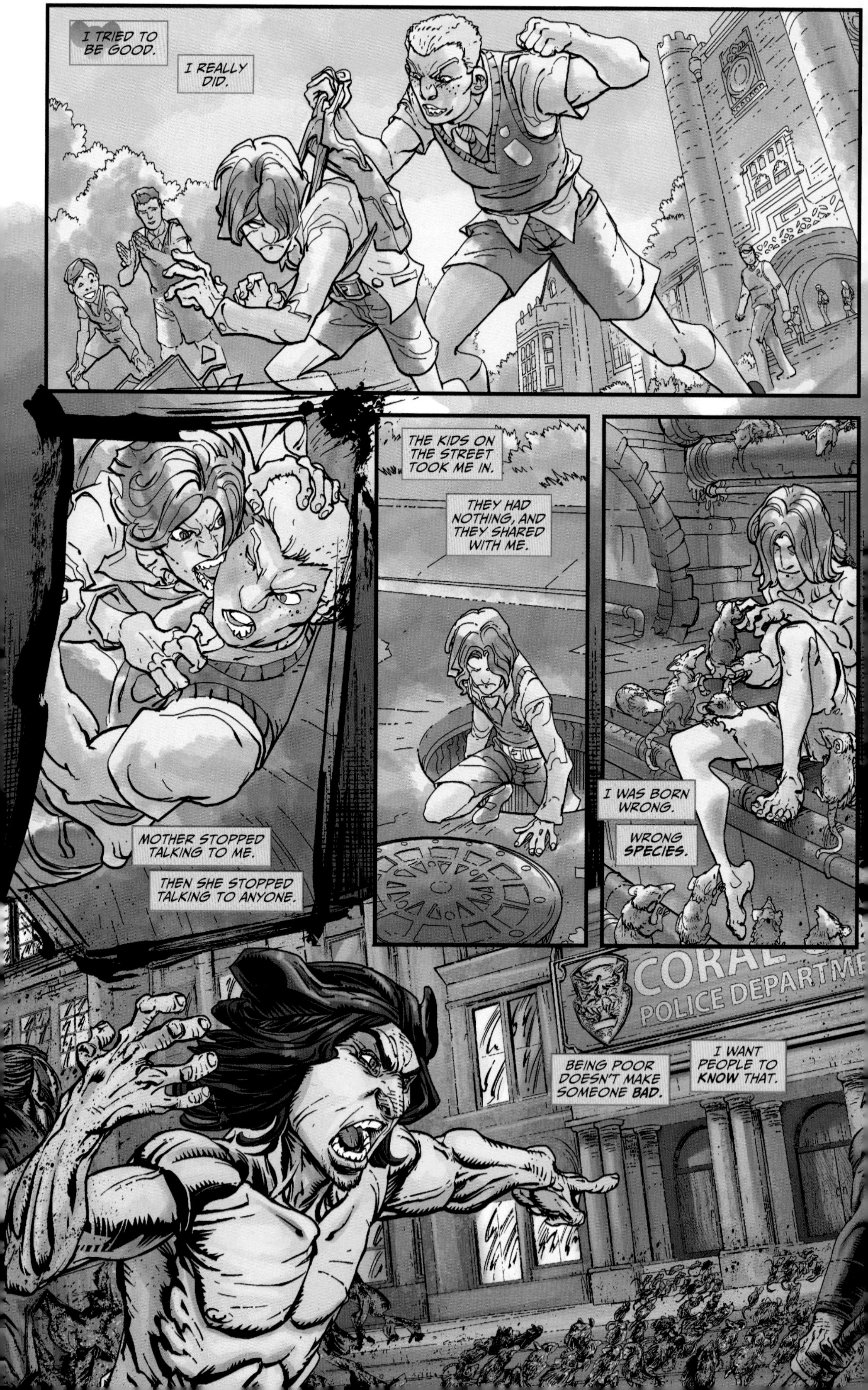
I TRIED TO BE GOOD.
I REALLY DID.
MOTHER STOPPED TALKING TO ME.
THEN SHE STOPPED TALKING TO ANYONE.
THE KIDS ON THE STREET TOOK ME IN.
THEY HAD NOTHING, AND THEY SHARED WITH ME.
I WAS BORN WRONG.
WRONG SPECIES.
CORAL
POLICE DEPARTM
BEING POOR DOESN'T MAKE SOMEONE BAD.
I WANT PEOPLE TO KNOW THAT.

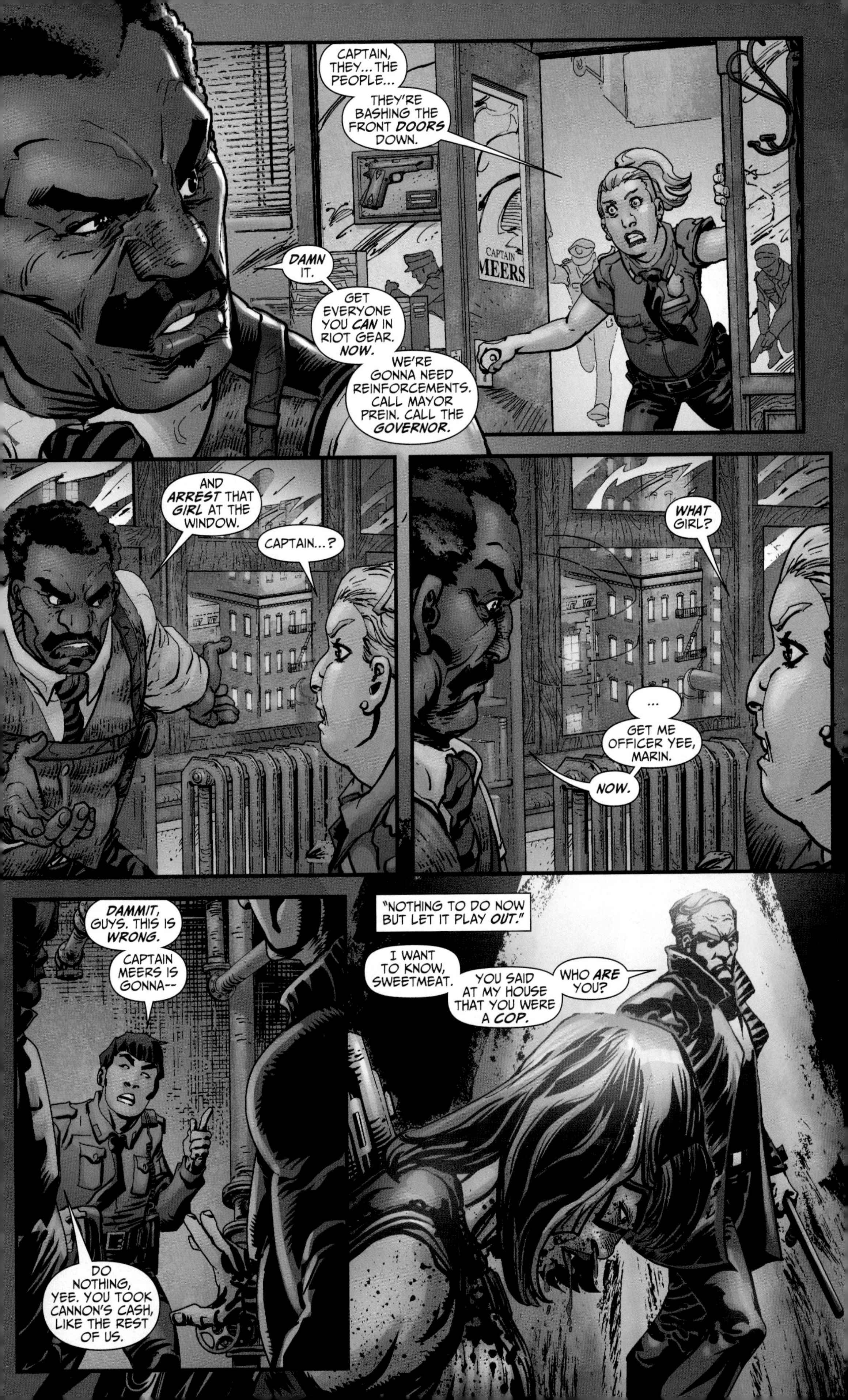
CAPTAIN, THEY... THE PEOPLE...
THEY'RE BASHING THE FRONT DOORS DOWN.
DAMN IT.
GET EVERYONE YOU CAN IN RIOT GEAR. NOW.
WE'RE GONNA NEED REINFORCEMENTS. CALL MAYOR PREIN. CALL THE GOVERNOR.
AND ARREST THAT GIRL AT THE WINDOW.
CAPTAIN...?
WHAT GIRL?
...
GET ME OFFICER YEE, MARIN.
NOW.
DAMMIT, GUYS. THIS IS WRONG.
CAPTAIN MEERS IS GONNA--
DO NOTHING, YEE. YOU TOOK CANNON'S CASH, LIKE THE REST OF US.
"NOTHING TO DO NOW BUT LET IT PLAY OUT."
I WANT TO KNOW, SWEETMEAT.
YOU SAID AT MY HOUSE THAT YOU WERE A COP.
WHO ARE YOU?

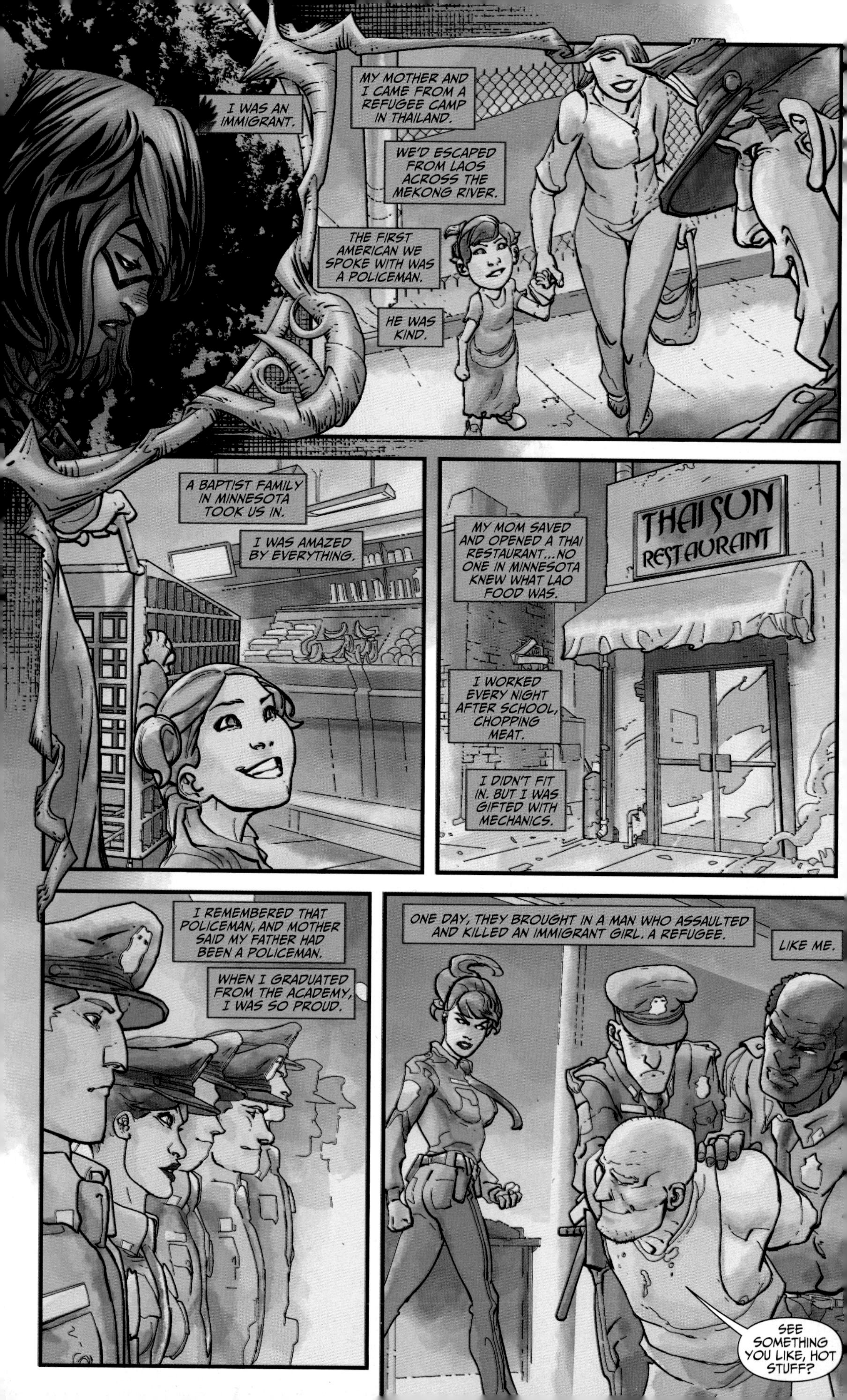
I WAS AN IMMIGRANT.
MY MOTHER AND I CAME FROM A REFUGEE CAMP IN THAILAND.
WE'D ESCAPED FROM LAOS ACROSS THE MEKONG RIVER.
THE FIRST AMERICAN WE SPOKE WITH WAS A POLICEMAN.
HE WAS KIND.
A BAPTIST FAMILY IN MINNESOTA TOOK US IN.
I WAS AMAZED BY EVERYTHING.
MY MOM SAVED AND OPENED A THAI RESTAURANT...NO ONE IN MINNESOTA KNEW WHAT LAO FOOD WAS.
THAI SUN RESTAURANT
I WORKED EVERY NIGHT AFTER SCHOOL, CHOPPING MEAT.
I DIDN'T FIT IN. BUT I WAS GIFTED WITH MECHANICS.
I REMEMBERED THAT POLICEMAN, AND MOTHER SAID MY FATHER HAD BEEN A POLICEMAN.
WHEN I GRADUATED FROM THE ACADEMY, I WAS SO PROUD.
ONE DAY, THEY BROUGHT IN A MAN WHO ASSAULTED AND KILLED AN IMMIGRANT GIRL. A REFUGEE.
LIKE ME.
SEE SOMETHING YOU LIKE, HOT STUFF?

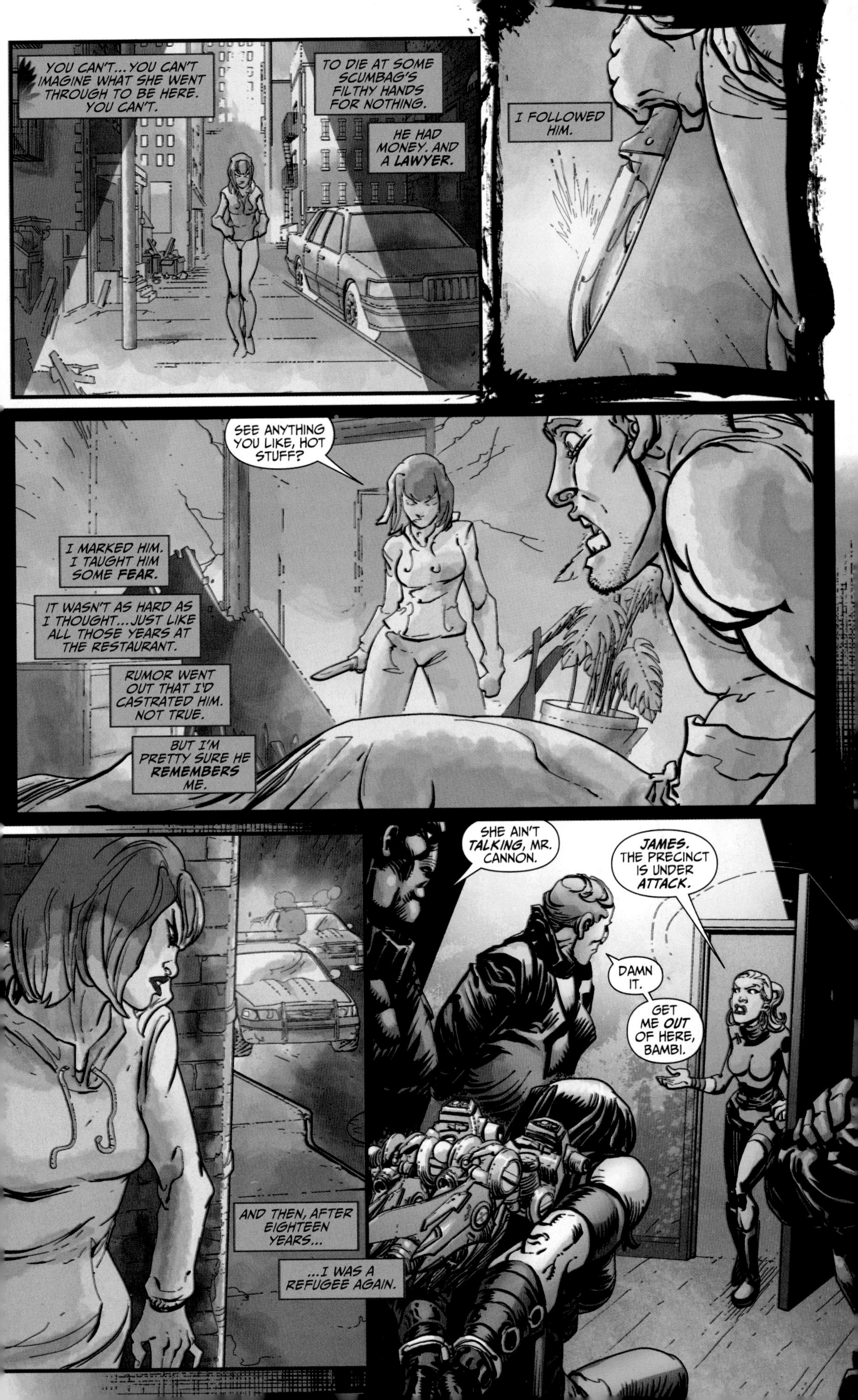
YOU CAN'T...YOU CAN'T IMAGINE WHAT SHE WENT THROUGH TO BE HERE. YOU CAN'T.
TO DIE AT SOME SCUMBAG'S FILTHY HANDS FOR NOTHING.
HE HAD MONEY. AND A LAWYER.
I FOLLOWED HIM.
SEE ANYTHING YOU LIKE, HOT STUFF?
I MARKED HIM. I TAUGHT HIM SOME FEAR.
IT WASN'T AS HARD AS I THOUGHT...JUST LIKE ALL THOSE YEARS AT THE RESTAURANT.
RUMOR WENT OUT THAT I'D CASTRATED HIM. NOT TRUE.
BUT I'M PRETTY SURE HE REMEMBERS ME.
AND THEN, AFTER EIGHTEEN YEARS...
...I WAS A REFUGEE AGAIN.
SHE AIN'T TALKING, MR. CANNON.
JAMES. THE PRECINCT IS UNDER ATTACK.
DAMN IT.
GET ME OUT OF HERE, BAMBI.

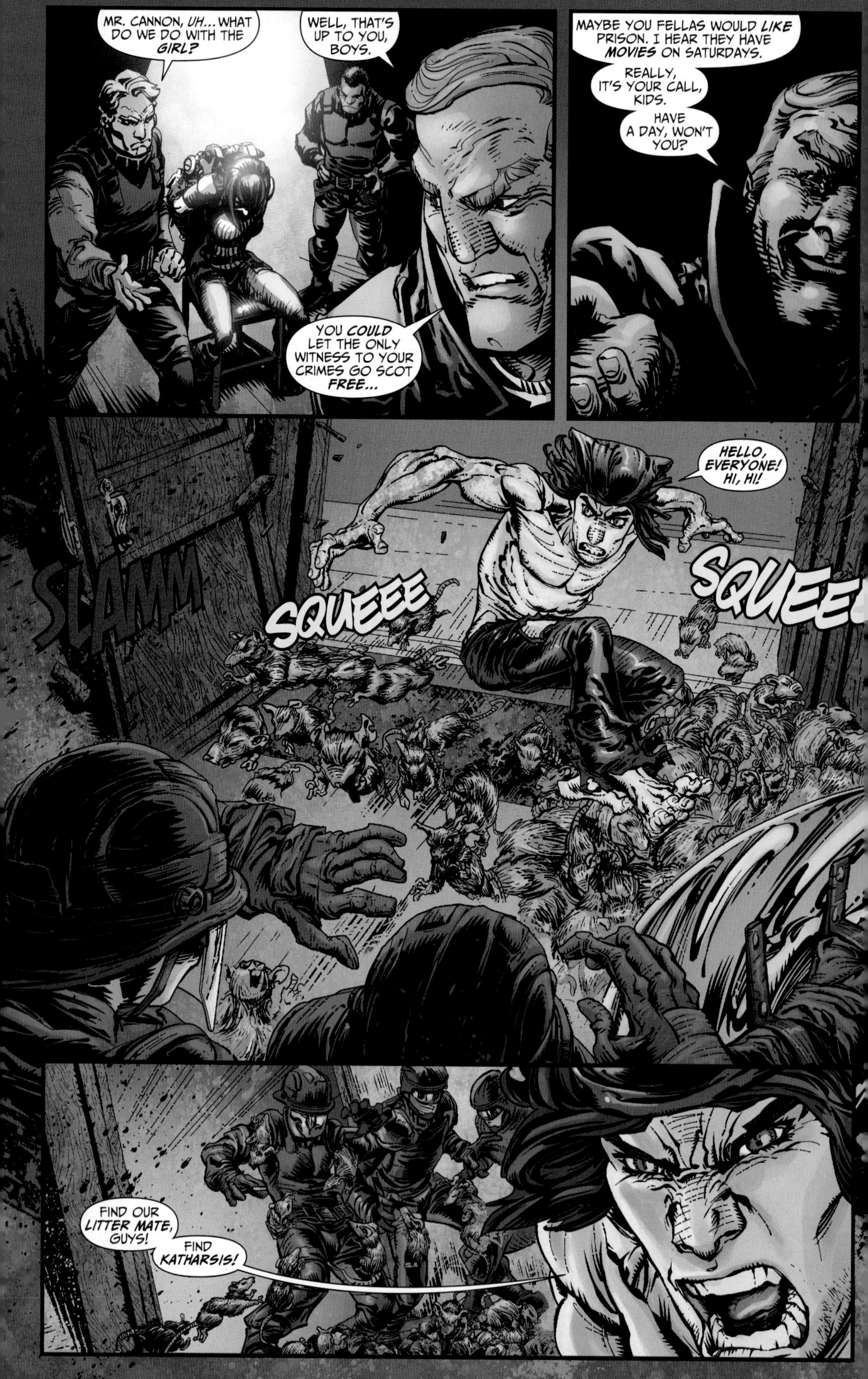
MR. CANNON, UH... WHAT DO WE DO WITH THE GIRL?
WELL, THAT'S UP TO YOU, BOYS.
YOU COULD LET THE ONLY WITNESS TO YOUR CRIMES GO SCOT FREE...
MAYBE YOU FELLAS WOULD LIKE PRISON. I HEAR THEY HAVE MOVIES ON SATURDAYS.
REALLY, IT'S YOUR CALL, KIDS.
HAVE A DAY, WON'T YOU?
SLAMM
HELLO, EVERYONE! HI, HI!
SQUEEE
FIND OUR LITTER MATE, GUYS!
FIND KATHARSIS!

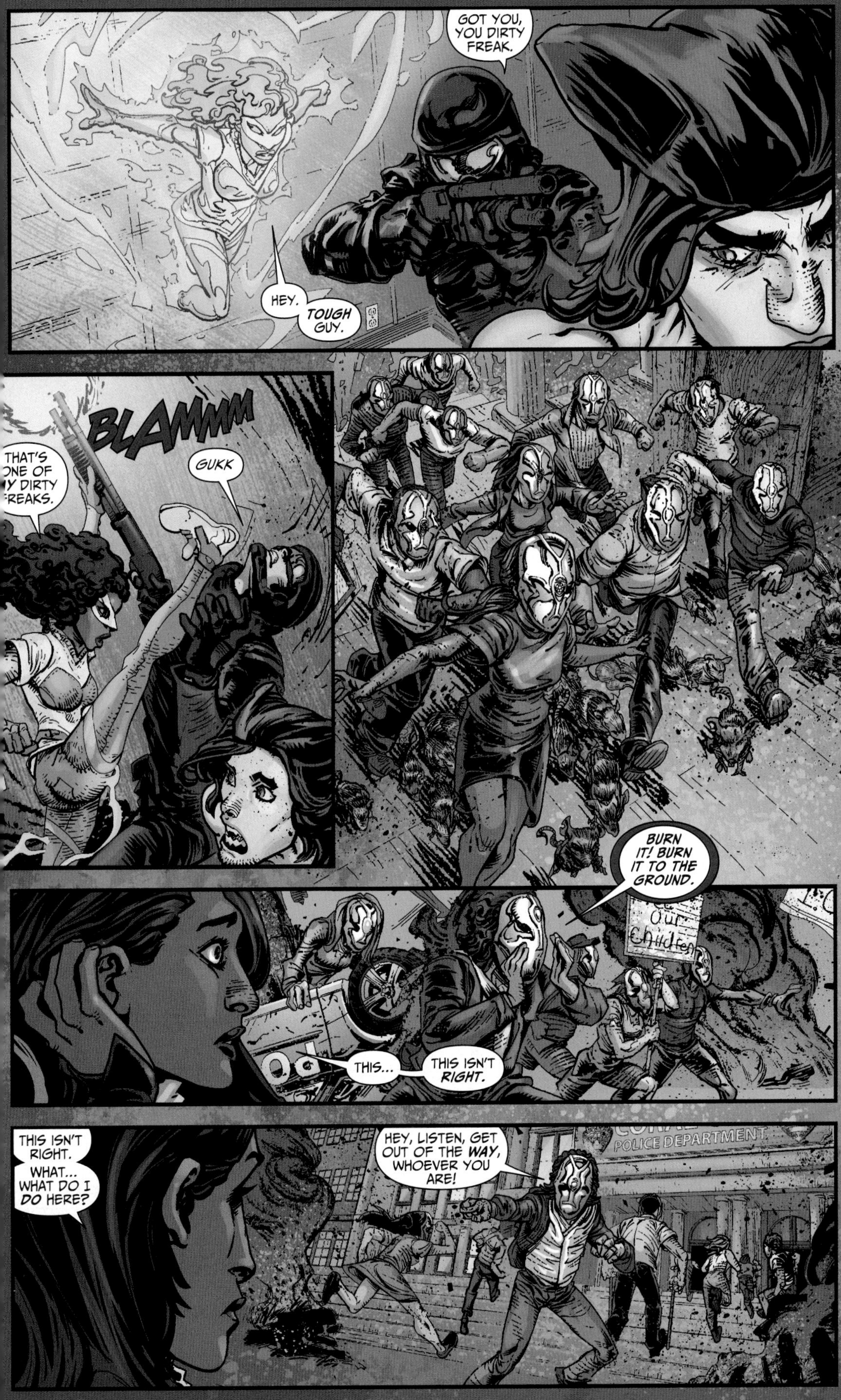

GOT YOU, YOU DIRTY FREAK.
HEY. TOUGH GUY.
BLAMMM
THAT'S ONE OF Y DIRTY FREAKS.
GUKK
BURN IT! BURN IT TO THE GROUND.
THIS...
THIS ISN'T RIGHT.
THIS ISN'T RIGHT. WHAT... WHAT DO I DO HERE?
HEY, LISTEN, GET OUT OF THE WAY, WHOEVER YOU ARE!
POLICE DEPARTMENT

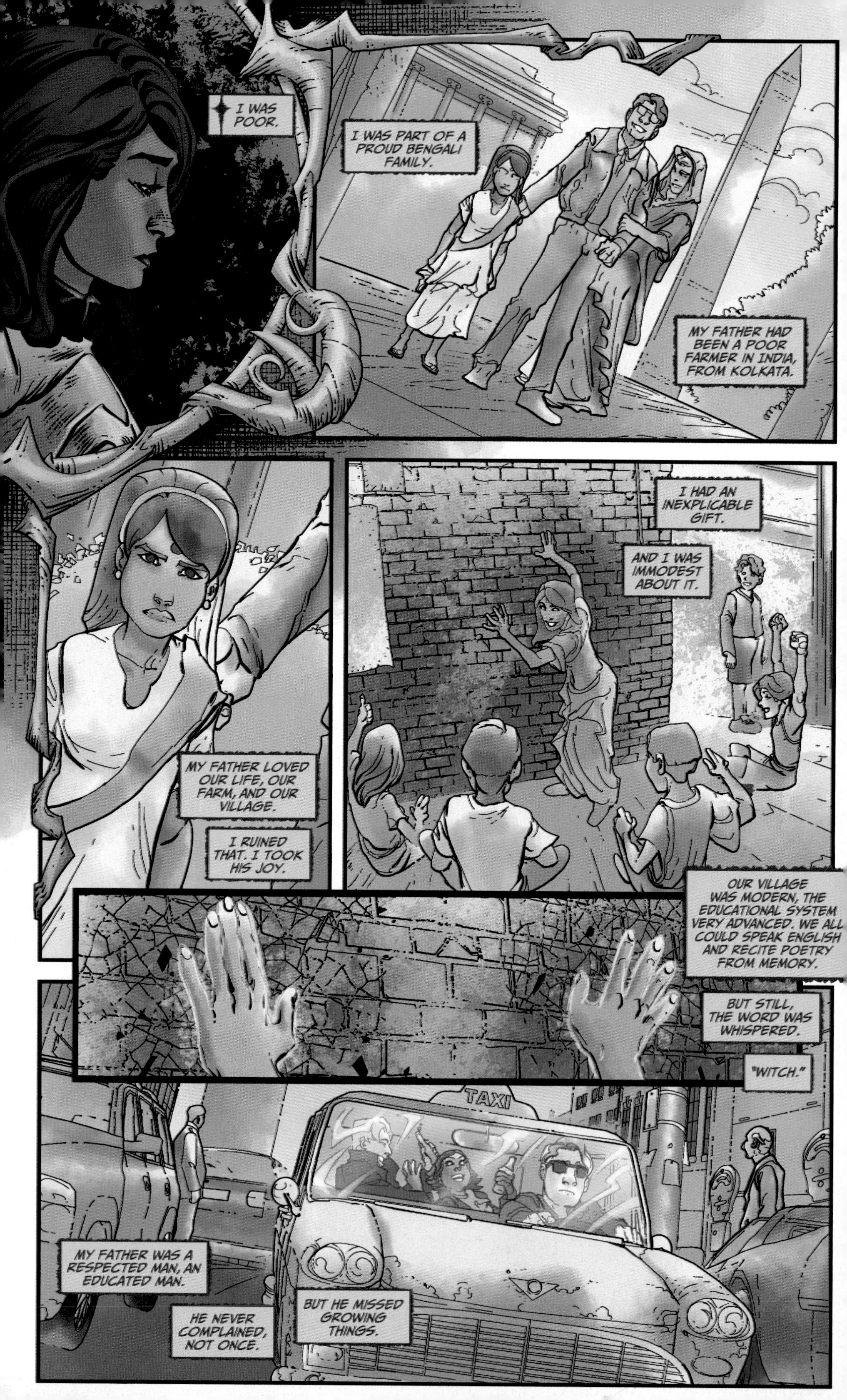
I WAS POOR.
I WAS PART OF A PROUD BENGALI FAMILY.
MY FATHER HAD BEEN A POOR FARMER IN INDIA, FROM KOLKATA.
MY FATHER LOVED OUR LIFE, OUR FARM, AND OUR VILLAGE.
I RUINED THAT. I TOOK HIS JOY.
I HAD AN INEXPLICABLE GIFT.
AND I WAS IMMODEST ABOUT IT.
OUR VILLAGE WAS MODERN, THE EDUCATIONAL SYSTEM VERY ADVANCED. WE ALL COULD SPEAK ENGLISH AND RECITE POETRY FROM MEMORY.
BUT STILL, THE WORD WAS WHISPERED.
"WITCH."
TAXI
MY FATHER WAS A RESPECTED MAN, AN EDUCATED MAN.
HE NEVER COMPLAINED, NOT ONCE.
BUT HE MISSED GROWING THINGS.

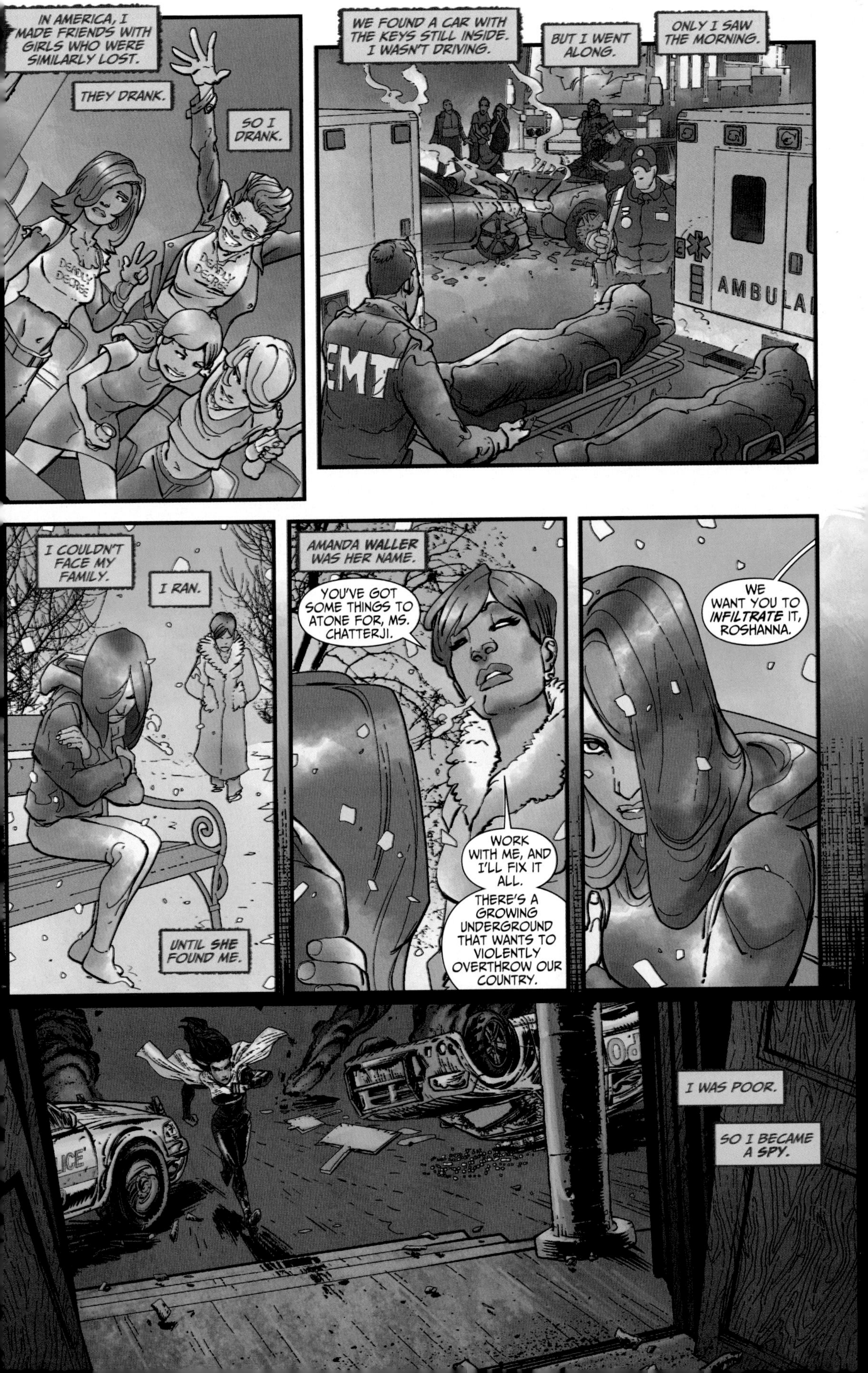
IN AMERICA, I MADE FRIENDS WITH GIRLS WHO WERE SIMILARLY LOST.
THEY DRANK.
SO I DRANK.
DEADLY DEGREE
WE FOUND A CAR WITH THE KEYS STILL INSIDE. I WASN'T DRIVING.
BUT I WENT ALONG.
ONLY I SAW THE MORNING.
EMT
AMBULA
I COULDN'T FACE MY FAMILY.
I RAN.
UNTIL SHE FOUND ME.
AMANDA WALLER WAS HER NAME.
YOU'VE GOT SOME THINGS TO ATONE FOR, MS. CHATTERJI.
WORK WITH ME, AND I'LL FIX IT ALL.
THERE'S A GROWING UNDERGROUND THAT WANTS TO VIOLENTLY OVERTHROW OUR COUNTRY.
WE WANT YOU TO INFILTRATE IT, ROSHANNA.
I WAS POOR.
SO I BECAME A SPY.
POLICE

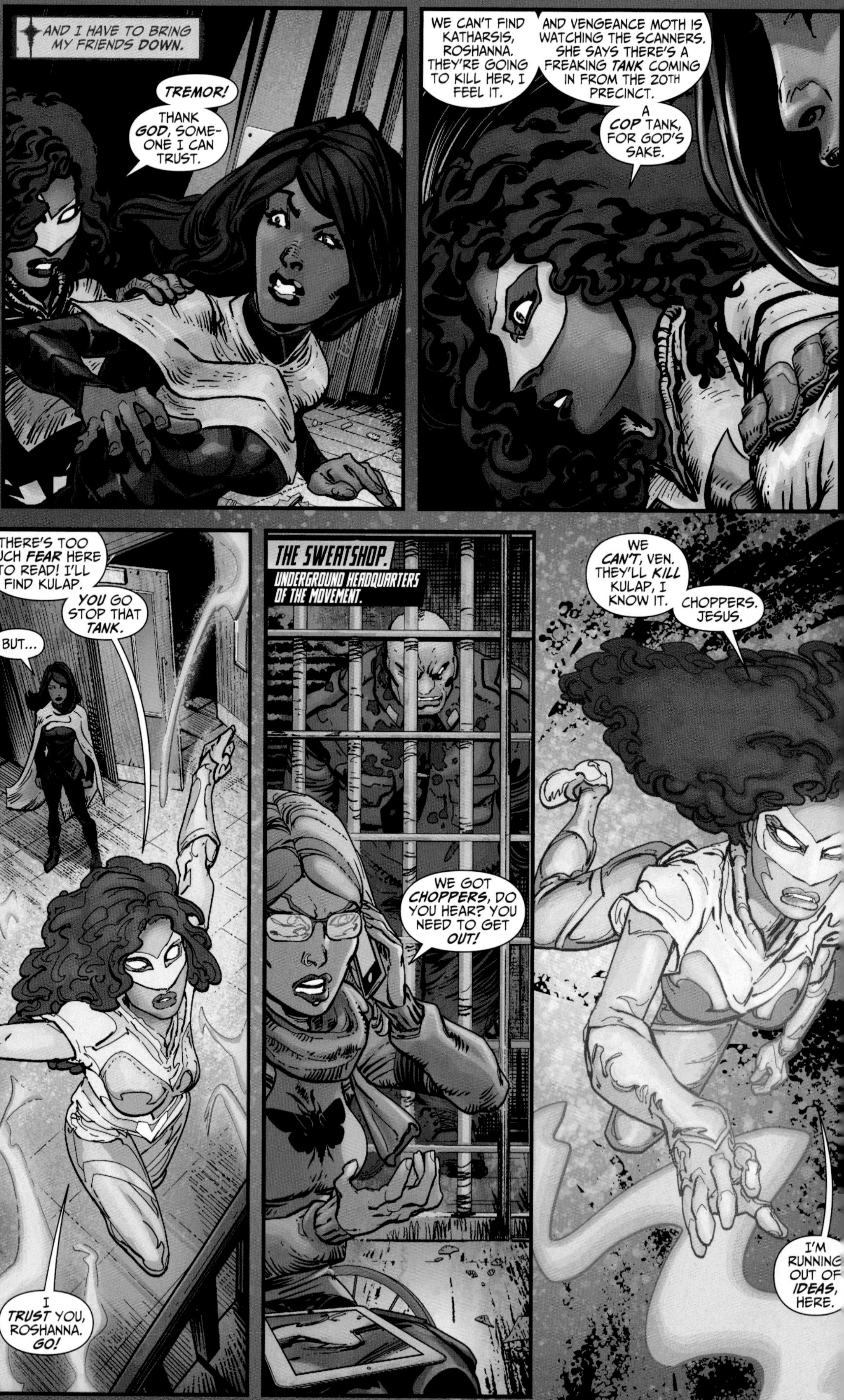
AND I HAVE TO BRING MY FRIENDS DOWN.
TREMOR!
THANK GOD, SOME-ONE I CAN TRUST.
WE CAN'T FIND KATHARSIS, ROSHANNA. THEY'RE GOING TO KILL HER, I FEEL IT.
AND VENGEANCE MOTH IS WATCHING THE SCANNERS. SHE SAYS THERE'S A FREAKING TANK COMING IN FROM THE 20TH PRECINCT.
A COP TANK, FOR GOD'S SAKE.
THERE'S TOO MUCH FEAR HERE TO READ! I'LL FIND KULAP.
YOU GO STOP THAT TANK.
BUT...
I TRUST YOU, ROSHANNA. GO!
THE SWEATSHOP.
UNDERGROUND HEADQUARTERS OF THE MOVEMENT.
WE GOT CHOPPERS, DO YOU HEAR? YOU NEED TO GET OUT!
WE CAN'T, VEN. THEY'LL KILL KULAP, I KNOW IT.
CHOPPERS. JESUS.
I'M RUNNING OUT OF IDEAS, HERE.

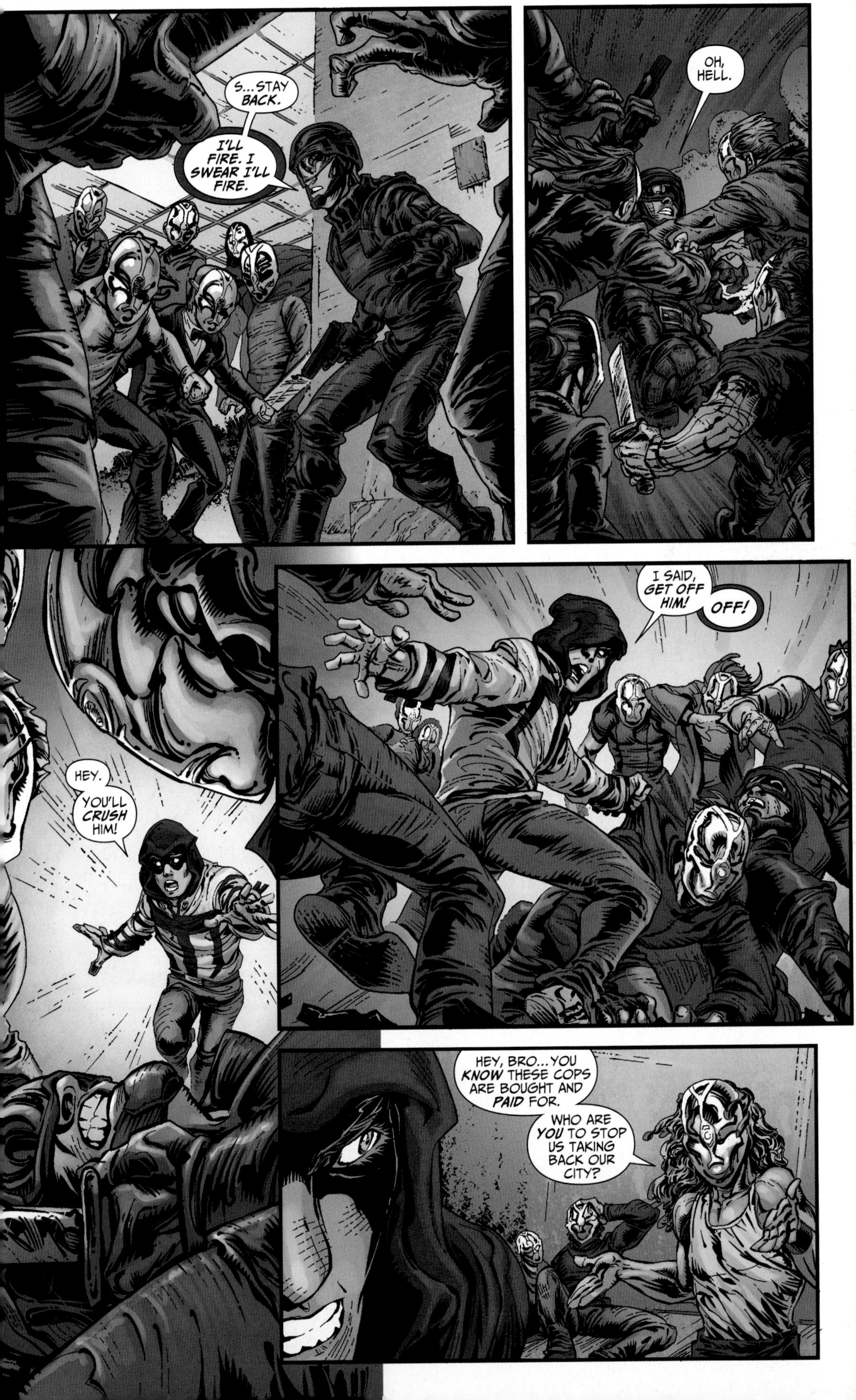
S...STAY BACK.
I'LL FIRE. I SWEAR I'LL FIRE.
OH, HELL.
HEY.
YOU'LL CRUSH HIM!
I SAID, GET OFF HIM!
OFF!
HEY, BRO...YOU KNOW THESE COPS ARE BOUGHT AND PAID FOR.
WHO ARE YOU TO STOP US TAKING BACK OUR CITY?

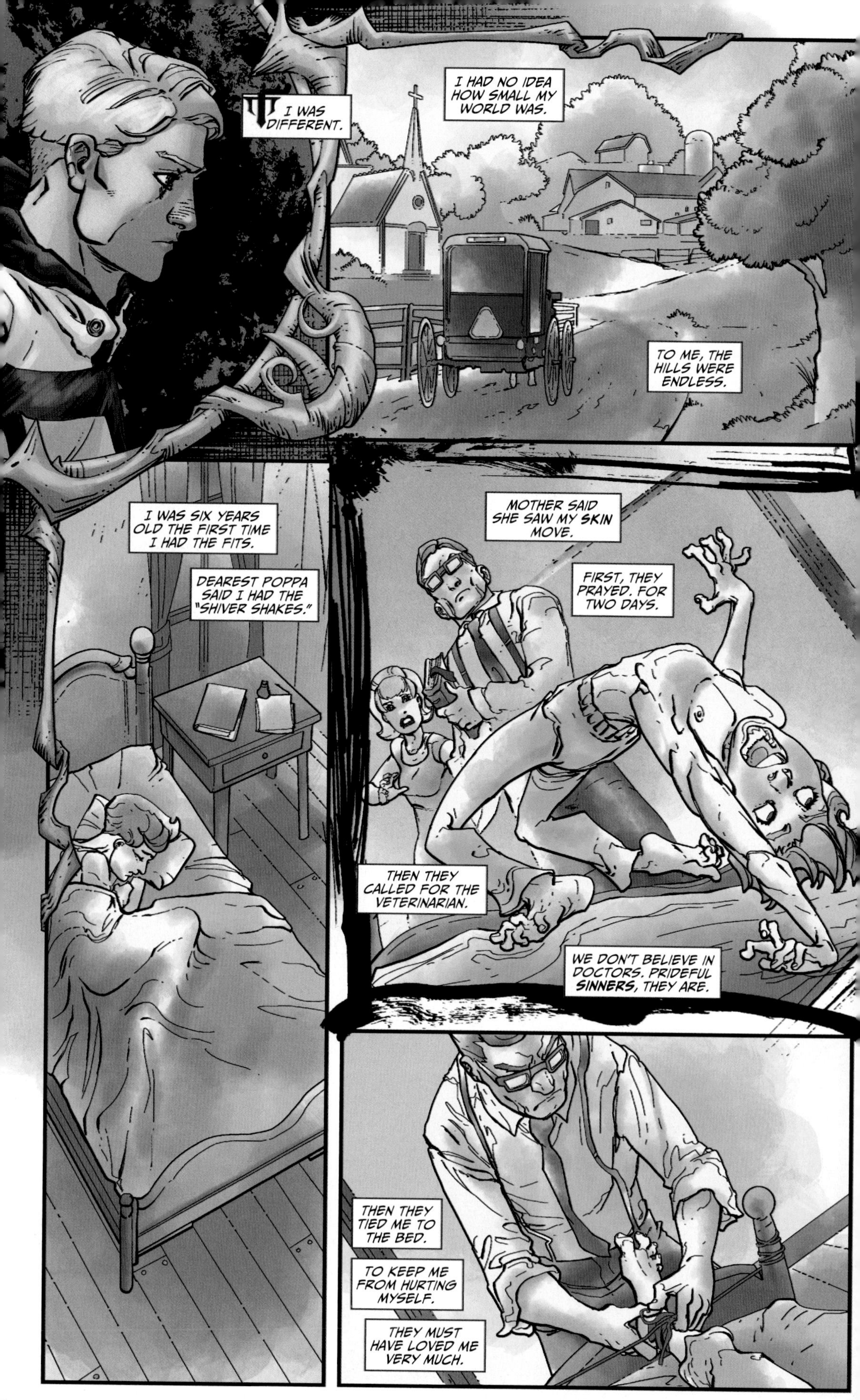
I WAS DIFFERENT.
I HAD NO IDEA HOW SMALL MY WORLD WAS.
TO ME, THE HILLS WERE ENDLESS.
I WAS SIX YEARS OLD THE FIRST TIME I HAD THE FITS.
DEAREST POPPA SAID I HAD THE "SHIVER SHAKES."
MOTHER SAID SHE SAW MY SKIN MOVE.
FIRST, THEY PRAYED. FOR TWO DAYS.
THEN THEY CALLED FOR THE VETERINARIAN.
WE DON'T BELIEVE IN DOCTORS. PRIDEFUL SINNERS, THEY ARE.
THEN THEY TIED ME TO THE BED.
TO KEEP ME FROM HURTING MYSELF.
THEY MUST HAVE LOVED ME VERY MUCH.

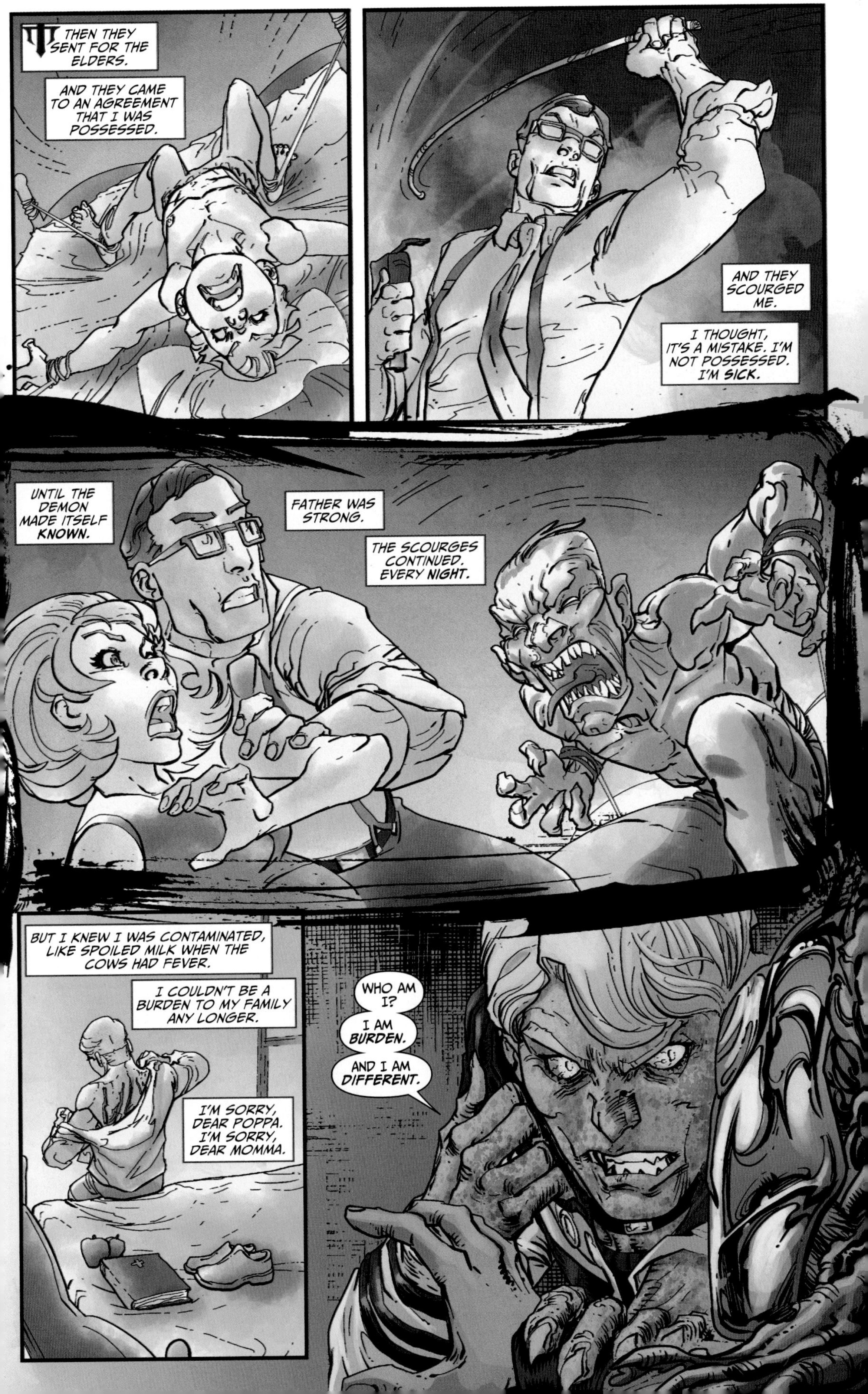
THEN THEY SENT FOR THE ELDERS.
AND THEY CAME TO AN AGREEMENT THAT I WAS POSSESSED.
AND THEY SCOURGED ME.
I THOUGHT, IT'S A MISTAKE. I'M NOT POSSESSED. I'M SICK.
UNTIL THE DEMON MADE ITSELF KNOWN.
FATHER WAS STRONG.
THE SCOURGES CONTINUED. EVERY NIGHT.
BUT I KNEW I WAS CONTAMINATED, LIKE SPOILED MILK WHEN THE COWS HAD FEVER.
I COULDN'T BE A BURDEN TO MY FAMILY ANY LONGER.
I'M SORRY, DEAR POPPA. I'M SORRY, DEAR MOMMA.
WHO AM I?
I AM BURDEN.
AND I AM DIFFERENT.

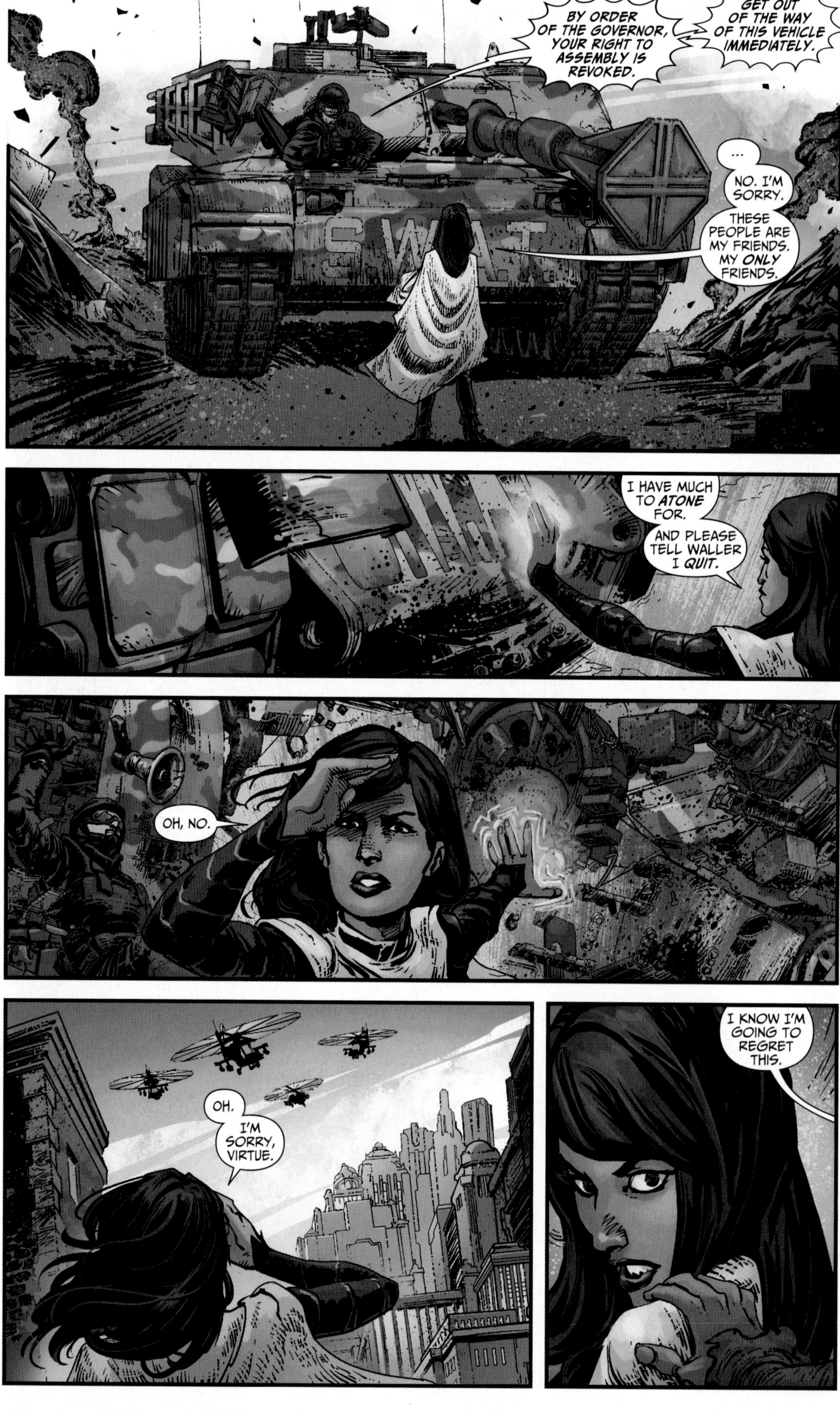
BY ORDER OF THE GOVERNOR, YOUR RIGHT TO ASSEMBLY IS REVOKED.
GET OUT OF THE WAY OF THIS VEHICLE IMMEDIATELY.
...
NO. I'M SORRY.
THESE PEOPLE ARE MY FRIENDS. MY ONLY FRIENDS.
I HAVE MUCH TO ATONE FOR.
AND PLEASE TELL WALLER I QUIT.
OH, NO.
OH.
I'M SORRY, VIRTUE.
I KNOW I'M GOING TO REGRET THIS.

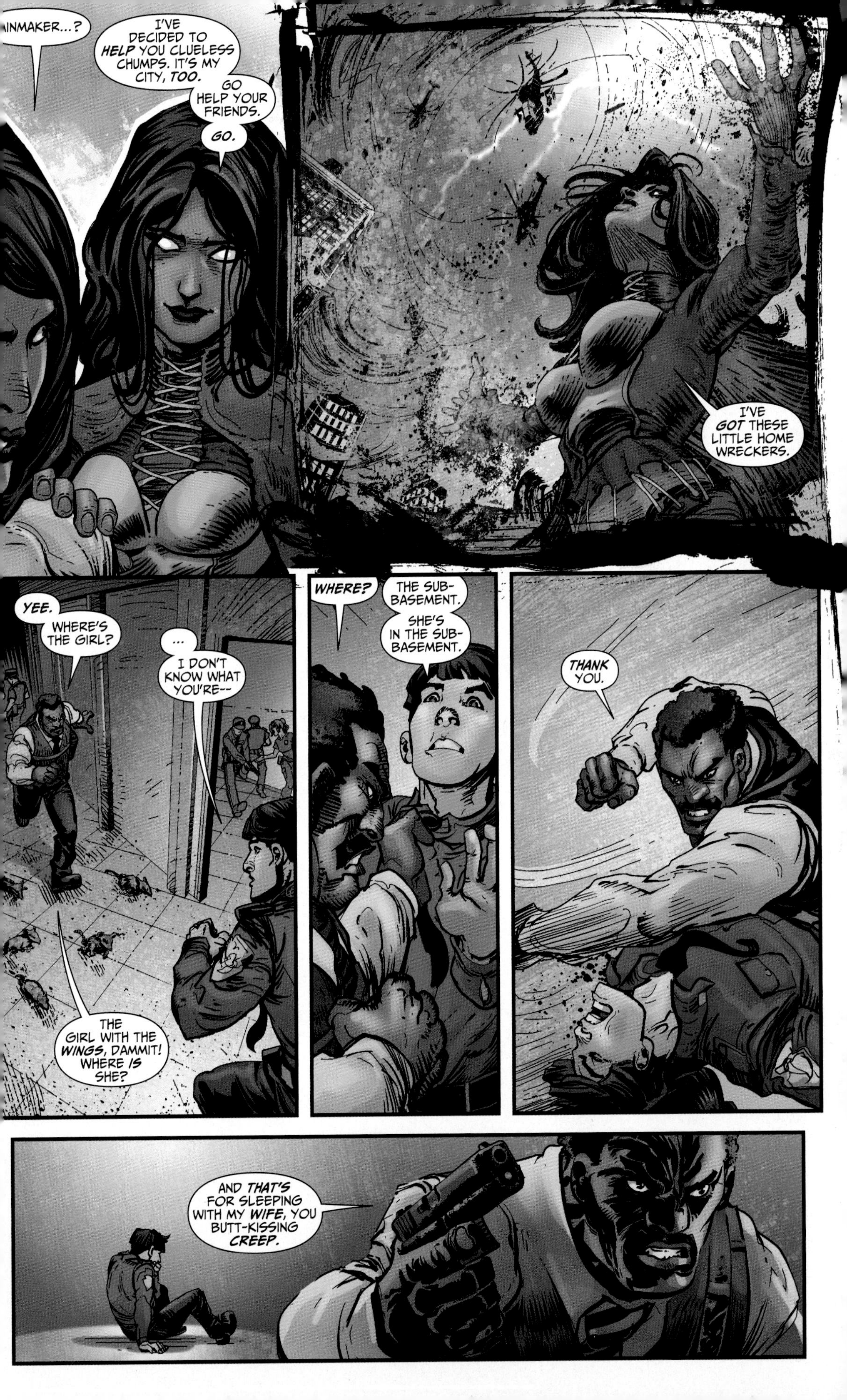

INMAKER...?
I'VE DECIDED TO HELP YOU CLUELESS CHUMPS. IT'S MY CITY, TOO.
GO HELP YOUR FRIENDS.
GO.
I'VE GOT THESE LITTLE HOME WRECKERS.
YEE.
WHERE'S THE GIRL?
...
I DON'T KNOW WHAT YOU'RE--
THE GIRL WITH THE WINGS, DAMMIT! WHERE IS SHE?
WHERE?
THE SUB-BASEMENT.
SHE'S IN THE SUB-BASEMENT.
THANK YOU.
AND THAT'S FOR SLEEPING WITH MY WIFE, YOU BUTT-KISSING CREEP.

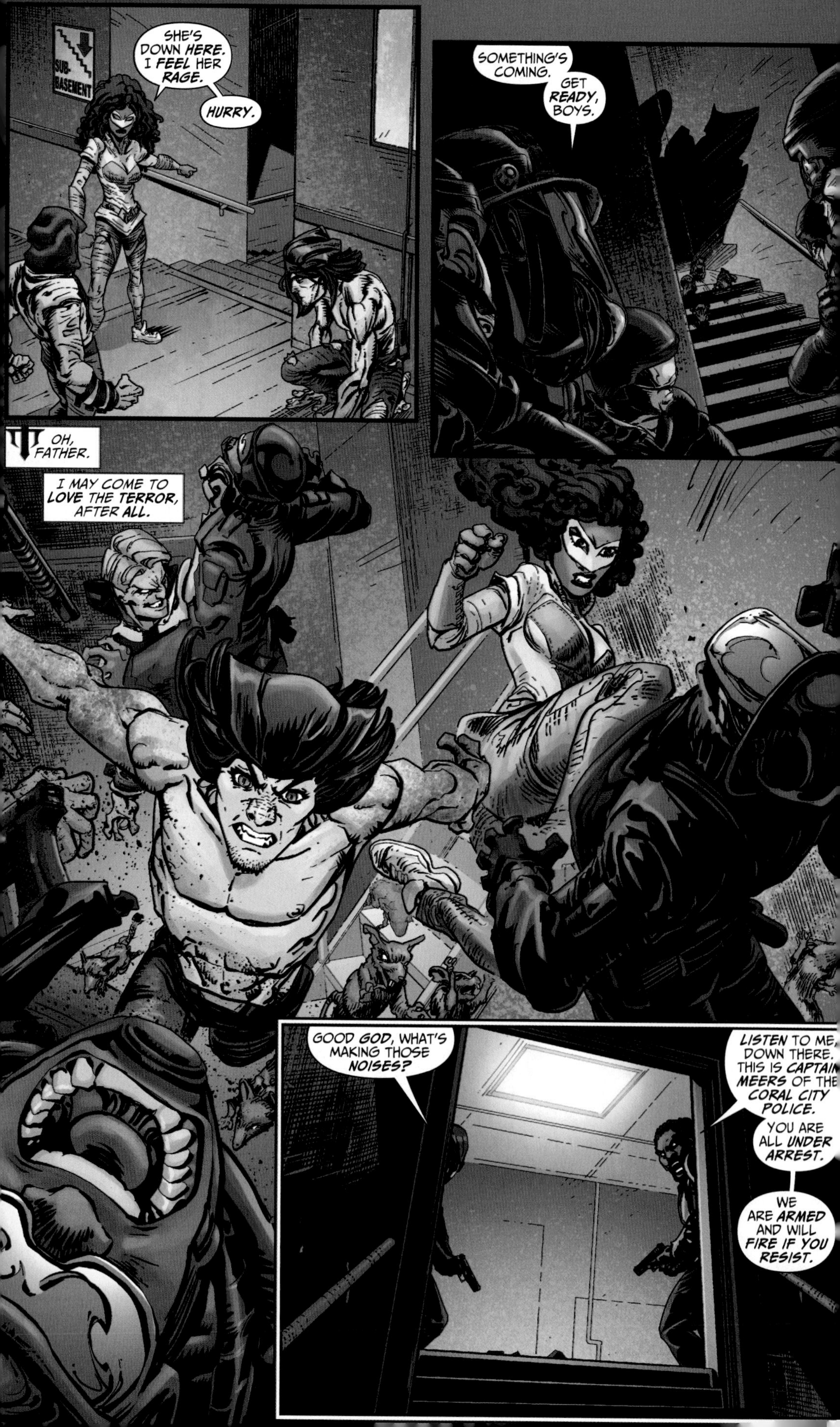
SUB-BASEMENT
SHE'S DOWN HERE. I FEEL HER RAGE.
HURRY.
SOMETHING'S COMING.
GET READY, BOYS.
OH, FATHER.
I MAY COME TO LOVE THE TERROR, AFTER ALL.
GOOD GOD, WHAT'S MAKING THOSE NOISES?
LISTEN TO ME, DOWN THERE. THIS IS CAPTAIN MEERS OF THE CORAL CITY POLICE.
YOU ARE ALL UNDER ARREST.
WE ARE ARMED AND WILL FIRE IF YOU RESIST.

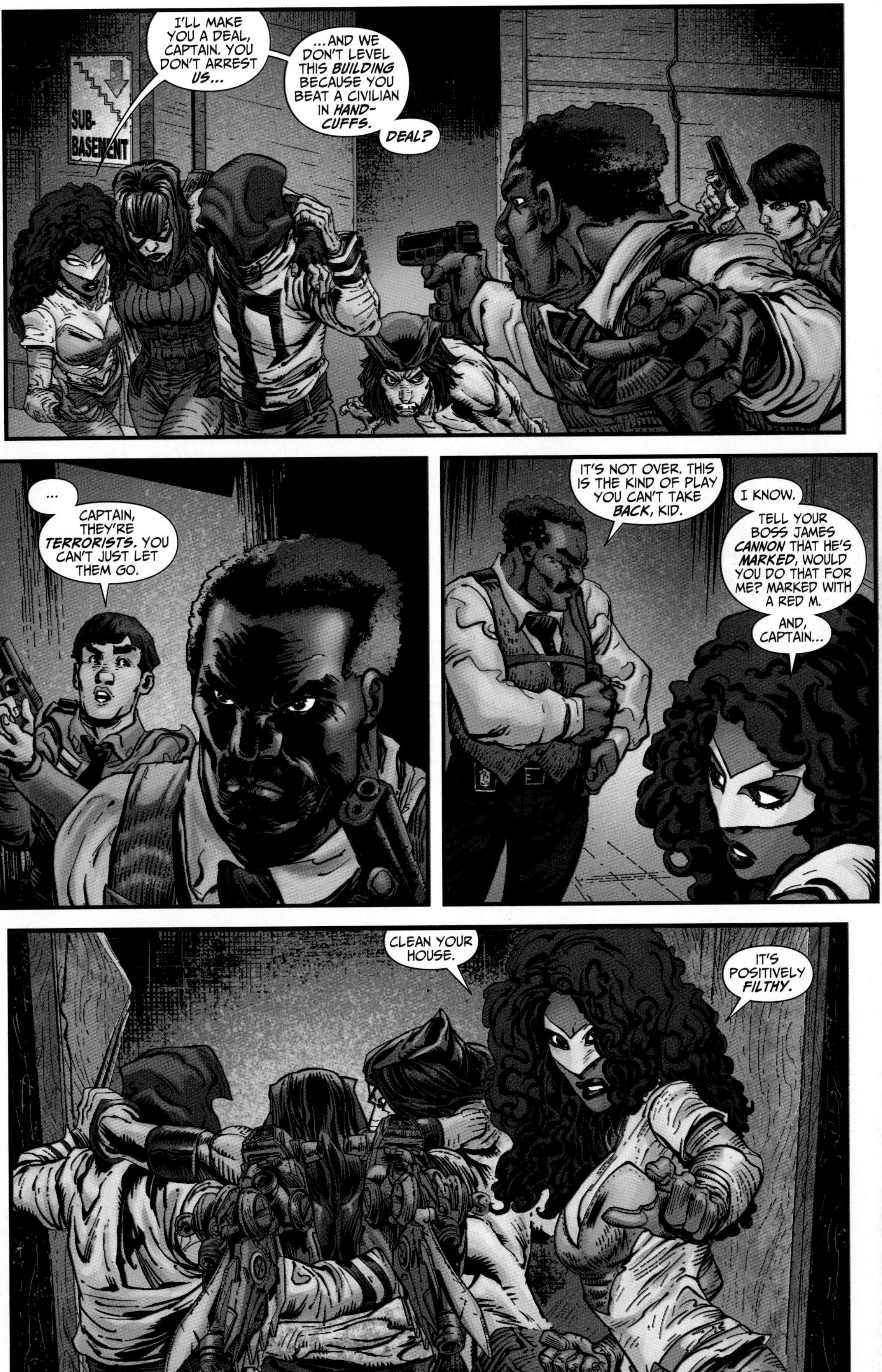

SUB-BASEMENT
I'LL MAKE YOU A DEAL, CAPTAIN. YOU DON'T ARREST *US*...
...AND WE DON'T LEVEL THIS *BUILDING* BECAUSE YOU BEAT A CIVILIAN IN *HAND-CUFFS*.
DEAL?
...
CAPTAIN, THEY'RE *TERRORISTS*. YOU CAN'T JUST LET THEM GO.
IT'S NOT OVER. THIS IS THE KIND OF PLAY YOU CAN'T TAKE *BACK*, KID.
I KNOW.
TELL YOUR BOSS JAMES *CANNON* THAT HE'S *MARKED*, WOULD YOU DO THAT FOR ME? MARKED WITH A RED M.
AND, CAPTAIN...
CLEAN YOUR HOUSE.
IT'S POSITIVELY *FILTHY*.

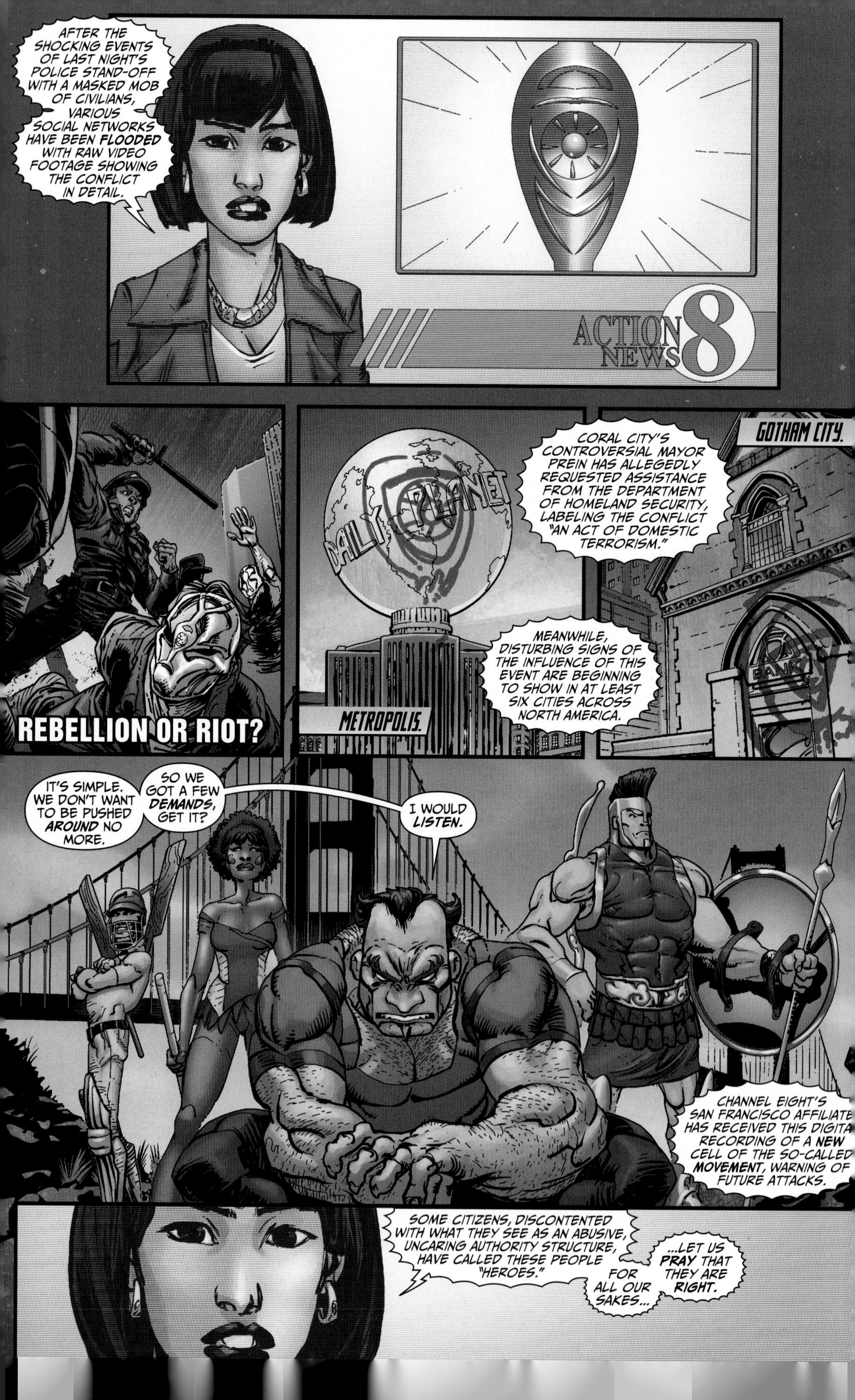
AFTER THE SHOCKING EVENTS OF LAST NIGHT'S POLICE STAND-OFF WITH A MASKED MOB OF CIVILIANS, VARIOUS SOCIAL NETWORKS HAVE BEEN FLOODED WITH RAW VIDEO FOOTAGE SHOWING THE CONFLICT IN DETAIL.
ACTION NEWS 8
REBELLION OR RIOT?
DAILY PLANET
METROPOLIS.
GOTHAM CITY.
CORAL CITY'S CONTROVERSIAL MAYOR PREIN HAS ALLEGEDLY REQUESTED ASSISTANCE FROM THE DEPARTMENT OF HOMELAND SECURITY, LABELING THE CONFLICT "AN ACT OF DOMESTIC TERRORISM."
MEANWHILE, DISTURBING SIGNS OF THE INFLUENCE OF THIS EVENT ARE BEGINNING TO SHOW IN AT LEAST SIX CITIES ACROSS NORTH AMERICA.
BANK
IT'S SIMPLE. WE DON'T WANT TO BE PUSHED AROUND NO MORE.
SO WE GOT A FEW DEMANDS, GET IT?
I WOULD LISTEN.
CHANNEL EIGHT'S SAN FRANCISCO AFFILIATE HAS RECEIVED THIS DIGITA RECORDING OF A NEW CELL OF THE SO-CALLED MOVEMENT, WARNING OF FUTURE ATTACKS.
SOME CITIZENS, DISCONTENTED WITH WHAT THEY SEE AS AN ABUSIVE, UNCARING AUTHORITY STRUCTURE, HAVE CALLED THESE PEOPLE "HEROES."
FOR ALL OUR SAKES...
...LET US PRAY THAT THEY ARE RIGHT.

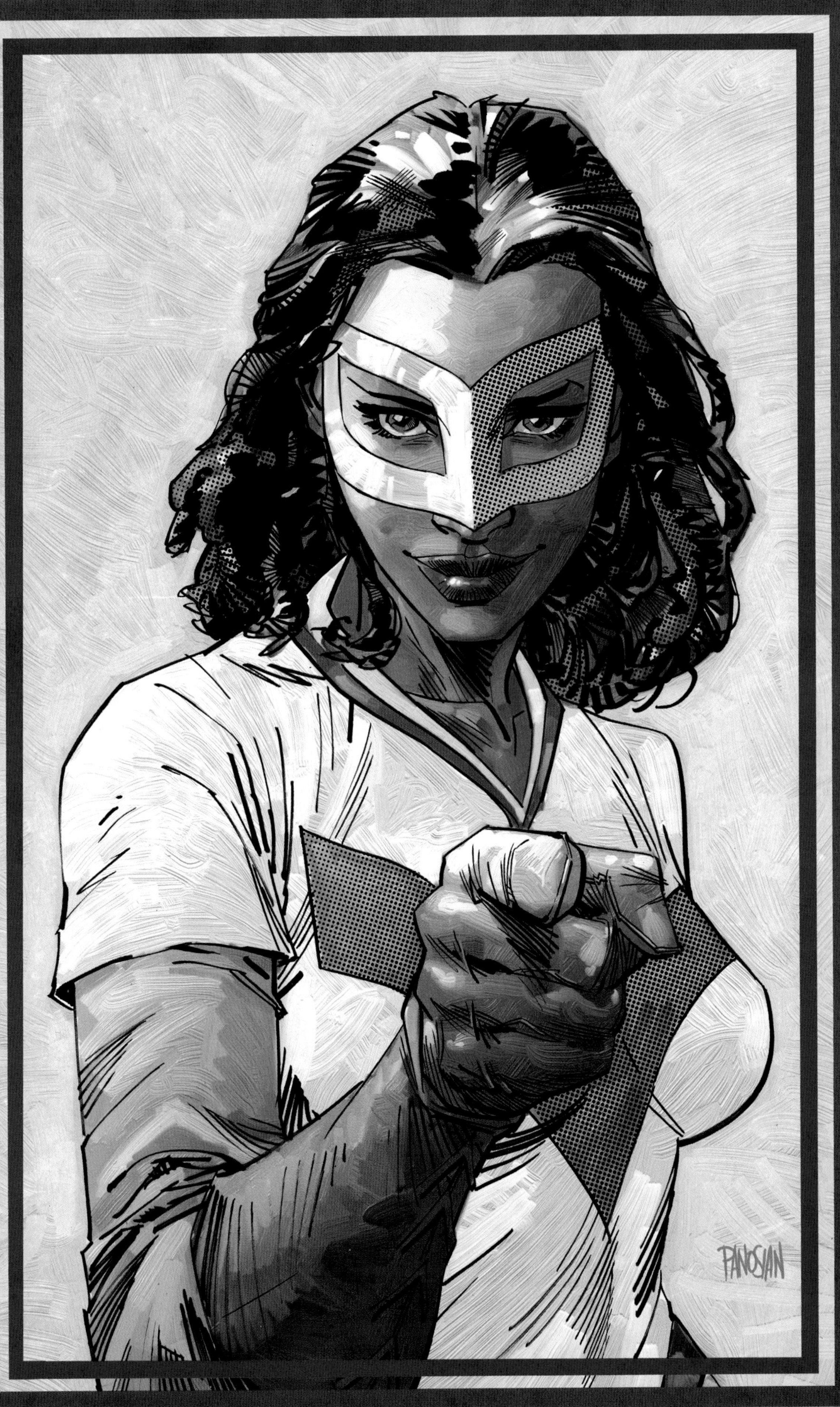
PANOSIAN

The Movement #5 cover by Dan Panosian

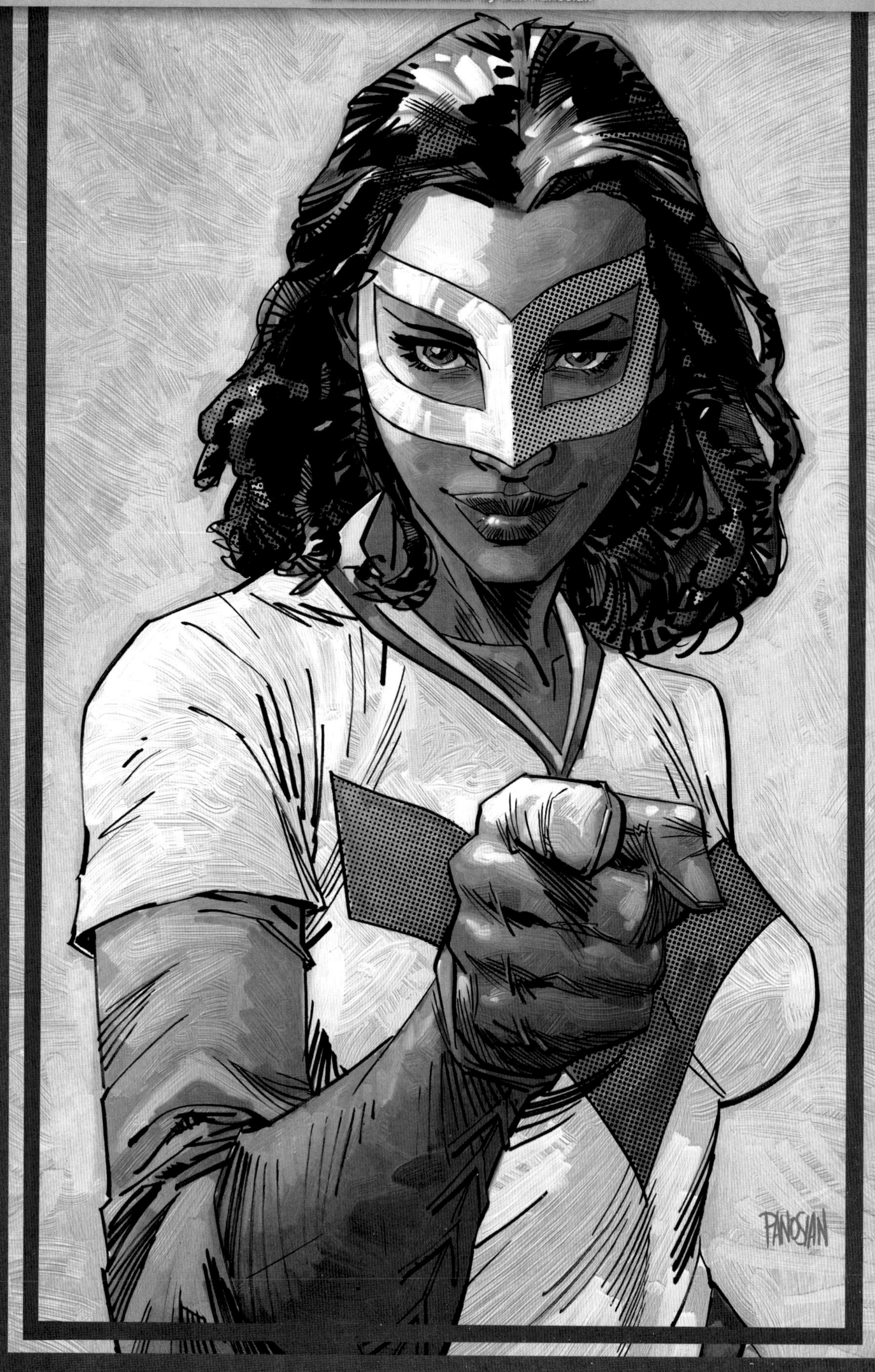
PANOSIAN

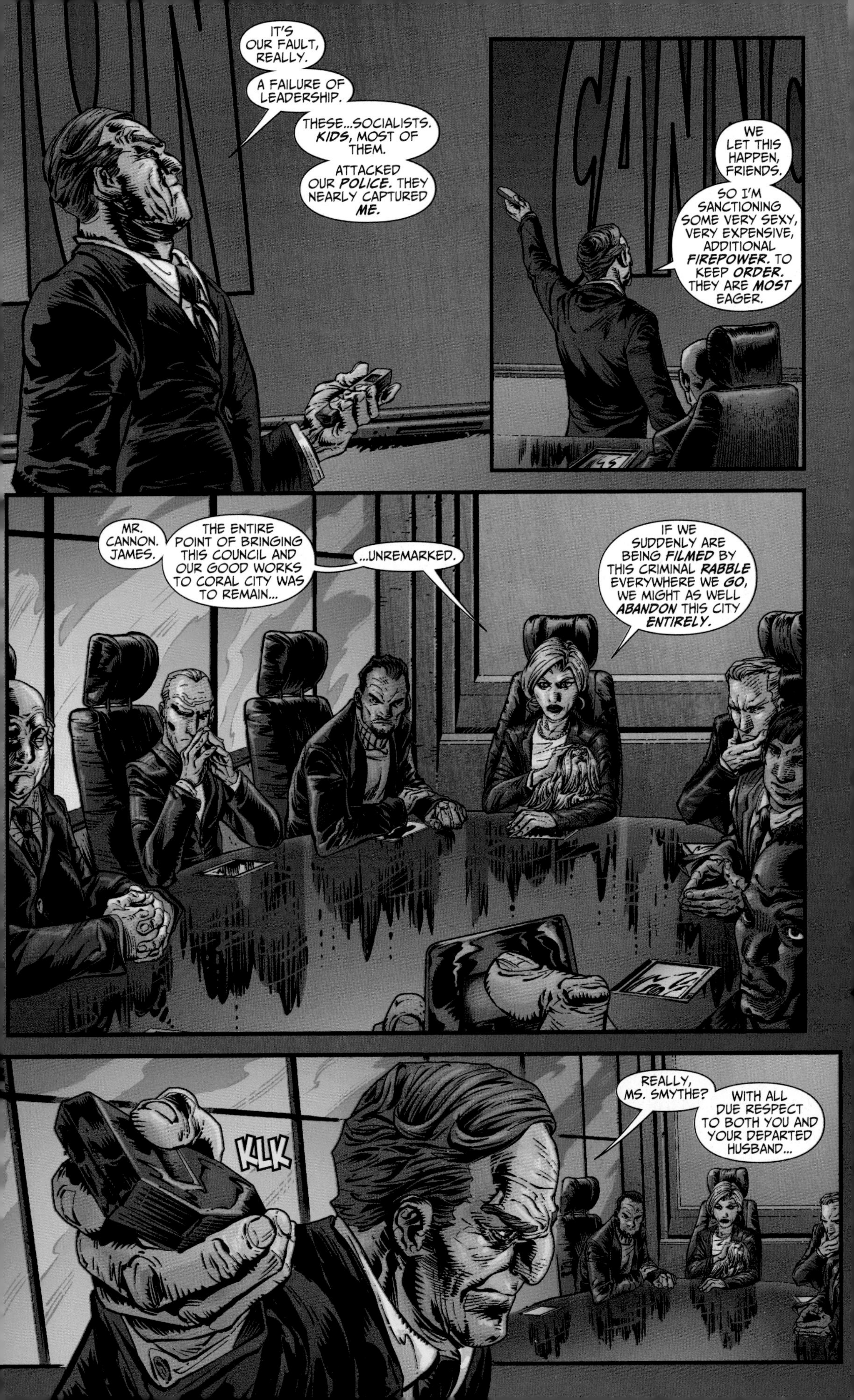
IT'S OUR FAULT, REALLY.
A FAILURE OF LEADERSHIP.
THESE...SOCIALISTS. KIDS, MOST OF THEM.
ATTACKED OUR POLICE. THEY NEARLY CAPTURED ME.
WE LET THIS HAPPEN, FRIENDS.
SO I'M SANCTIONING SOME VERY SEXY, VERY EXPENSIVE, ADDITIONAL FIREPOWER. TO KEEP ORDER. THEY ARE MOST EAGER.
MR. CANNON. JAMES.
THE ENTIRE POINT OF BRINGING THIS COUNCIL AND OUR GOOD WORKS TO CORAL CITY WAS TO REMAIN...
...UNREMARKED.
IF WE SUDDENLY ARE BEING FILMED BY THIS CRIMINAL RABBLE EVERYWHERE WE GO, WE MIGHT AS WELL ABANDON THIS CITY ENTIRELY.
KLK
REALLY, MS. SMYTHE?
WITH ALL DUE RESPECT TO BOTH YOU AND YOUR DEPARTED HUSBAND...

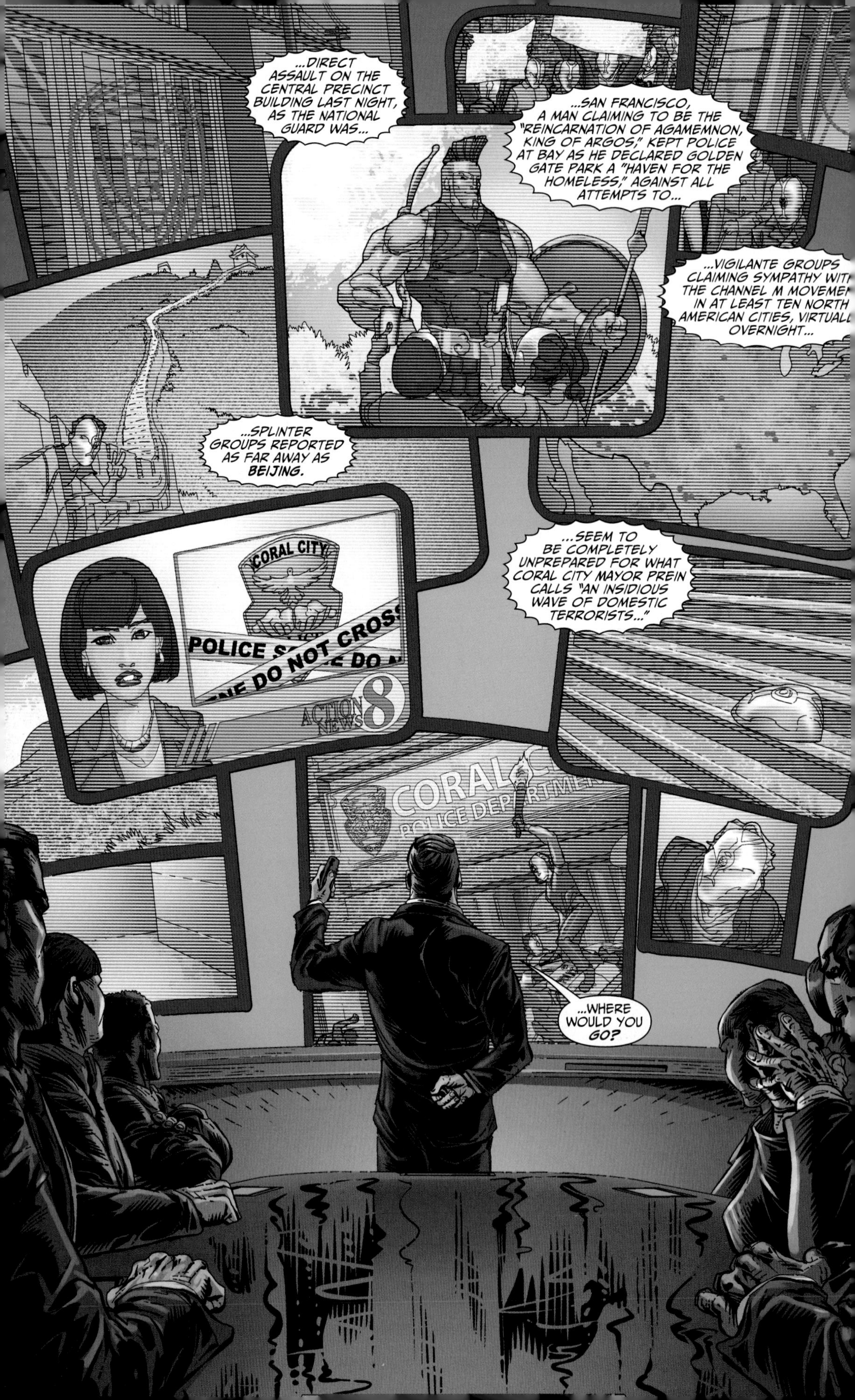
...DIRECT ASSAULT ON THE CENTRAL PRECINCT BUILDING LAST NIGHT, AS THE NATIONAL GUARD WAS...
...SAN FRANCISCO, A MAN CLAIMING TO BE THE "REINCARNATION OF AGAMEMNON, KING OF ARGOS," KEPT POLICE AT BAY AS HE DECLARED GOLDEN GATE PARK A "HAVEN FOR THE HOMELESS," AGAINST ALL ATTEMPTS TO...
...VIGILANTE GROUPS CLAIMING SYMPATHY WITH THE CHANNEL M MOVEMENT IN AT LEAST TEN NORTH AMERICAN CITIES, VIRTUALL OVERNIGHT...
...SPLINTER GROUPS REPORTED AS FAR AWAY AS BEIJING.
CORAL CITY
POLICE SC NE DO NOT CROSS
ACTION NEWS 8
...SEEM TO BE COMPLETELY UNPREPARED FOR WHAT CORAL CITY MAYOR PREIN CALLS "AN INSIDIOUS WAVE OF DOMESTIC TERRORISTS..."
CORAL C POLICE DEPARTME
...WHERE WOULD YOU GO?

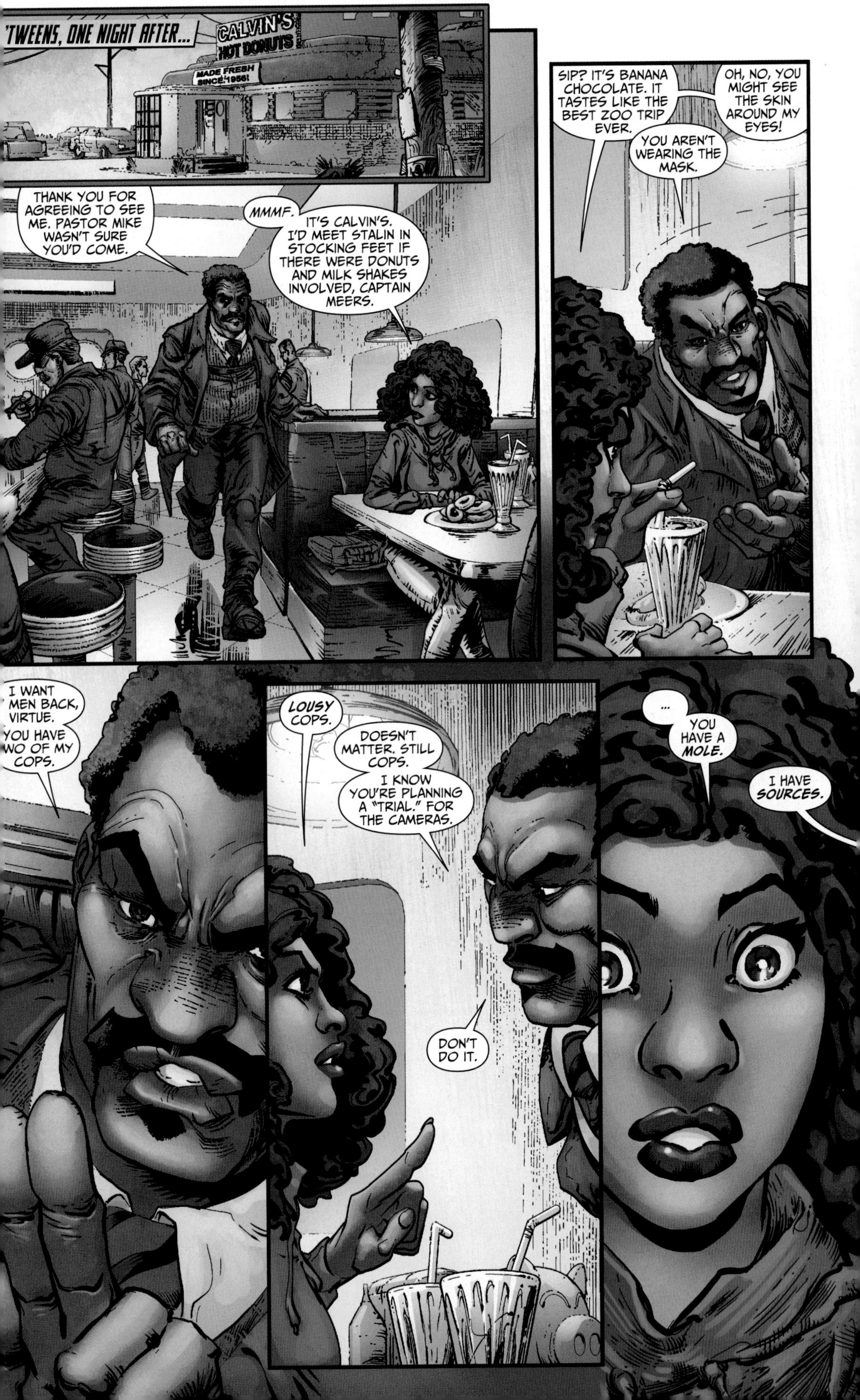
'TWEENS, ONE NIGHT AFTER...
CALVIN'S
HOT DONUTS
MADE FRESH SINCE 1956!
THANK YOU FOR AGREEING TO SEE ME. PASTOR MIKE WASN'T SURE YOU'D COME.
MMMF.
IT'S CALVIN'S. I'D MEET STALIN IN STOCKING FEET IF THERE WERE DONUTS AND MILK SHAKES INVOLVED, CAPTAIN MEERS.
SIP? IT'S BANANA CHOCOLATE. IT TASTES LIKE THE BEST ZOO TRIP EVER.
YOU AREN'T WEARING THE MASK.
OH, NO, YOU MIGHT SEE THE SKIN AROUND MY EYES!
I WANT MEN BACK, VIRTUE.
YOU HAVE WO OF MY COPS.
LOUSY COPS.
DOESN'T MATTER. STILL COPS.
I KNOW YOU'RE PLANNING A "TRIAL." FOR THE CAMERAS.
DON'T DO IT.
...
YOU HAVE A MOLE.
I HAVE SOURCES.

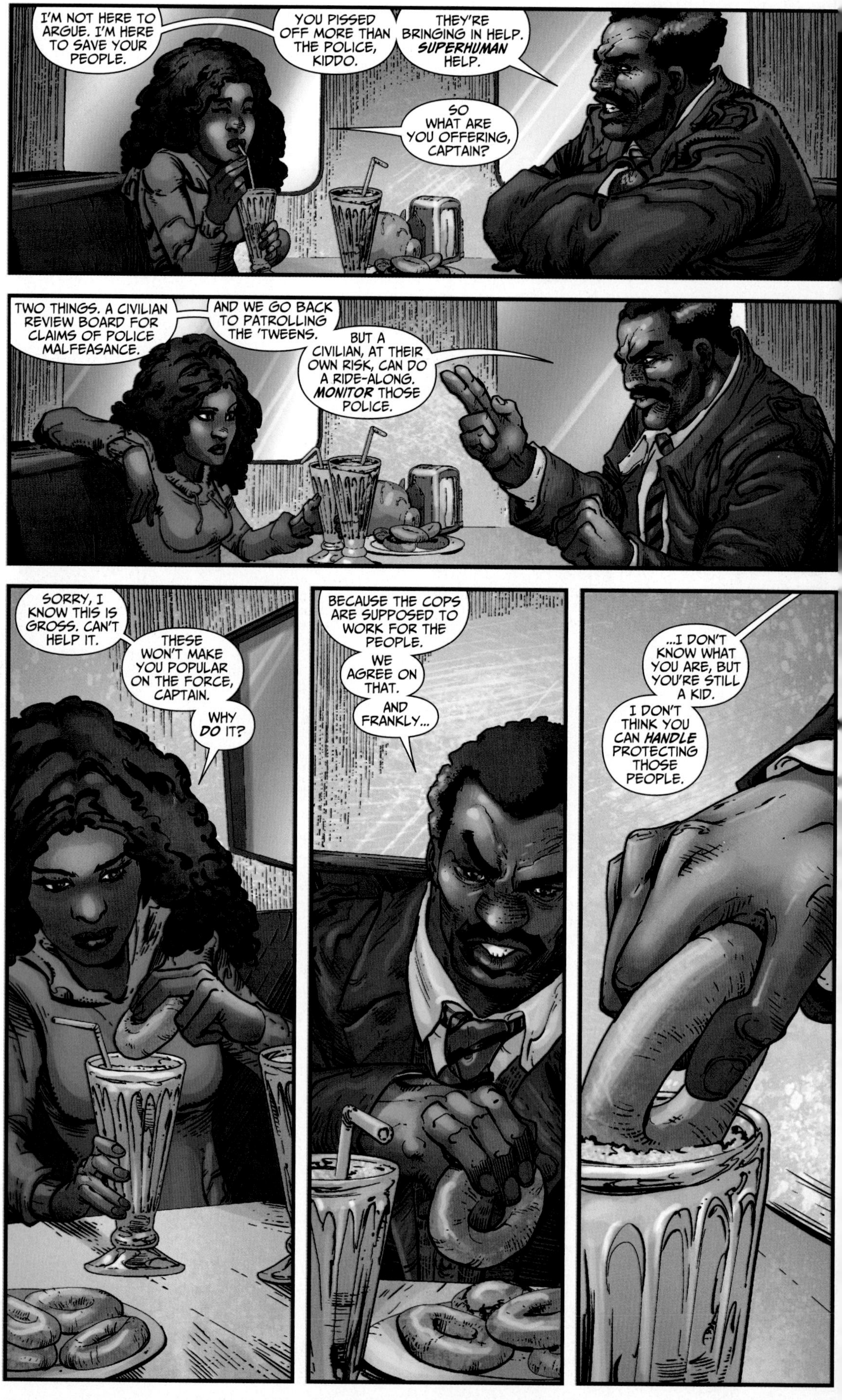
I'M NOT HERE TO ARGUE. I'M HERE TO SAVE YOUR PEOPLE.
YOU PISSED OFF MORE THAN THE POLICE, KIDDO.
THEY'RE BRINGING IN HELP. SUPERHUMAN HELP.
SO WHAT ARE YOU OFFERING, CAPTAIN?
TWO THINGS. A CIVILIAN REVIEW BOARD FOR CLAIMS OF POLICE MALFEASANCE.
AND WE GO BACK TO PATROLLING THE 'TWEENS.
BUT A CIVILIAN, AT THEIR OWN RISK, CAN DO A RIDE-ALONG. MONITOR THOSE POLICE.
SORRY, I KNOW THIS IS GROSS. CAN'T HELP IT.
THESE WON'T MAKE YOU POPULAR ON THE FORCE, CAPTAIN.
WHY DO IT?
BECAUSE THE COPS ARE SUPPOSED TO WORK FOR THE PEOPLE.
WE AGREE ON THAT.
AND FRANKLY...
...I DON'T KNOW WHAT YOU ARE, BUT YOU'RE STILL A KID.
I DON'T THINK YOU CAN HANDLE PROTECTING THOSE PEOPLE.

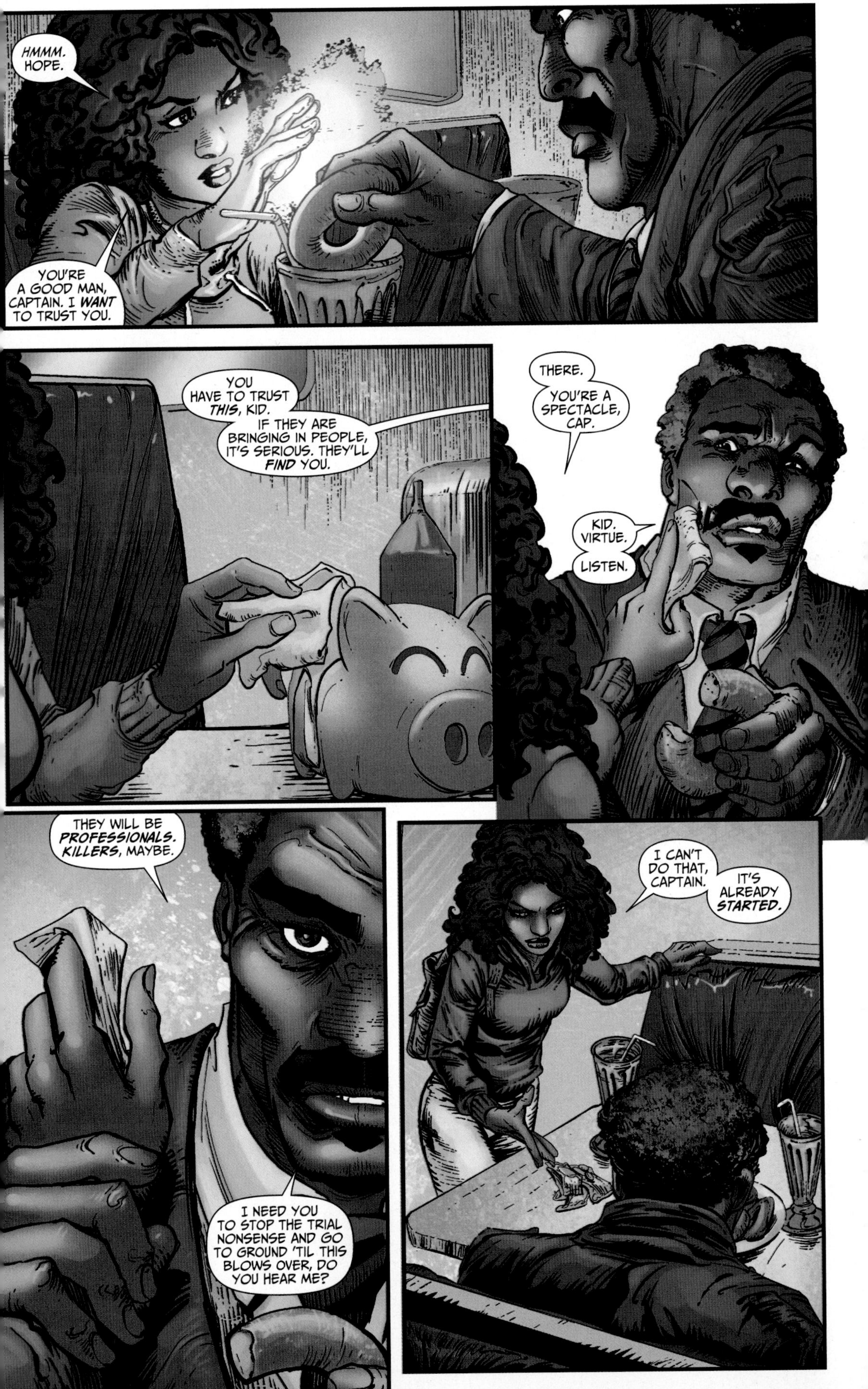
HMMM. HOPE.
YOU'RE A GOOD MAN, CAPTAIN. I *WANT* TO TRUST YOU.
YOU HAVE TO TRUST *THIS*, KID.
IF THEY ARE BRINGING IN PEOPLE, IT'S SERIOUS. THEY'LL *FIND* YOU.
THERE.
YOU'RE A SPECTACLE, CAP.
KID. VIRTUE.
LISTEN.
THEY WILL BE ***PROFESSIONALS. KILLERS***, MAYBE.
I NEED YOU TO STOP THE TRIAL NONSENSE AND GO TO GROUND 'TIL THIS BLOWS OVER, DO YOU HEAR ME?
I CAN'T DO THAT, CAPTAIN.
IT'S ALREADY ***STARTED.***

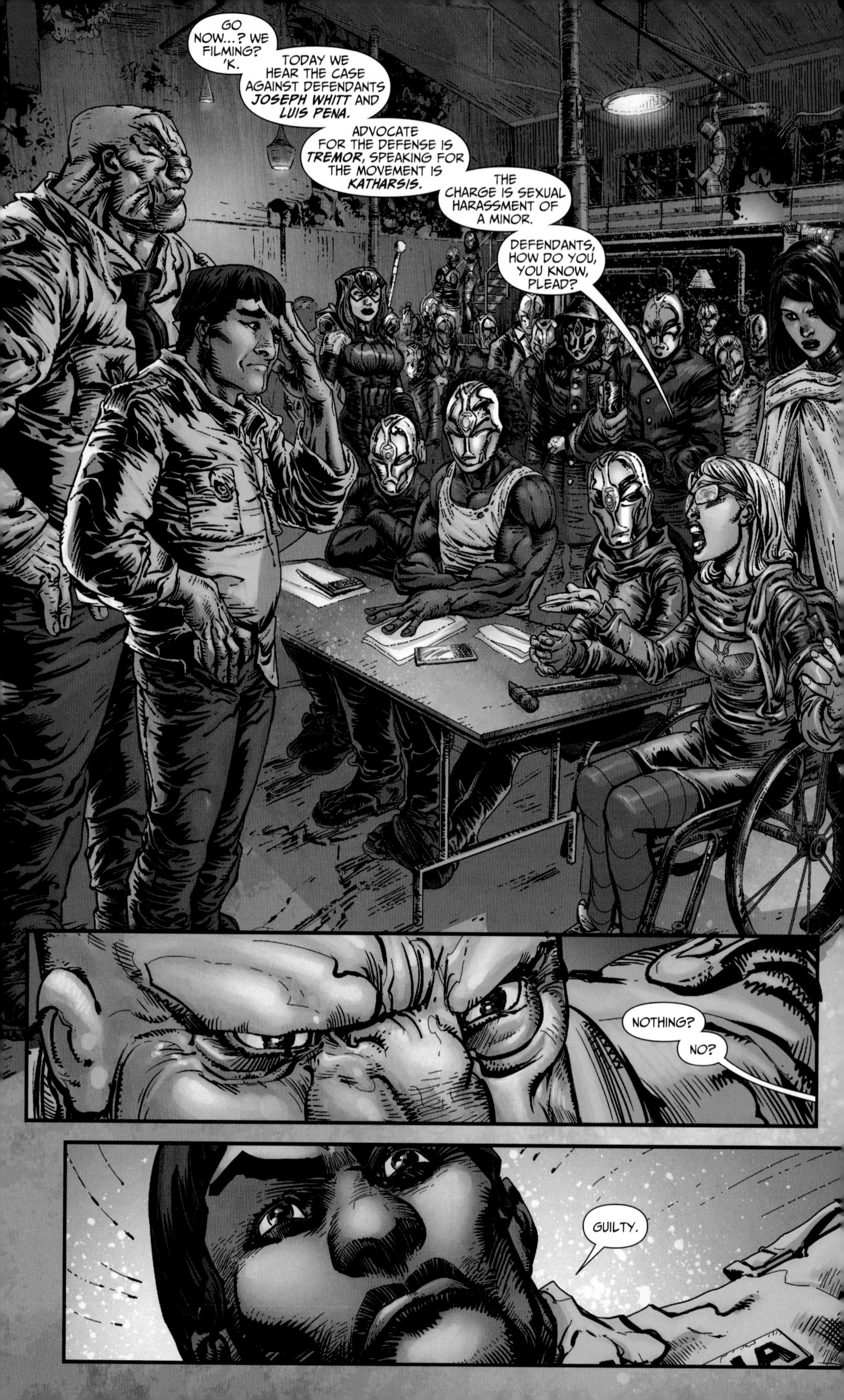
GO NOW...? WE FILMING? 'K.
TODAY WE HEAR THE CASE AGAINST DEFENDANTS JOSEPH WHITT AND LUIS PENA.
ADVOCATE FOR THE DEFENSE IS TREMOR, SPEAKING FOR THE MOVEMENT IS KATHARSIS.
THE CHARGE IS SEXUAL HARASSMENT OF A MINOR.
DEFENDANTS, HOW DO YOU, YOU KNOW, PLEAD?
NOTHING?
NO?
GUILTY.

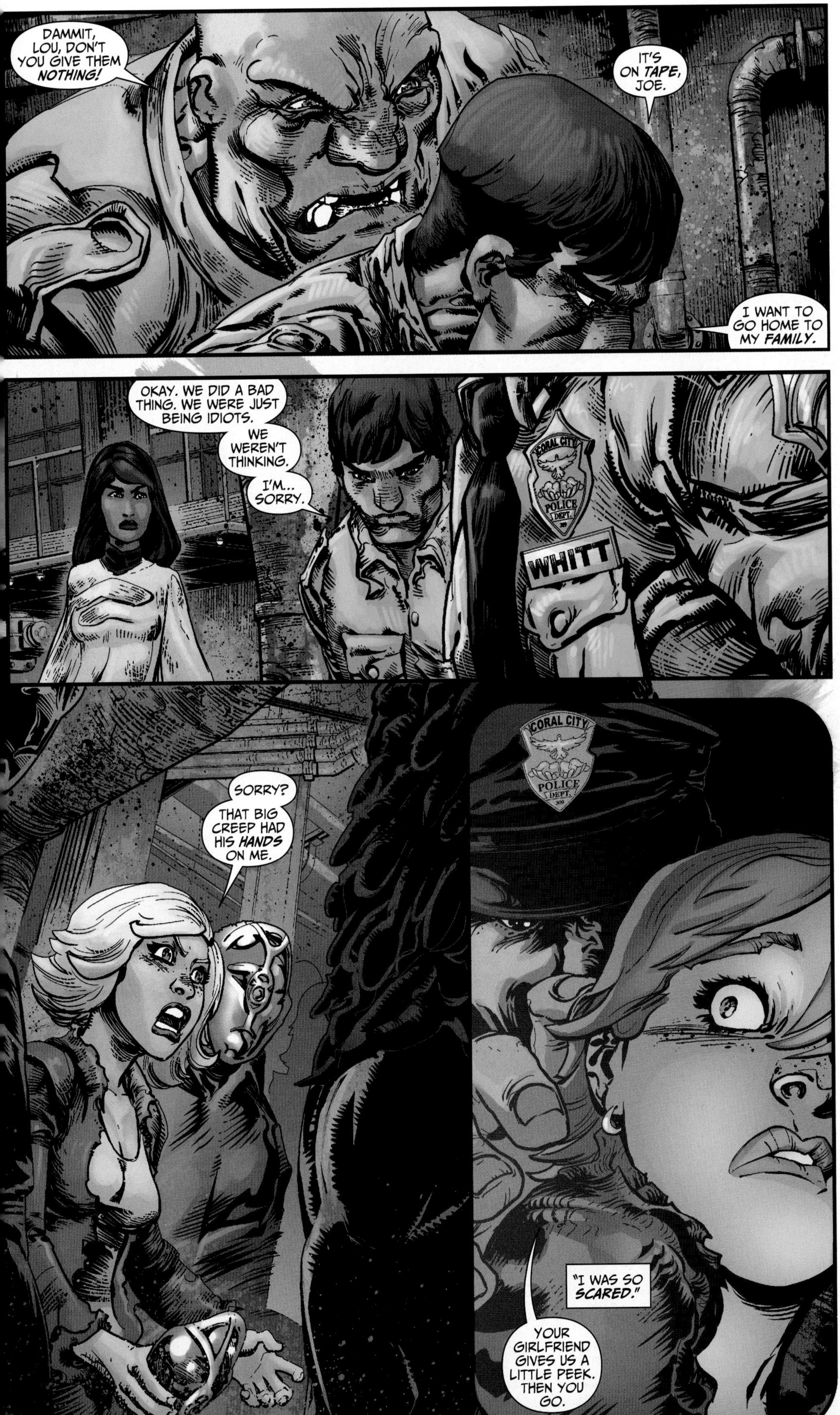

DAMMIT, LOU, DON'T YOU GIVE THEM NOTHING!
IT'S ON TAPE, JOE.
I WANT TO GO HOME TO MY FAMILY.
OKAY. WE DID A BAD THING. WE WERE JUST BEING IDIOTS.
WE WEREN'T THINKING.
I'M... SORRY.
CORAL CITY POLICE DEPT. 309
WHITT
SORRY?
THAT BIG CREEP HAD HIS HANDS ON ME.
CORAL CITY POLICE DEPT. 309
"I WAS SO SCARED."
YOUR GIRLFRIEND GIVES US A LITTLE PEEK. THEN YOU GO.

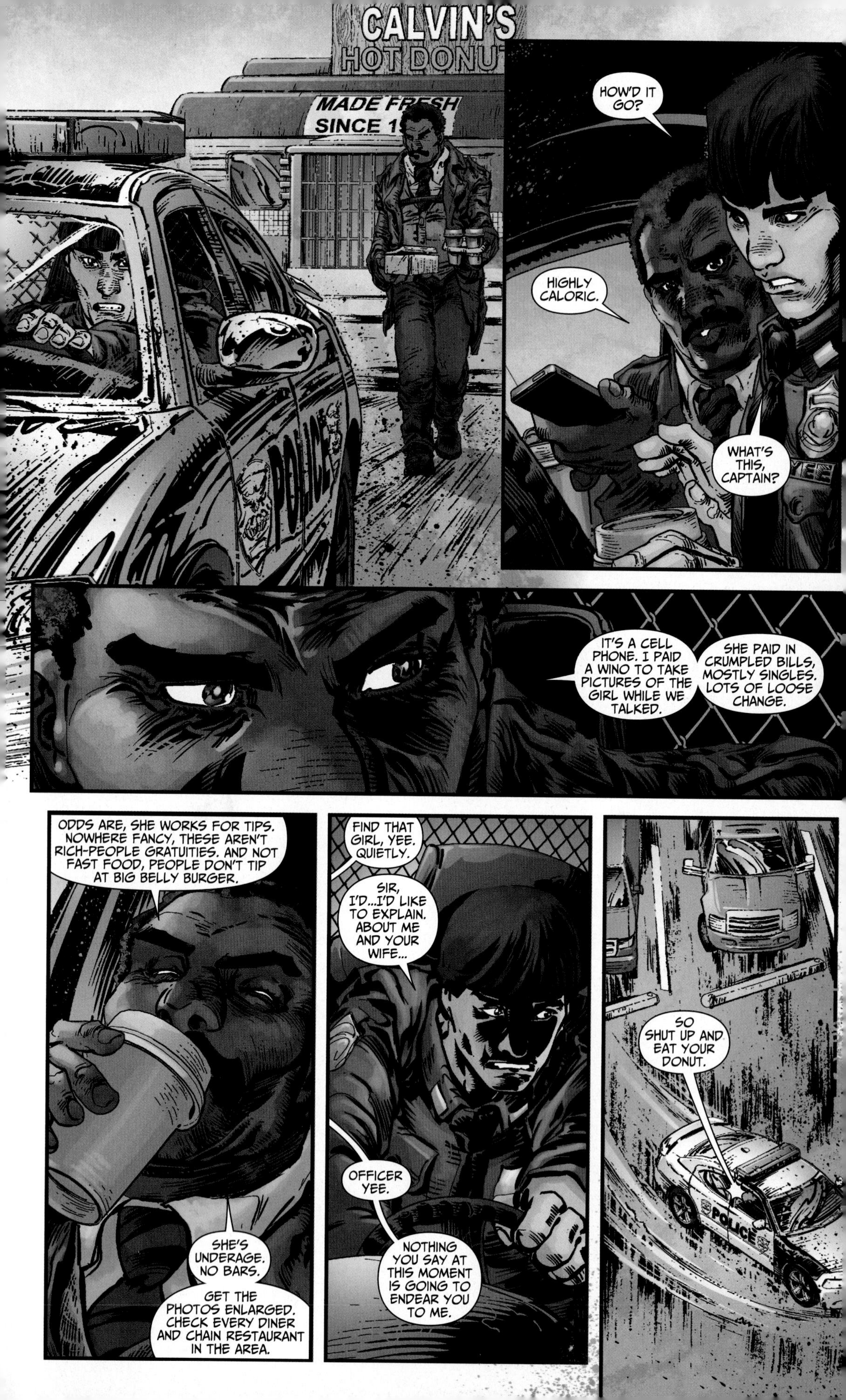
CALVIN'S
HOT DONUT
MADE FRESH
SINCE 1
POLICE
HOW'D IT GO?
HIGHLY CALORIC.
WHAT'S THIS, CAPTAIN?
YEE
IT'S A CELL PHONE. I PAID A WINO TO TAKE PICTURES OF THE GIRL WHILE WE TALKED.
SHE PAID IN CRUMPLED BILLS, MOSTLY SINGLES. LOTS OF LOOSE CHANGE.
ODDS ARE, SHE WORKS FOR TIPS. NOWHERE FANCY, THESE AREN'T RICH-PEOPLE GRATUITIES. AND NOT FAST FOOD, PEOPLE DON'T TIP AT BIG BELLY BURGER.
SHE'S UNDERAGE. NO BARS.
GET THE PHOTOS ENLARGED. CHECK EVERY DINER AND CHAIN RESTAURANT IN THE AREA.
FIND THAT GIRL, YEE. QUIETLY.
SIR, I'D...I'D LIKE TO EXPLAIN. ABOUT ME AND YOUR WIFE...
OFFICER YEE.
NOTHING YOU SAY AT THIS MOMENT IS GOING TO ENDEAR YOU TO ME.
SO SHUT UP AND EAT YOUR DONUT.
POLICE

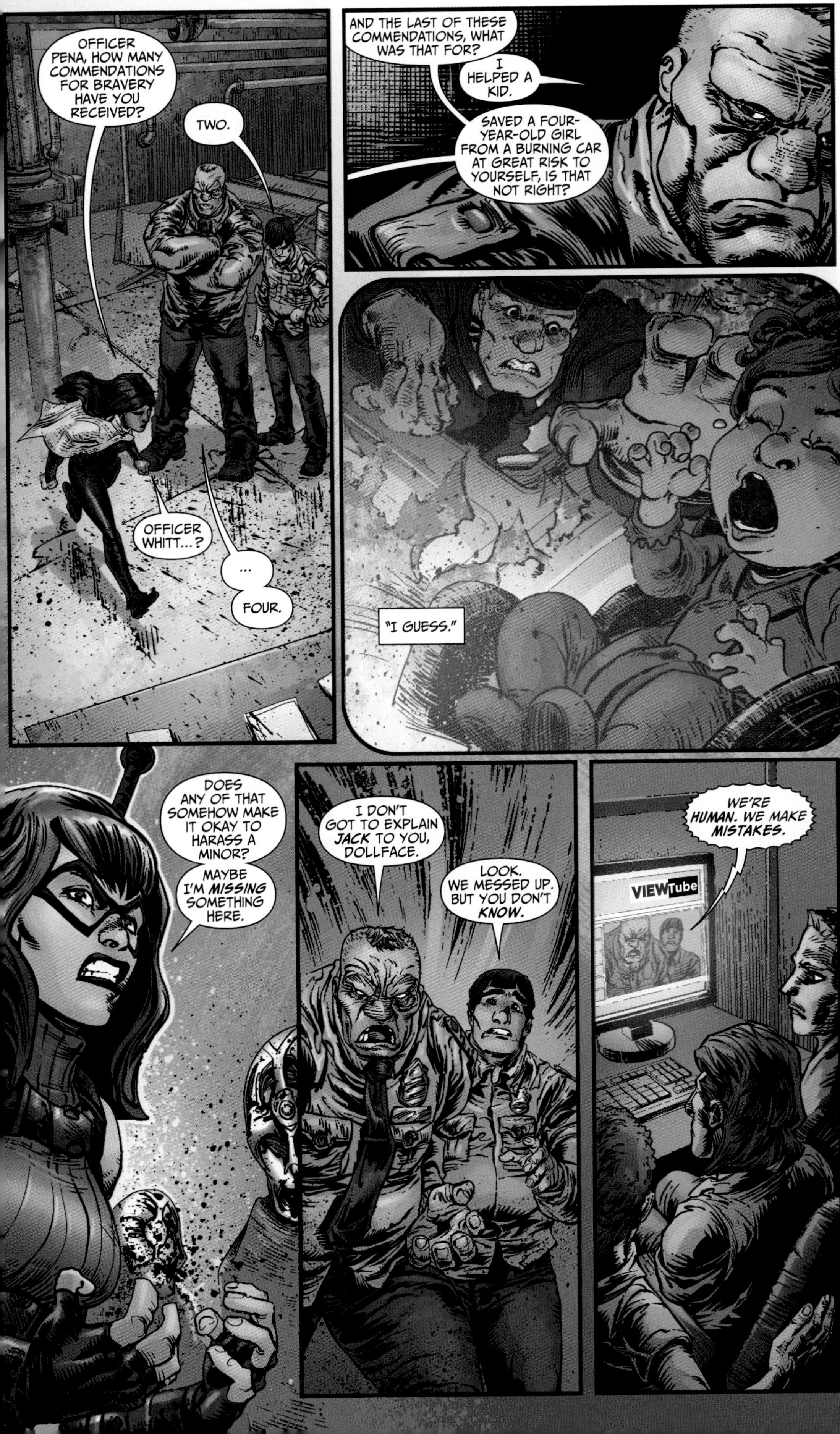
OFFICER PENA, HOW MANY COMMENDATIONS FOR BRAVERY HAVE YOU RECEIVED?
TWO.
OFFICER WHITT...?
...
FOUR.
AND THE LAST OF THESE COMMENDATIONS, WHAT WAS THAT FOR?
I HELPED A KID.
SAVED A FOUR-YEAR-OLD GIRL FROM A BURNING CAR AT GREAT RISK TO YOURSELF, IS THAT NOT RIGHT?
"I GUESS."
DOES ANY OF THAT SOMEHOW MAKE IT OKAY TO HARASS A MINOR?
MAYBE I'M MISSING SOMETHING HERE.
I DON'T GOT TO EXPLAIN JACK TO YOU, DOLLFACE.
LOOK. WE MESSED UP. BUT YOU DON'T KNOW.
WE'RE HUMAN. WE MAKE MISTAKES.
VIEWTube

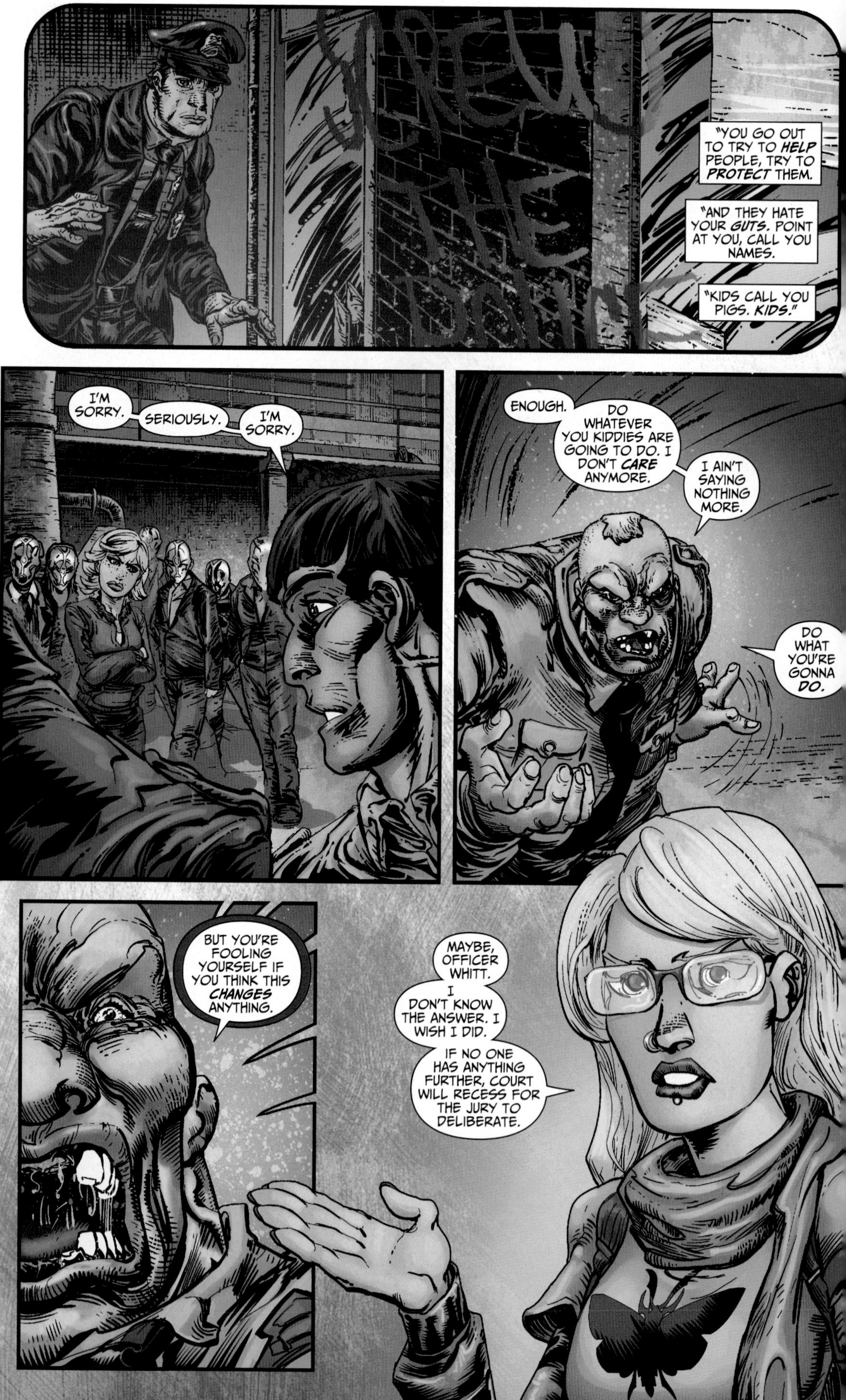

"YOU GO OUT TO TRY TO HELP PEOPLE, TRY TO PROTECT THEM.
"AND THEY HATE YOUR GUTS. POINT AT YOU, CALL YOU NAMES.
"KIDS CALL YOU PIGS. KIDS."
I'M SORRY.
SERIOUSLY.
I'M SORRY.
ENOUGH.
DO WHATEVER YOU KIDDIES ARE GOING TO DO. I DON'T CARE ANYMORE.
I AIN'T SAYING NOTHING MORE.
DO WHAT YOU'RE GONNA DO.
BUT YOU'RE FOOLING YOURSELF IF YOU THINK THIS CHANGES ANYTHING.
MAYBE, OFFICER WHITT.
I DON'T KNOW THE ANSWER. I WISH I DID.
IF NO ONE HAS ANYTHING FURTHER, COURT WILL RECESS FOR THE JURY TO DELIBERATE.

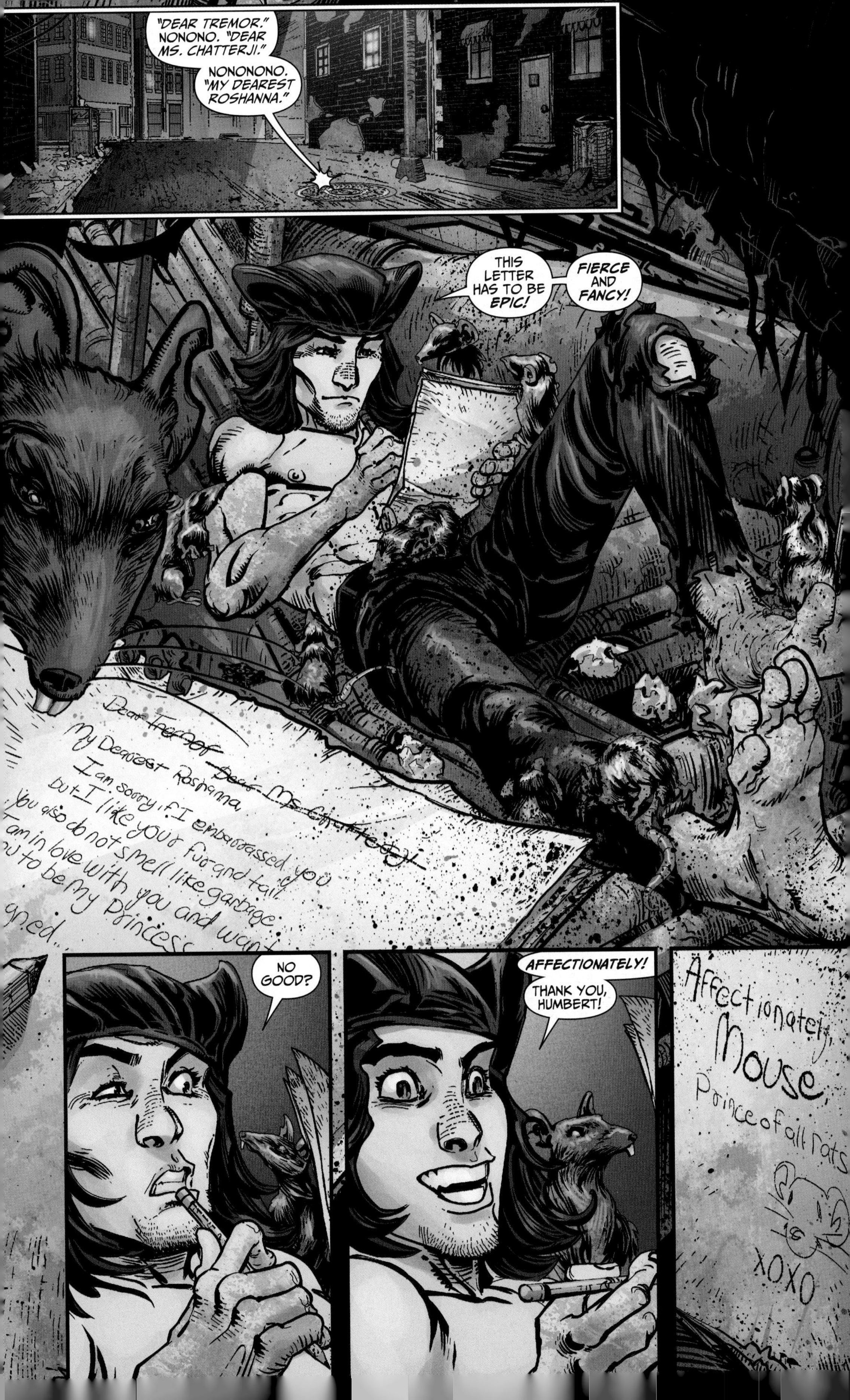

"DEAR TREMOR." NONONO. "DEAR MS. CHATTERJI."
NONONONO. "MY DEAREST ROSHANNA."
THIS LETTER HAS TO BE EPIC!
FIERCE AND FANCY!
~~Dear Tremor~~ ~~Dear Ms. Chatterji~~
My Dearest Roshanna,
I am sorry if I embarrassed you
but I like your fur and tail.
You also do not smell like garbage.
I am in love with you and want
ou to be my Princess
gned...
NO GOOD?
AFFECTIONATELY!
THANK YOU, HUMBERT!
Affectionately,
Mouse
Prince of all rats
XOXO

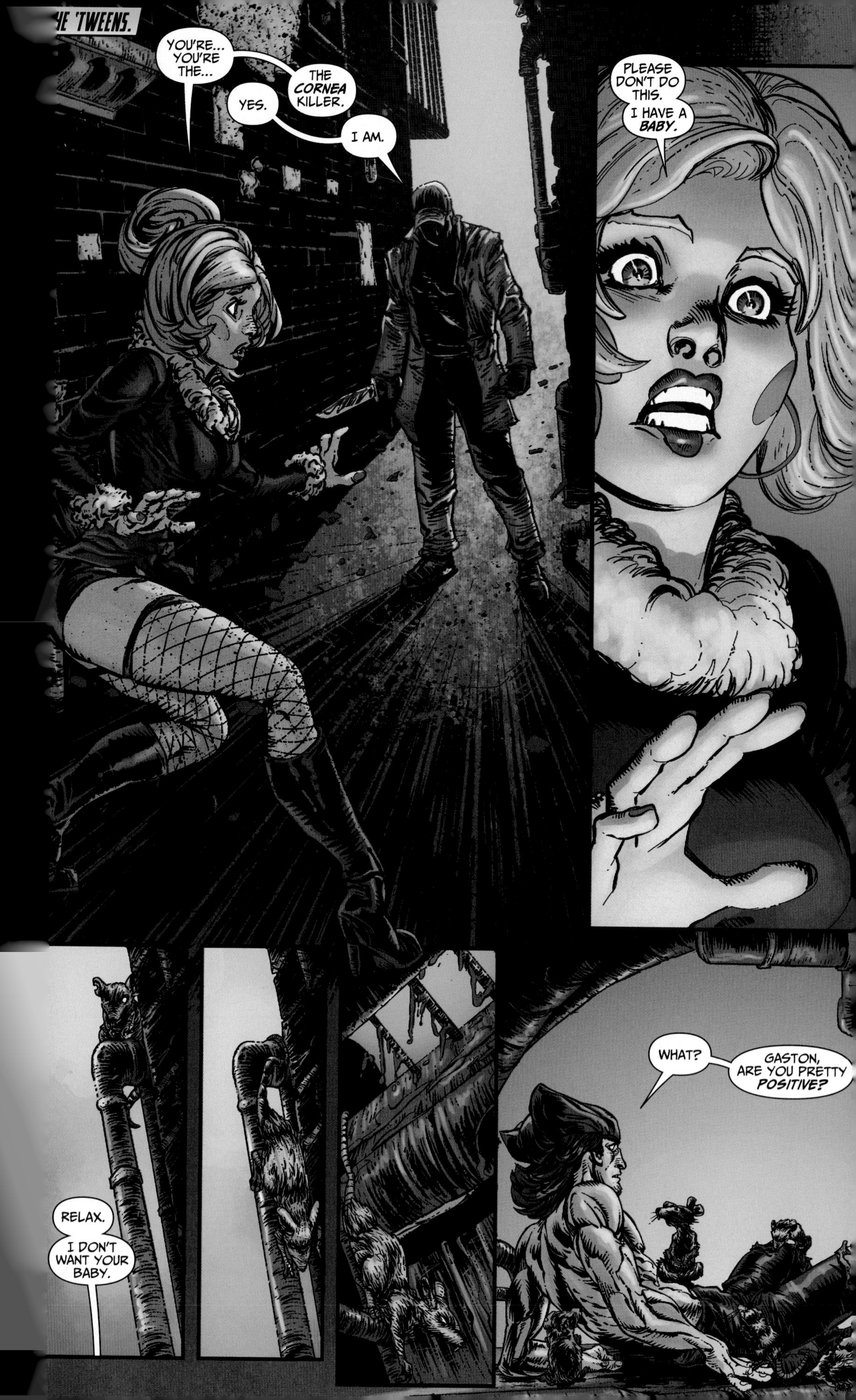
HE 'TWEENS.
YOU'RE... YOU'RE THE...
THE CORNEA KILLER.
YES.
I AM.
PLEASE DON'T DO THIS. I HAVE A BABY.
RELAX.
I DON'T WANT YOUR BABY.
WHAT?
GASTON, ARE YOU PRETTY POSITIVE?

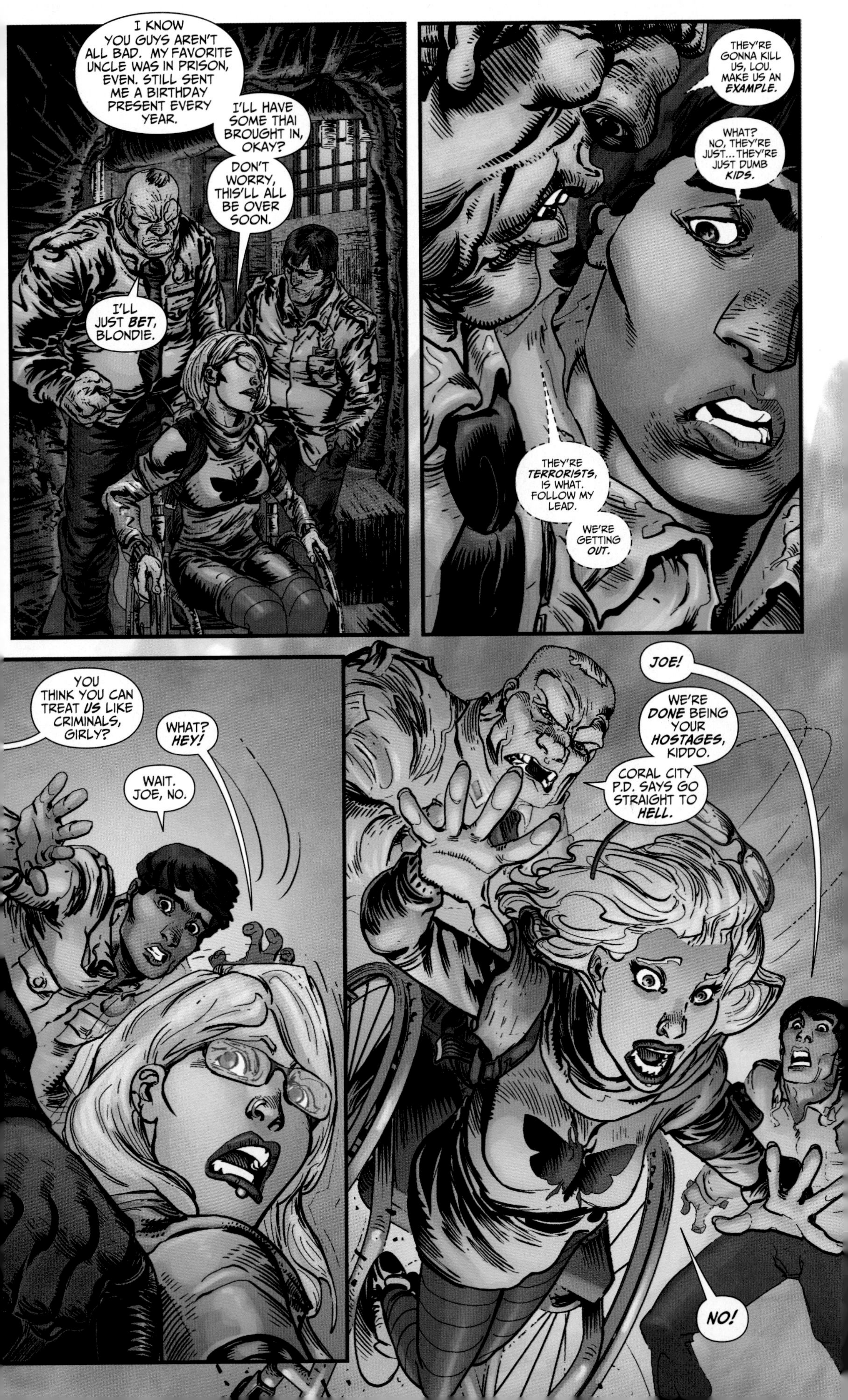
I KNOW YOU GUYS AREN'T ALL BAD. MY FAVORITE UNCLE WAS IN PRISON, EVEN. STILL SENT ME A BIRTHDAY PRESENT EVERY YEAR.
I'LL HAVE SOME THAI BROUGHT IN, OKAY?
DON'T WORRY, THIS'LL ALL BE OVER SOON.
I'LL JUST BET, BLONDIE.
THEY'RE GONNA KILL US, LOU. MAKE US AN EXAMPLE.
WHAT? NO, THEY'RE JUST... THEY'RE JUST DUMB KIDS.
THEY'RE TERRORISTS, IS WHAT. FOLLOW MY LEAD.
WE'RE GETTING OUT.
YOU THINK YOU CAN TREAT US LIKE CRIMINALS, GIRLY?
WHAT? HEY!
WAIT. JOE, NO.
JOE!
WE'RE DONE BEING YOUR HOSTAGES, KIDDO.
CORAL CITY P.D. SAYS GO STRAIGHT TO HELL.
NO!

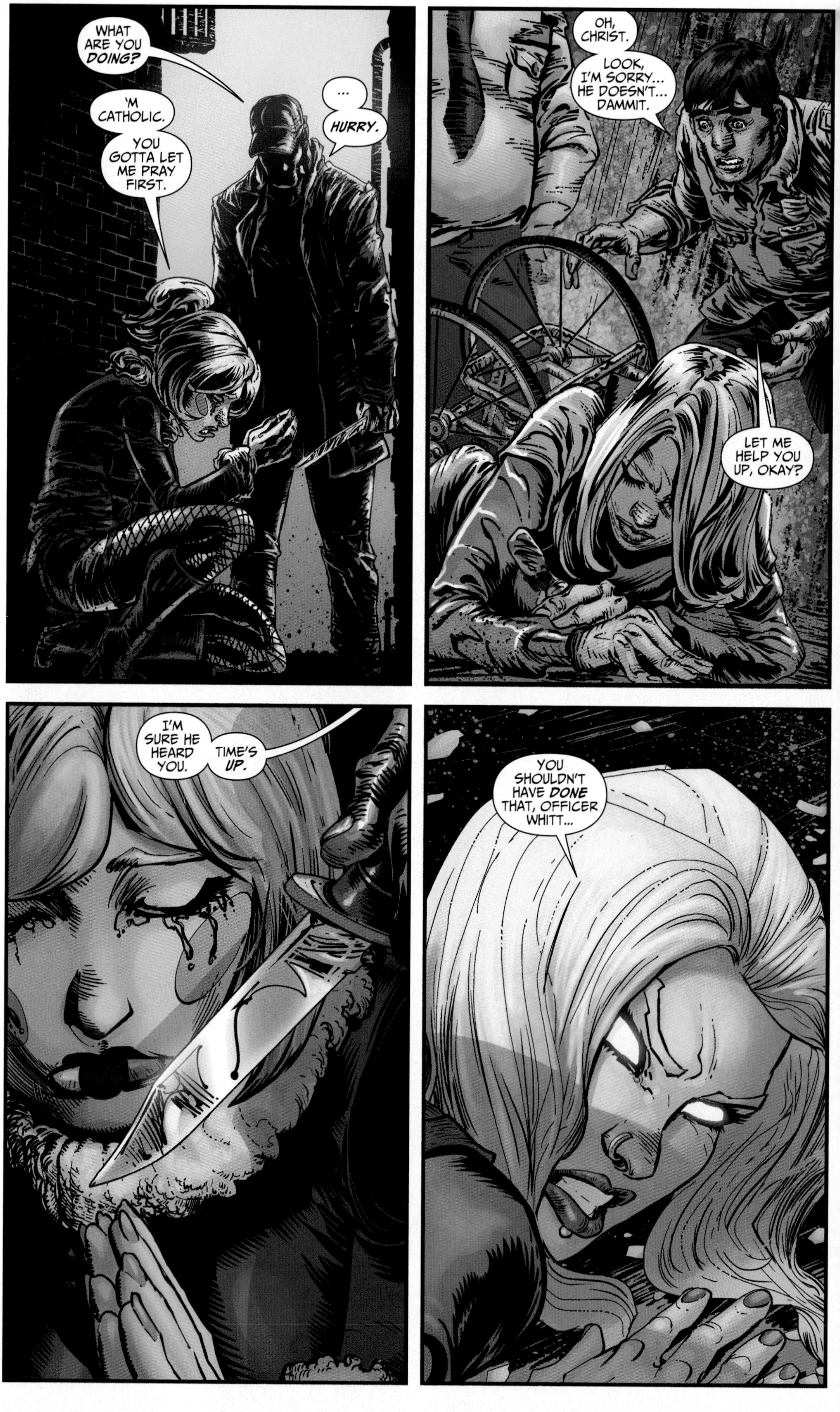

WHAT ARE YOU *DOING?*
'M CATHOLIC.
YOU GOTTA LET ME PRAY FIRST.
... *HURRY.*
OH, CHRIST.
LOOK, I'M SORRY... HE DOESN'T... DAMMIT.
LET ME HELP YOU UP, OKAY?
I'M SURE HE HEARD YOU.
TIME'S *UP.*
YOU SHOULDN'T HAVE *DONE* THAT, OFFICER WHITT...

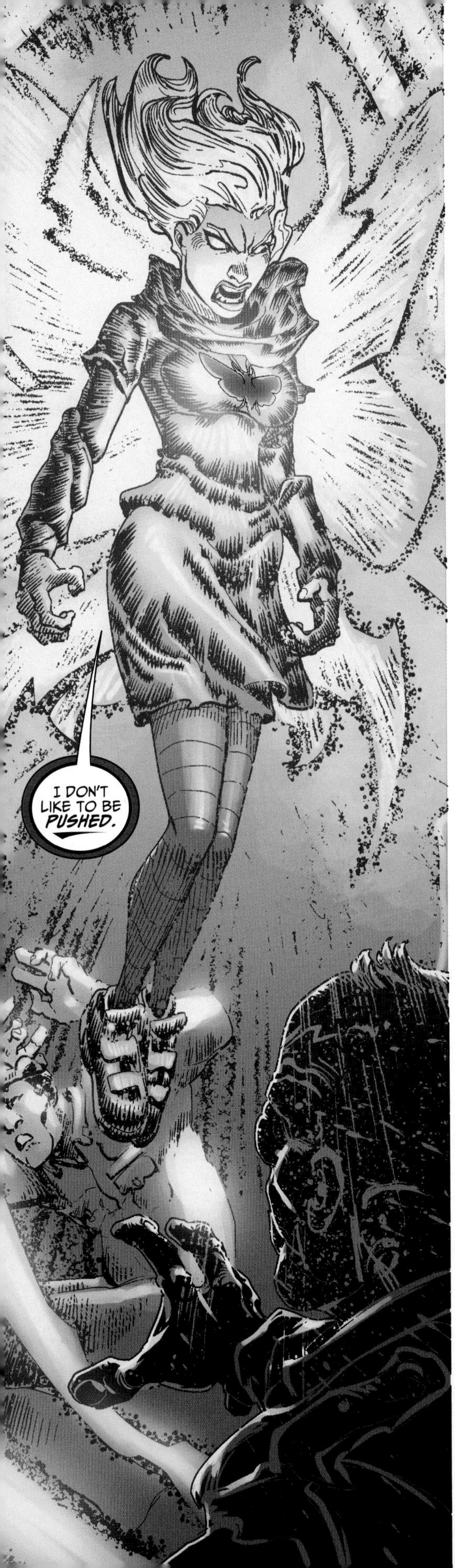
I DON'T LIKE TO BE PUSHED.

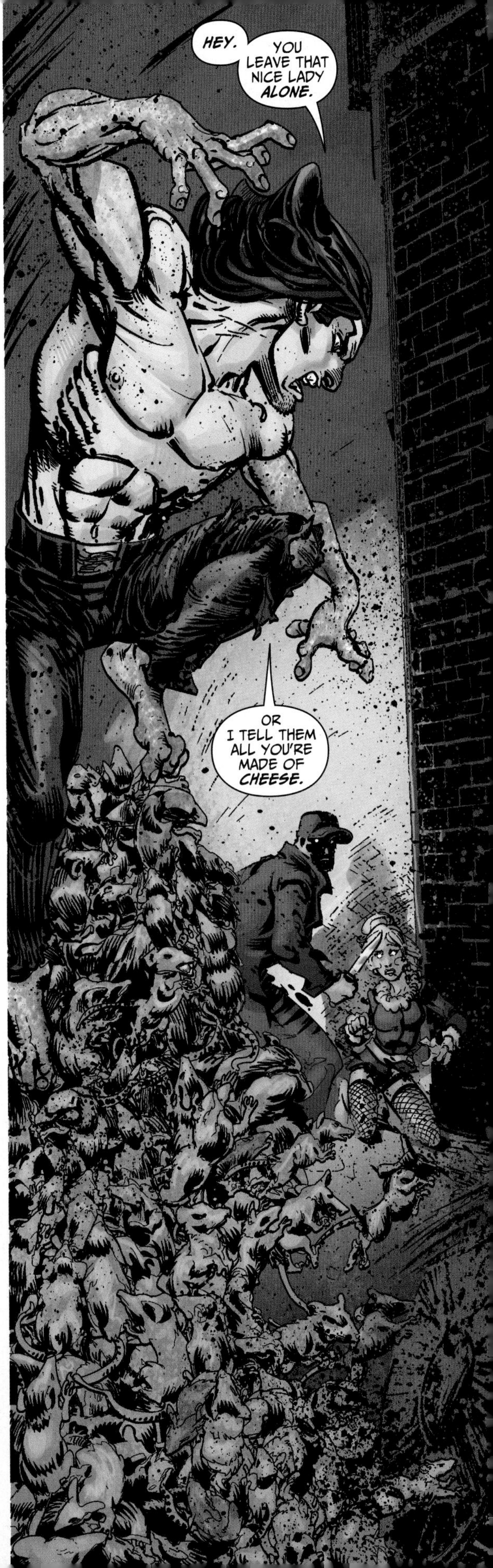
HEY.
YOU LEAVE THAT NICE LADY ALONE.
OR I TELL THEM ALL YOU'RE MADE OF CHEESE.

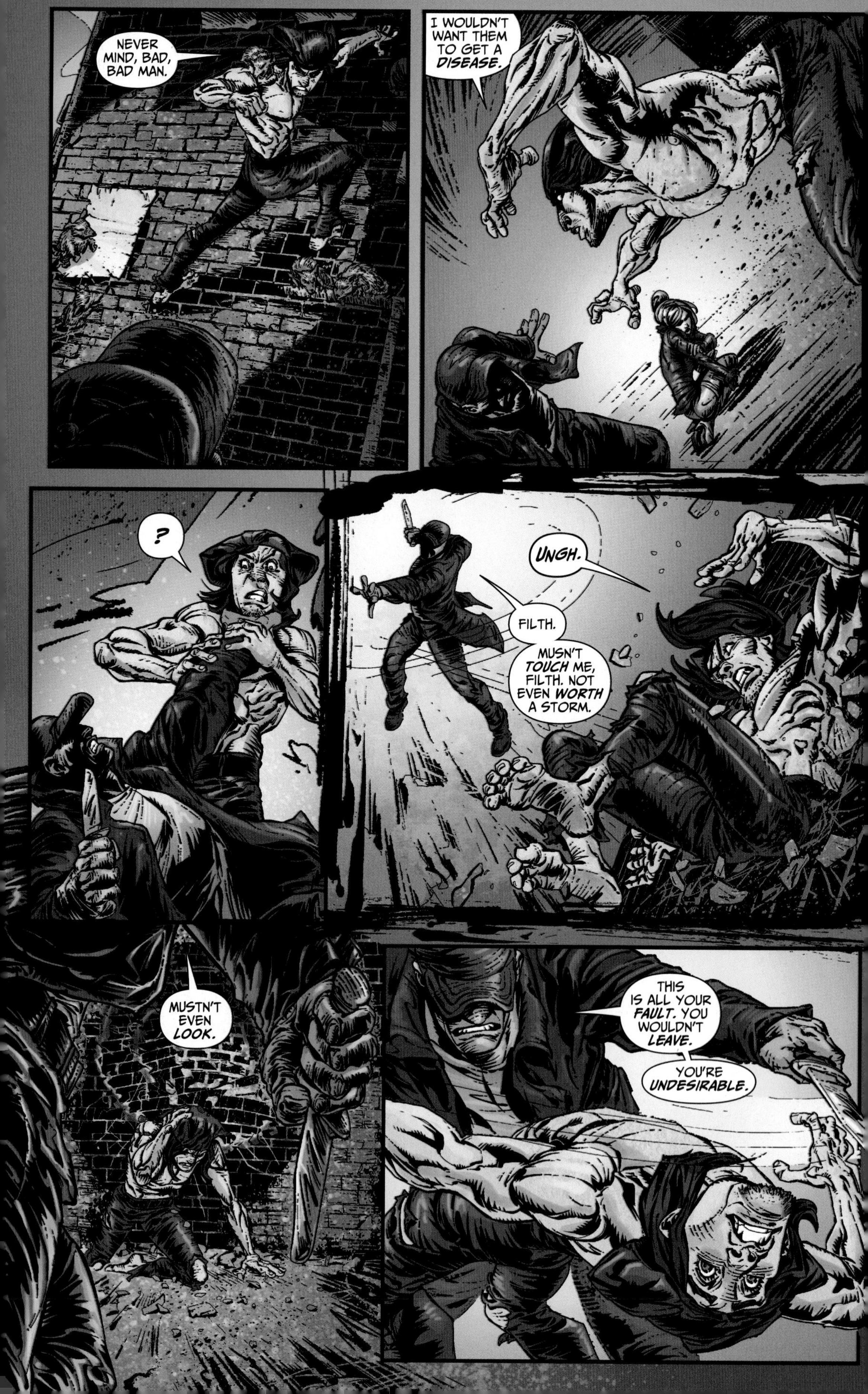
NEVER MIND, BAD, BAD MAN.
I WOULDN'T WANT THEM TO GET A DISEASE.
?
UNGH.
FILTH.
MUSN'T TOUCH ME, FILTH. NOT EVEN WORTH A STORM.
MUSTN'T EVEN LOOK.
THIS IS ALL YOUR FAULT. YOU WOULDN'T LEAVE.
YOU'RE UNDESIRABLE.

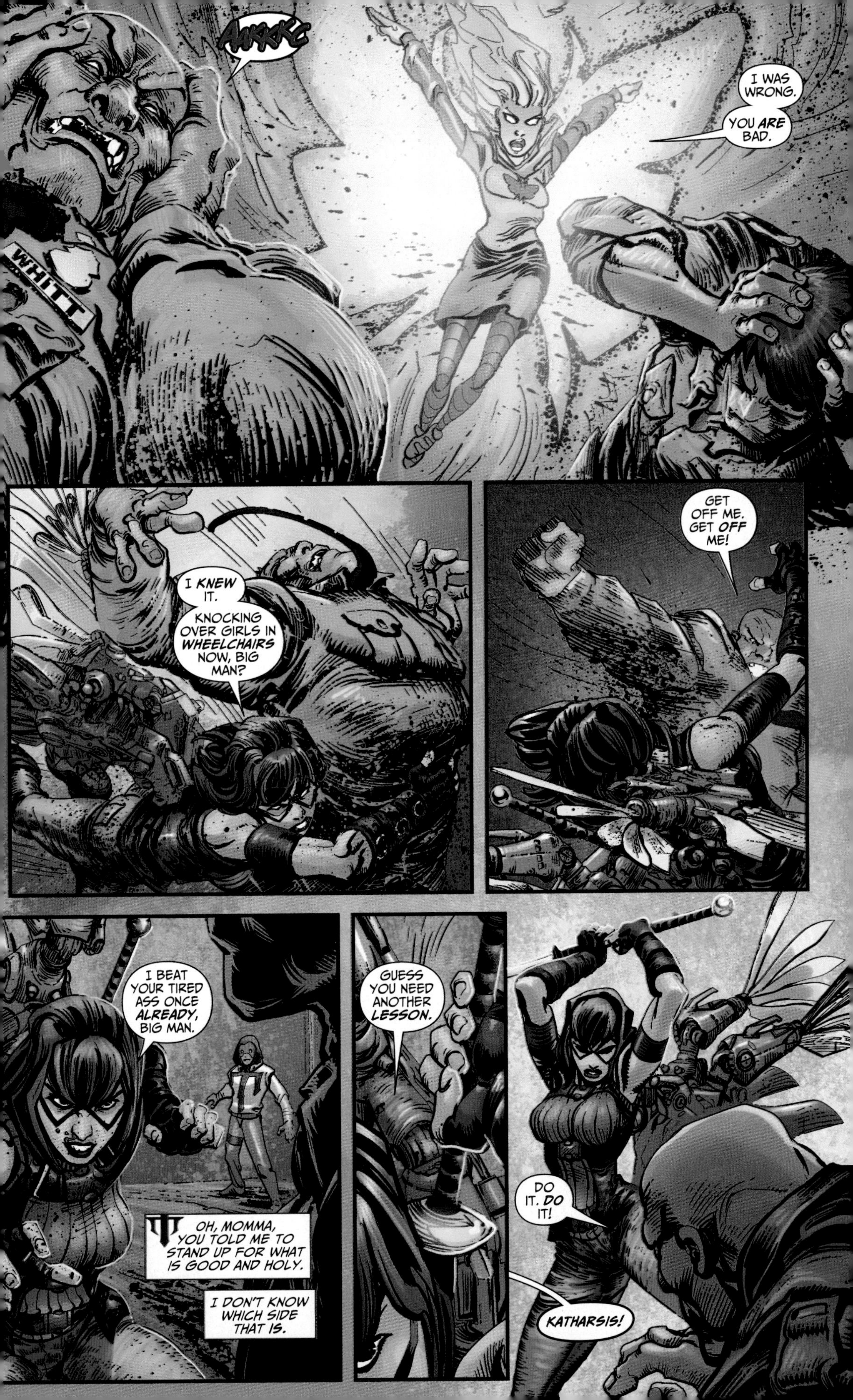
AAKKKC
WHITT
I WAS WRONG.
YOU ARE BAD.
I KNEW IT.
KNOCKING OVER GIRLS IN WHEELCHAIRS NOW, BIG MAN?
GET OFF ME. GET OFF ME!
I BEAT YOUR TIRED ASS ONCE ALREADY, BIG MAN.
OH, MOMMA, YOU TOLD ME TO STAND UP FOR WHAT IS GOOD AND HOLY.
I DON'T KNOW WHICH SIDE THAT IS.
GUESS YOU NEED ANOTHER LESSON.
DO IT. DO IT!
KATHARSIS!

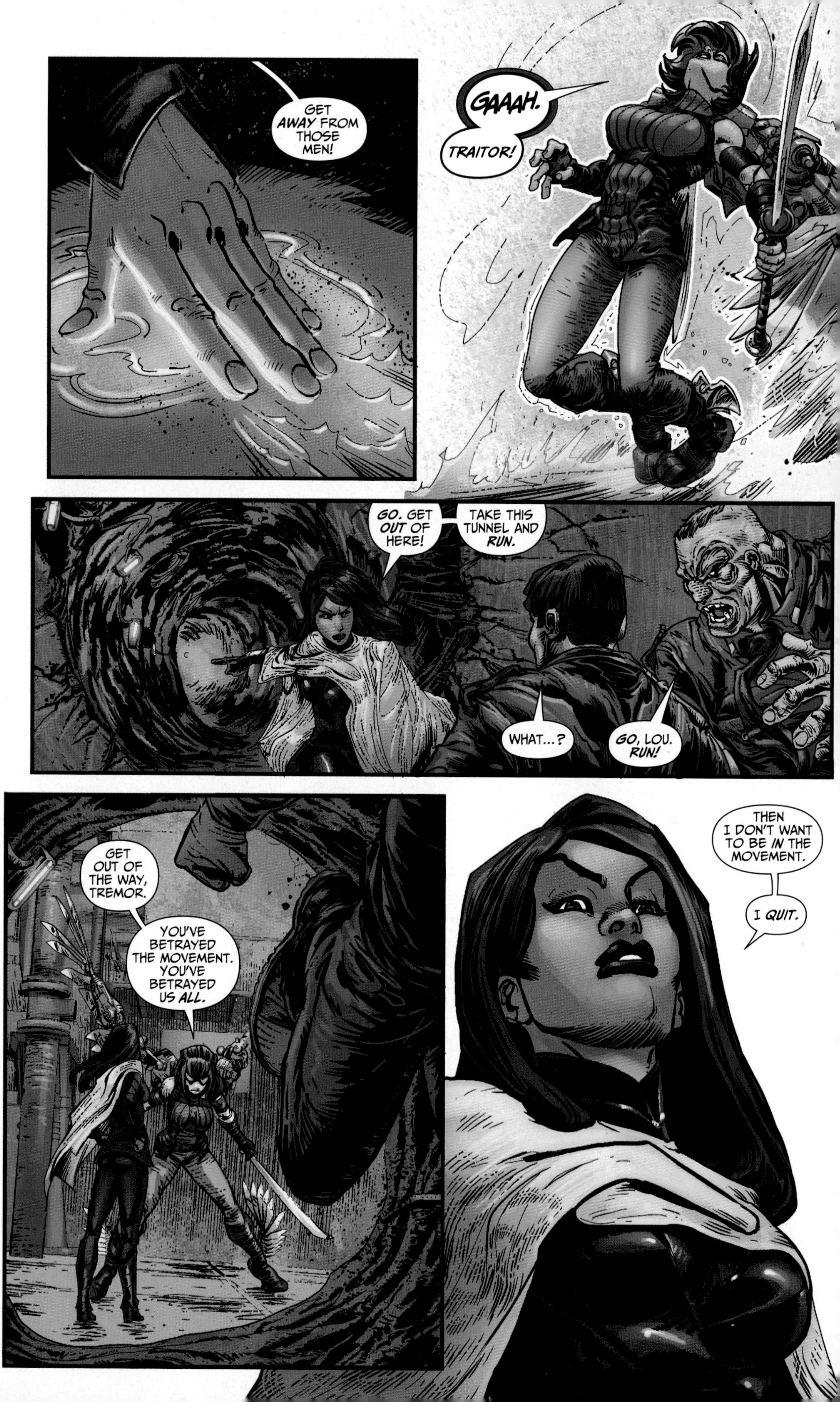
GET AWAY FROM THOSE MEN!
GAAAH.
TRAITOR!
GO. GET OUT OF HERE!
TAKE THIS TUNNEL AND RUN.
WHAT...?
GO, LOU. RUN!
GET OUT OF THE WAY, TREMOR.
YOU'VE BETRAYED THE MOVEMENT. YOU'VE BETRAYED US ALL.
THEN I DON'T WANT TO BE IN THE MOVEMENT.
I QUIT.

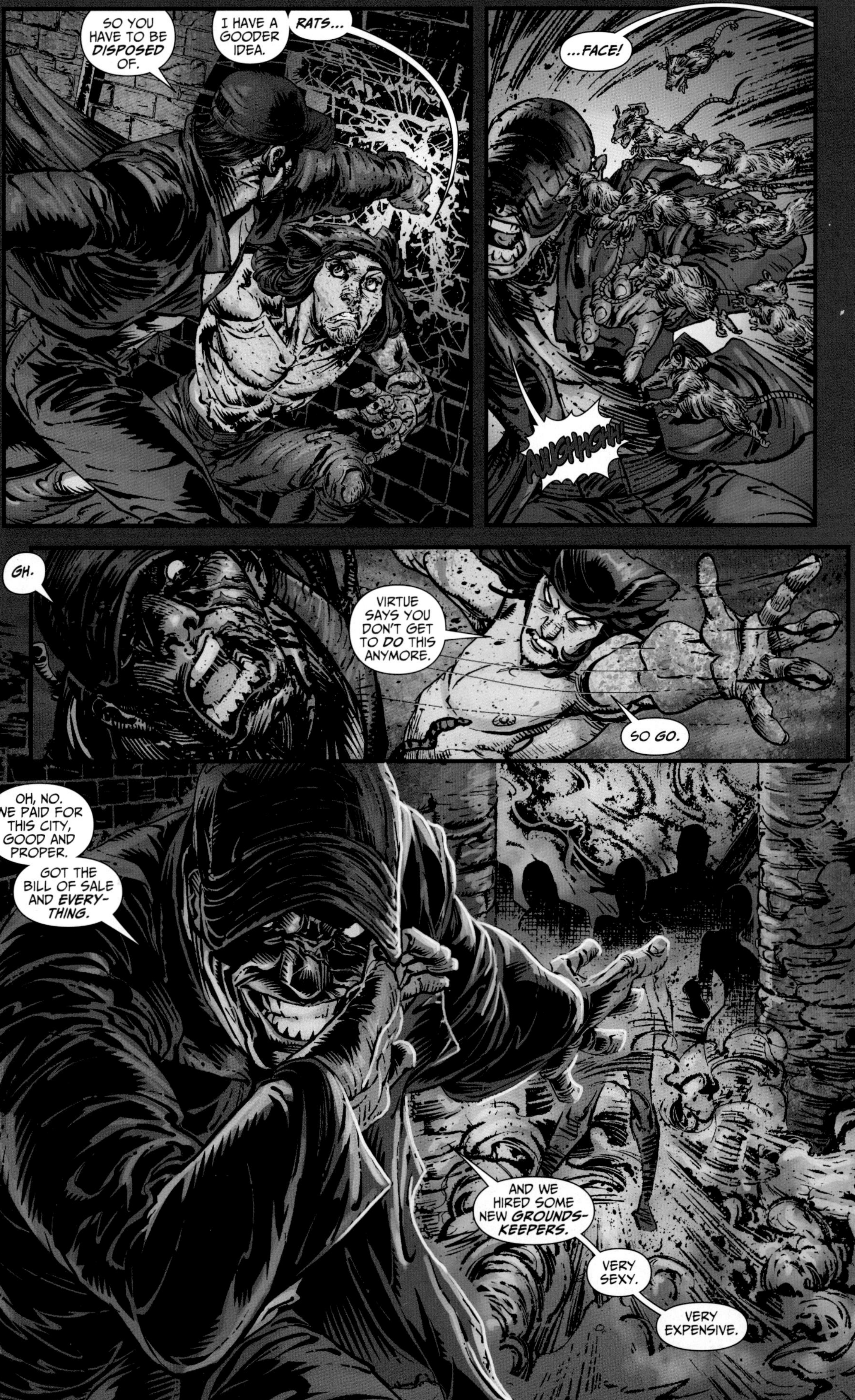

SO YOU HAVE TO BE DISPOSED OF.
I HAVE A GOODER IDEA.
RATS...
...FACE!
AAUGHHGHH!
GH.
VIRTUE SAYS YOU DON'T GET TO DO THIS ANYMORE.
SO GO.
OH, NO. WE PAID FOR THIS CITY, GOOD AND PROPER.
GOT THE BILL OF SALE AND EVERY-THING.
AND WE HIRED SOME NEW GROUNDS-KEEPERS.
VERY SEXY.
VERY EXPENSIVE.

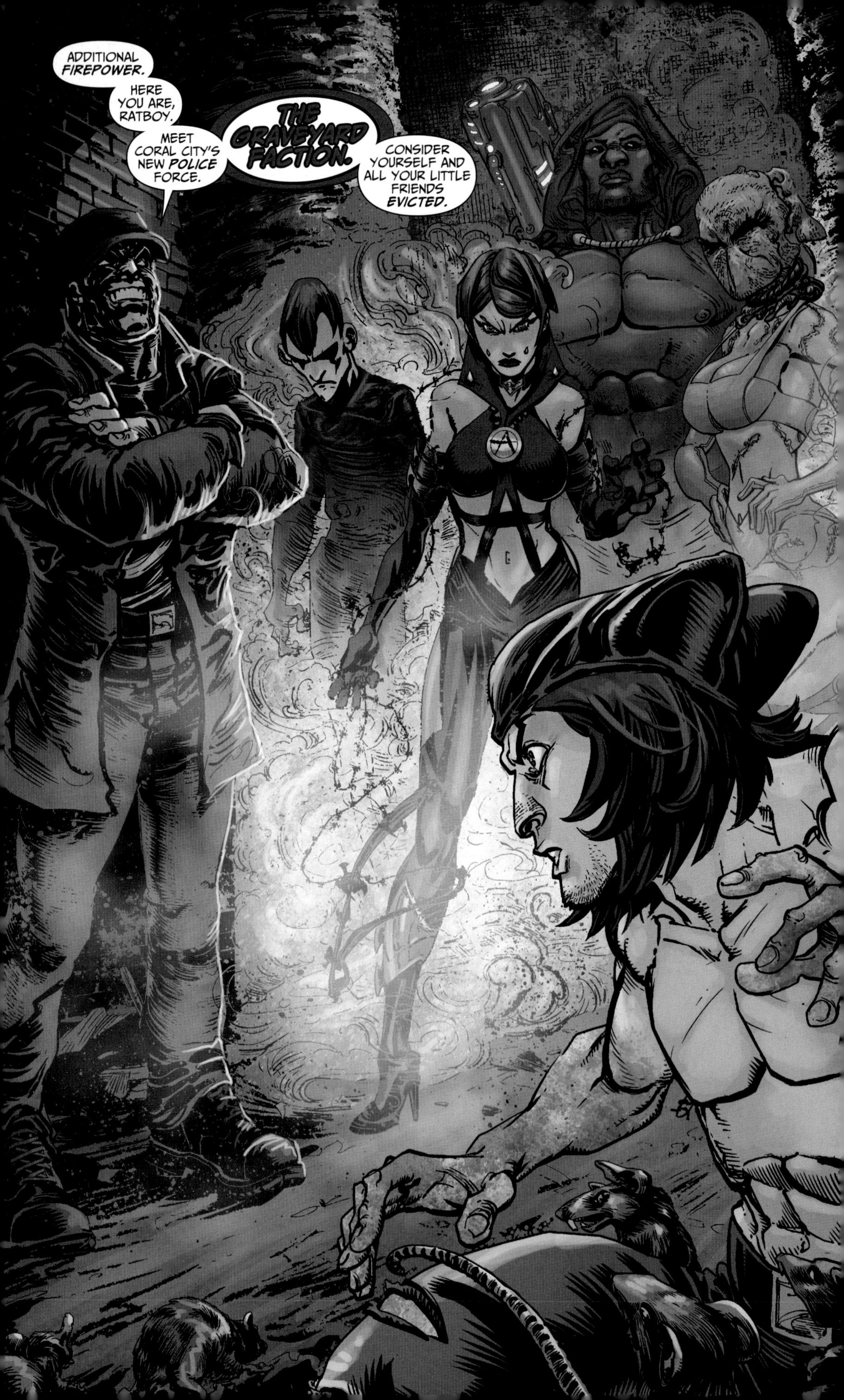

ADDITIONAL FIREPOWER.
HERE YOU ARE, RATBOY.
MEET CORAL CITY'S NEW POLICE FORCE.
THE GRAVEYARD FACTION.
CONSIDER YOURSELF AND ALL YOUR LITTLE FRIENDS EVICTED.

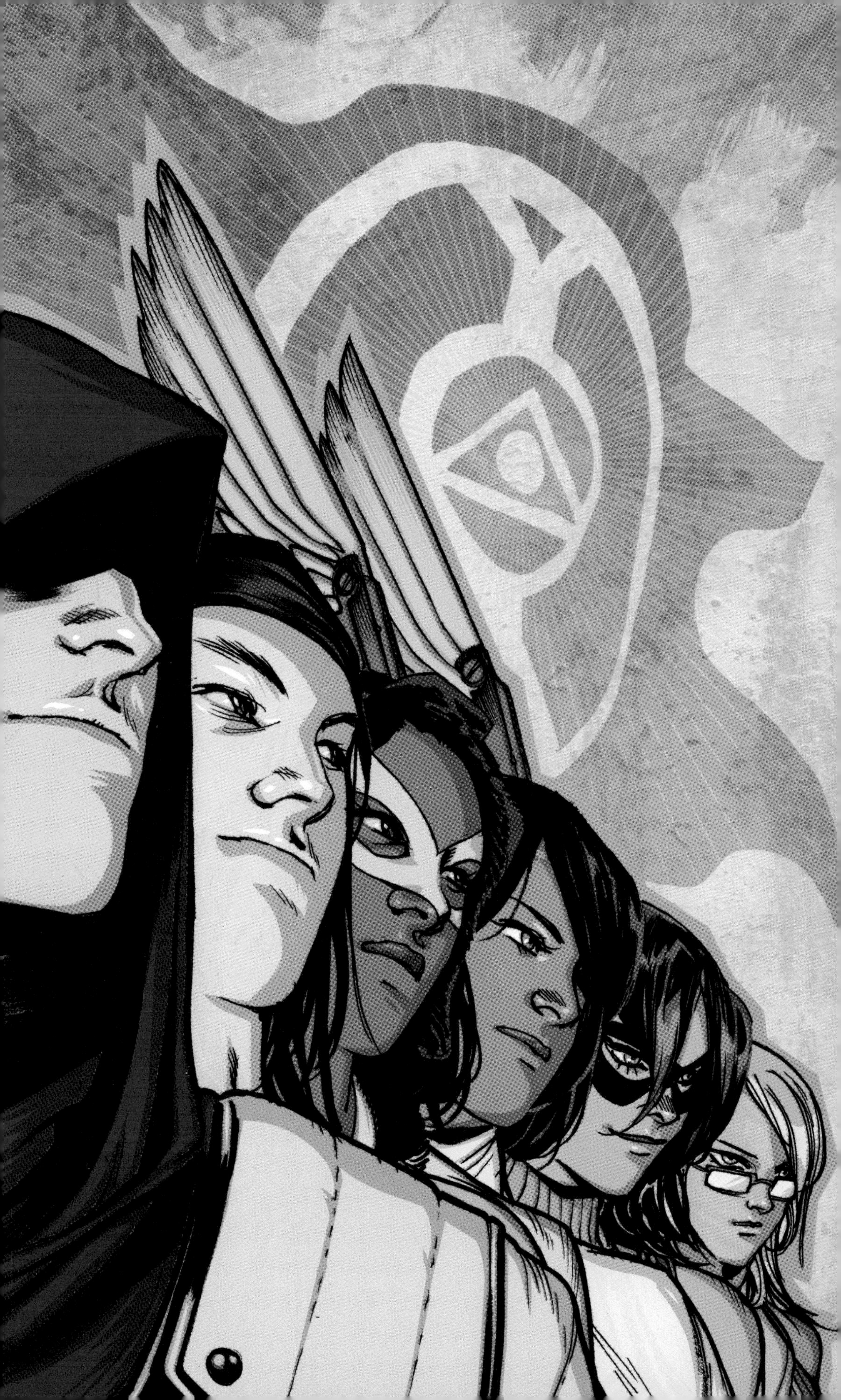

The Movement #6 cover by Rafael Albuquerque

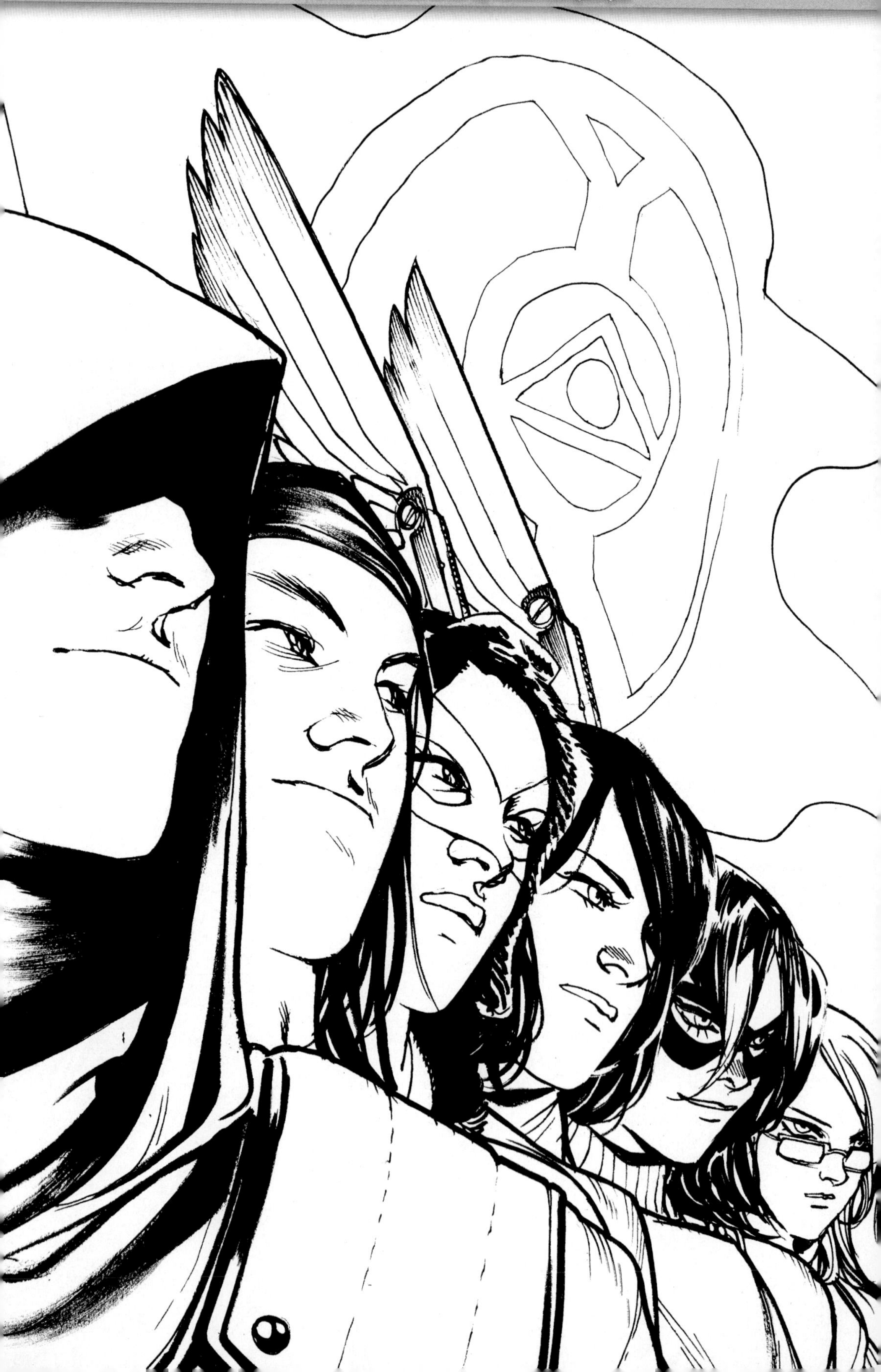

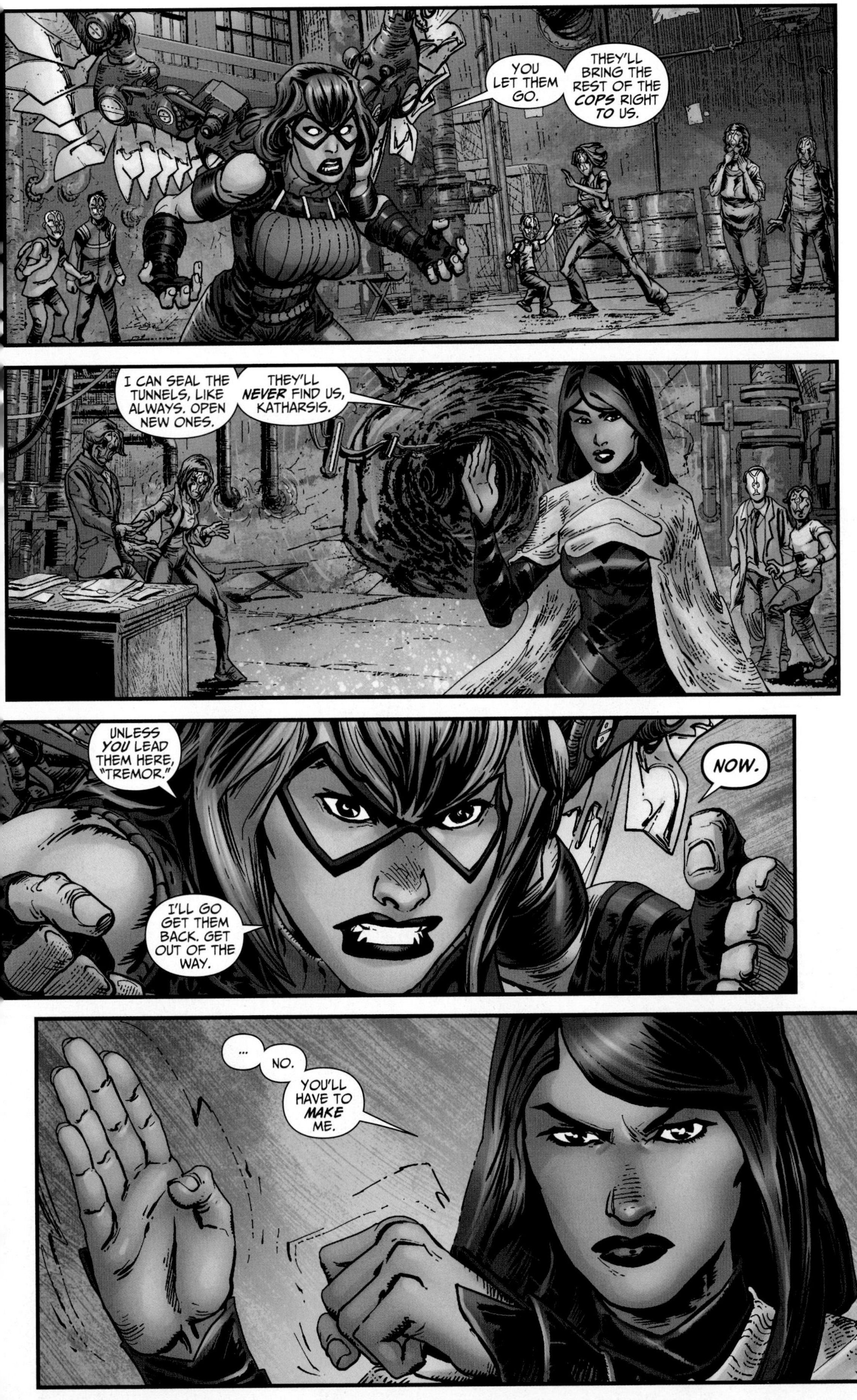
YOU LET THEM GO.
THEY'LL BRING THE REST OF THE COPS RIGHT TO US.
I CAN SEAL THE TUNNELS, LIKE ALWAYS. OPEN NEW ONES.
THEY'LL NEVER FIND US, KATHARSIS.
UNLESS YOU LEAD THEM HERE, "TREMOR."
NOW.
I'LL GO GET THEM BACK. GET OUT OF THE WAY.
...
NO.
YOU'LL HAVE TO MAKE ME.

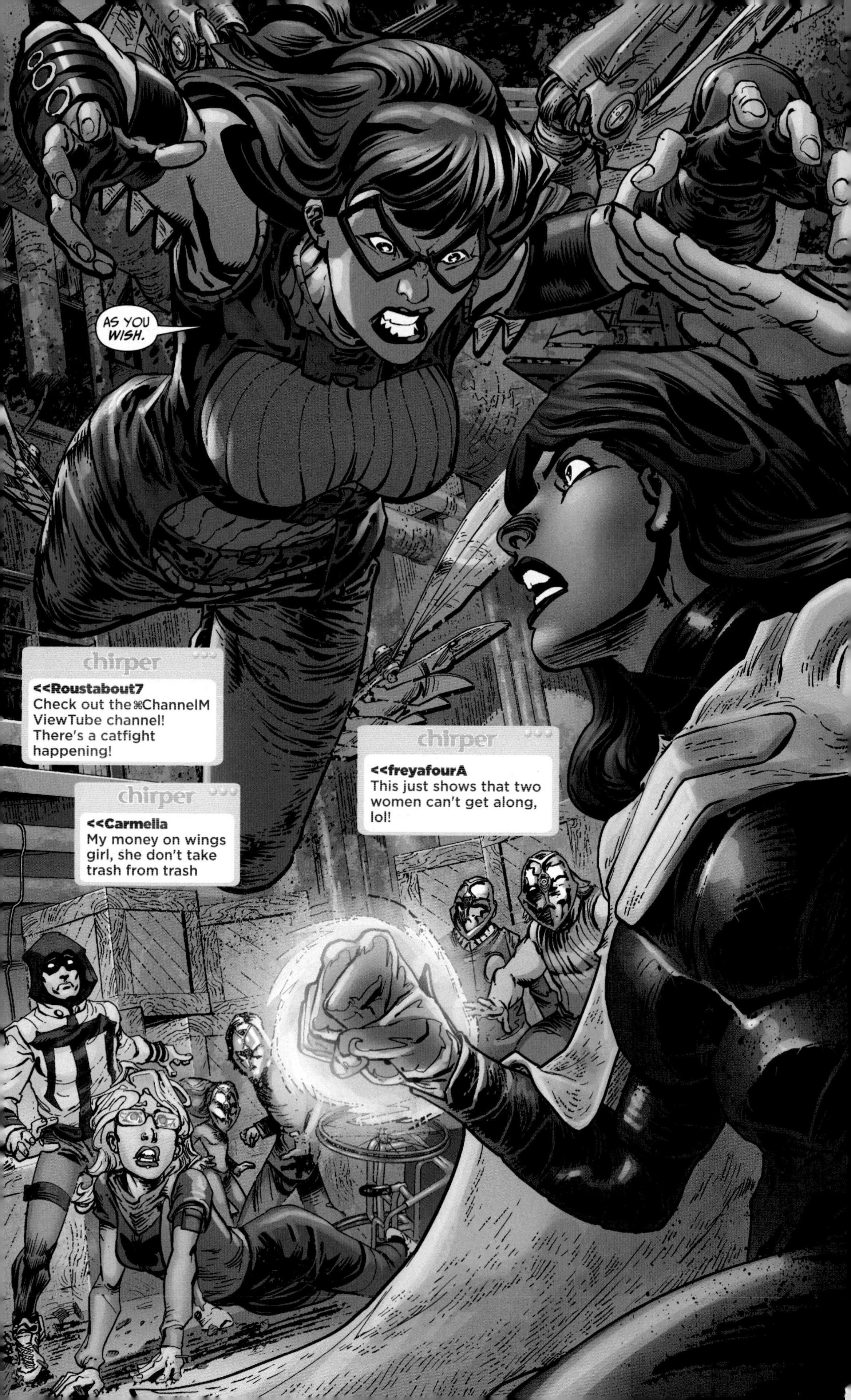

AS YOU WISH.
chirper
<<Roustabout7
Check out the ⌘ChannelM ViewTube channel! There's a catfight happening!
chirper
<<Carmella
My money on wings girl, she don't take trash from trash
chirper
<<freyafourA
This just shows that two women can't get along, lol!

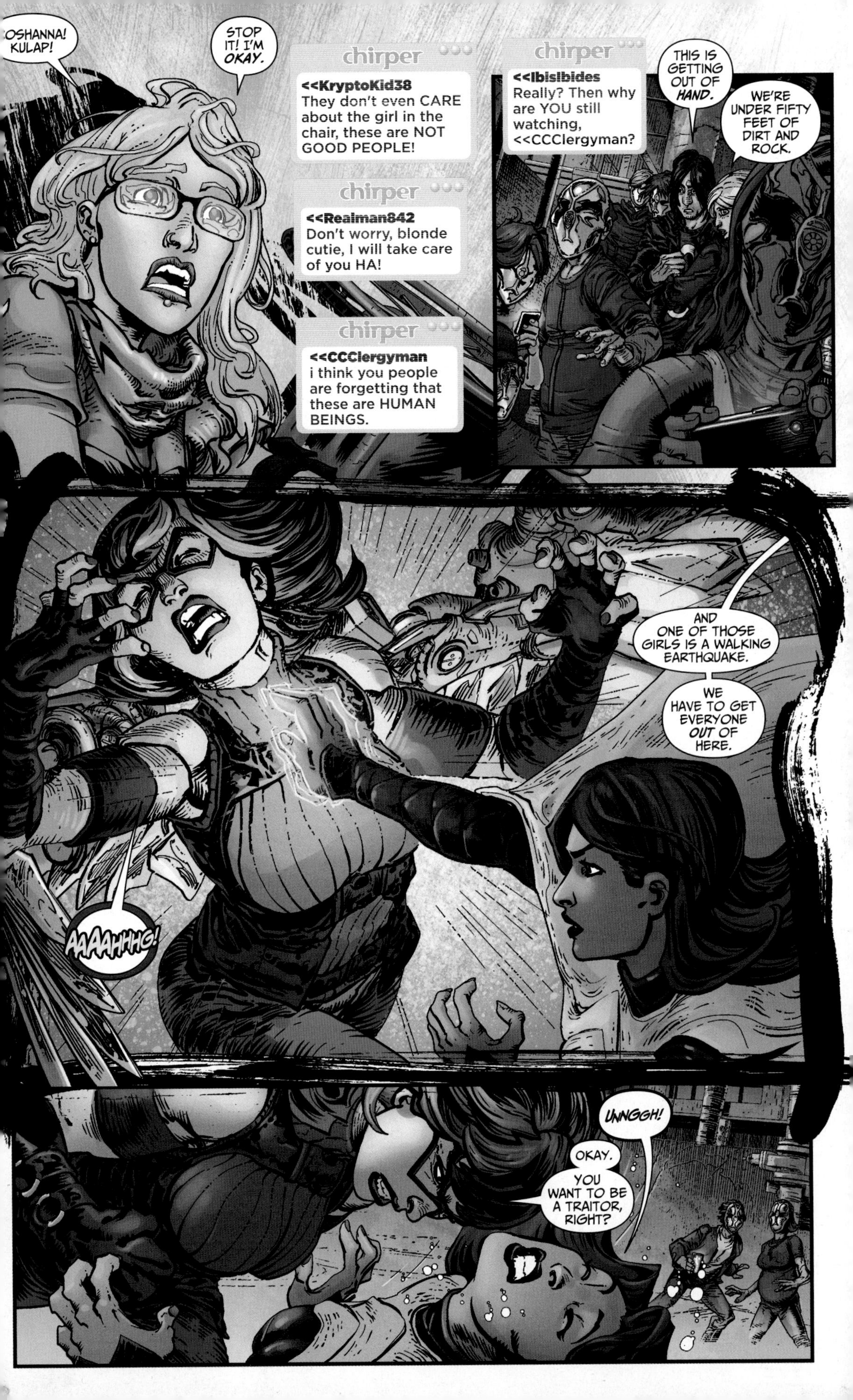
OSHANNA! KULAP!
STOP IT! I'M OKAY.
chirper
<<KryptoKid38 They don't even CARE about the girl in the chair, these are NOT GOOD PEOPLE!
chirper
<<Realman842 Don't worry, blonde cutie, I will take care of you HA!
chirper
<<CCClergyman i think you people are forgetting that these are HUMAN BEINGS.
chirper
<<Ibislbides Really? Then why are YOU still watching, <<CCClergyman?
THIS IS GETTING OUT OF HAND.
WE'RE UNDER FIFTY FEET OF DIRT AND ROCK.
AND ONE OF THOSE GIRLS IS A WALKING EARTHQUAKE.
WE HAVE TO GET EVERYONE OUT OF HERE.
AAAAHHHG!
UNNGGH!
OKAY.
YOU WANT TO BE A TRAITOR, RIGHT?

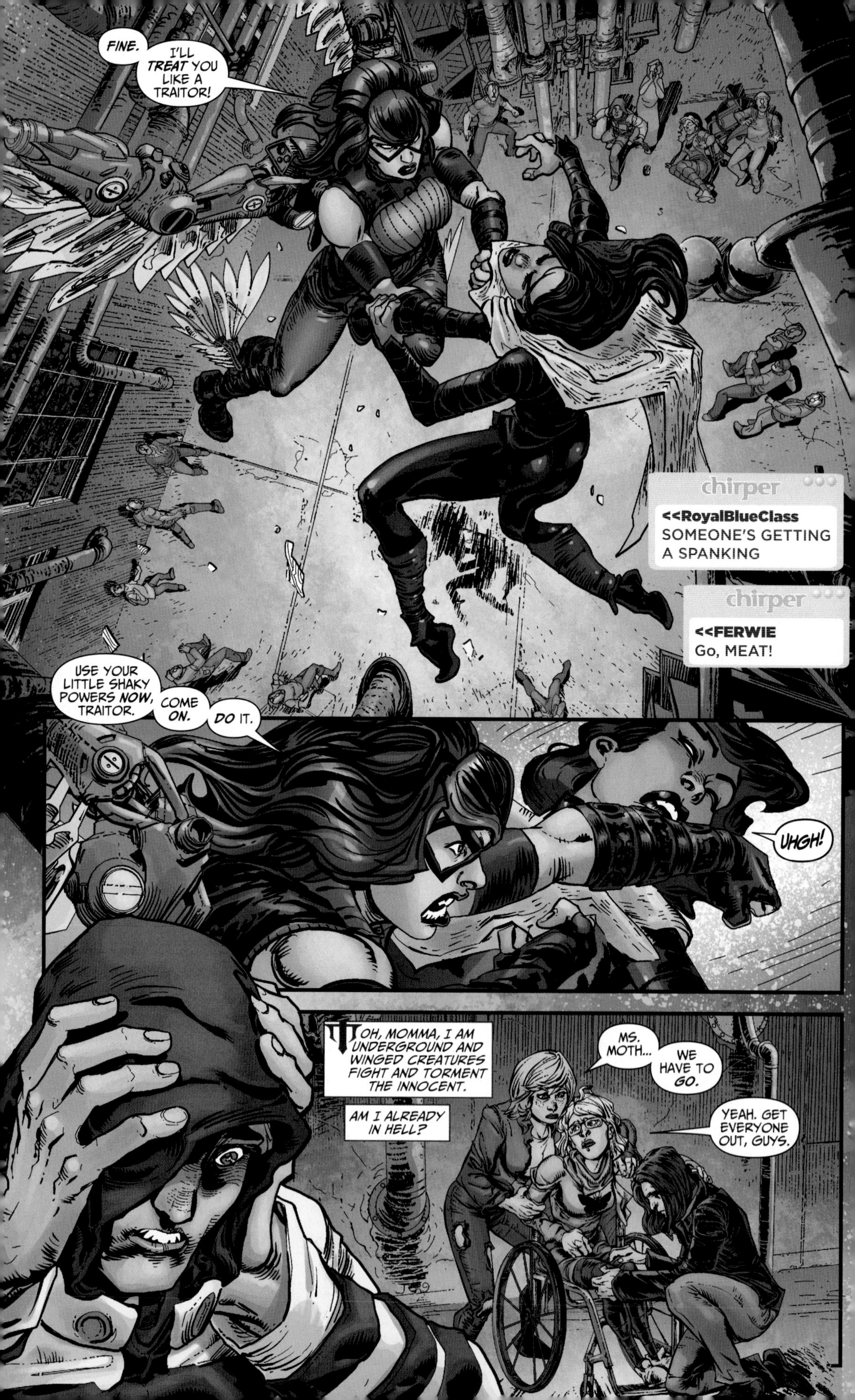
FINE.
I'LL TREAT YOU LIKE A TRAITOR!
chirper
<<RoyalBlueClass
SOMEONE'S GETTING A SPANKING
chirper
<<FERWIE
Go, MEAT!
USE YOUR LITTLE SHAKY POWERS NOW, TRAITOR.
COME ON.
DO IT.
UHGH!
OH, MOMMA, I AM UNDERGROUND AND WINGED CREATURES FIGHT AND TORMENT THE INNOCENT.
AM I ALREADY IN HELL?
MS. MOTH...
WE HAVE TO GO.
YEAH. GET EVERYONE OUT, GUYS.

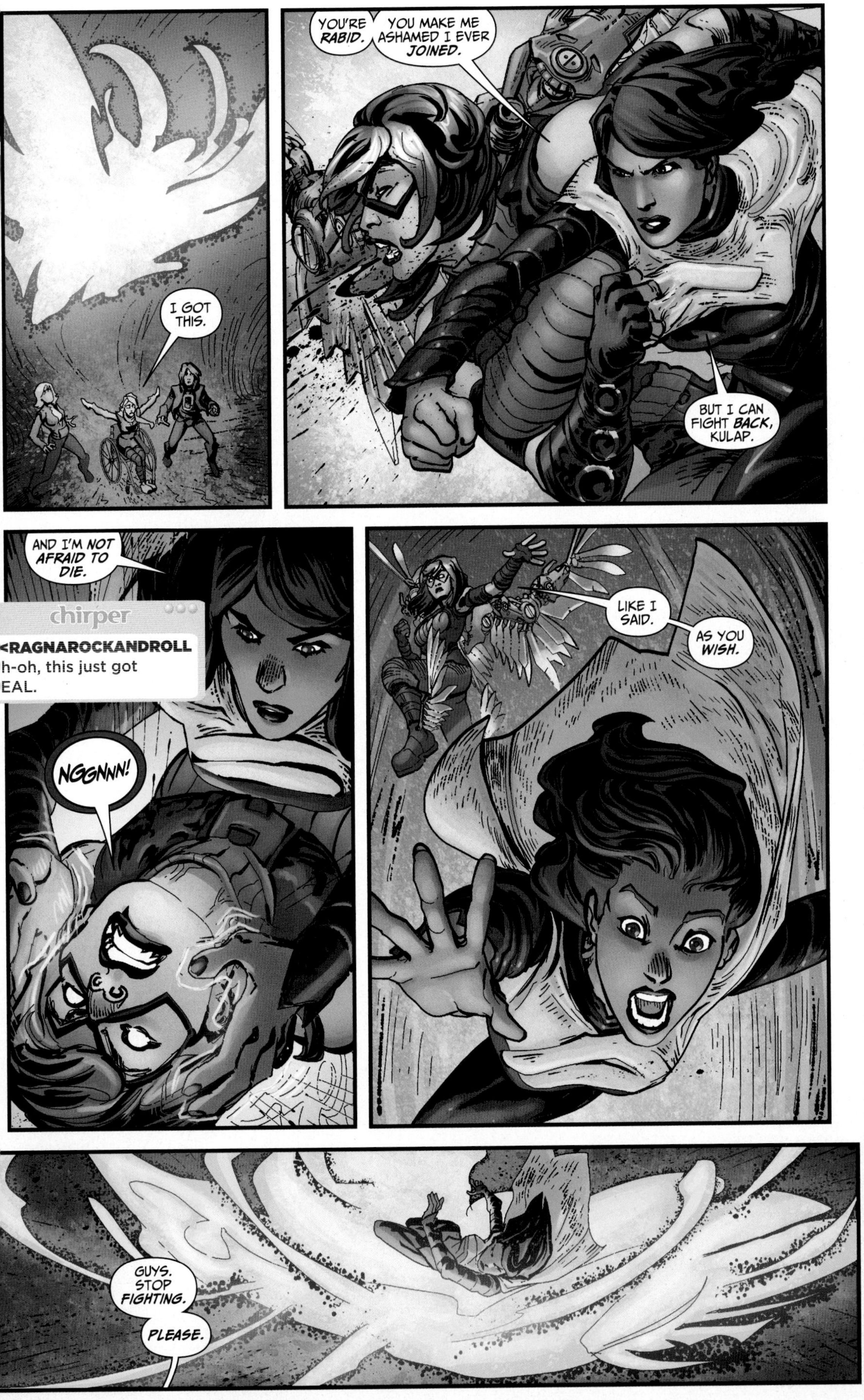
I GOT THIS.
YOU'RE RABID.
YOU MAKE ME ASHAMED I EVER JOINED.
BUT I CAN FIGHT BACK, KULAP.
AND I'M NOT AFRAID TO DIE.
chirper
<RAGNAROCKANDROLL
h-oh, this just got
EAL.
NGGNNN!
LIKE I SAID.
AS YOU WISH.
GUYS. STOP FIGHTING.
PLEASE.

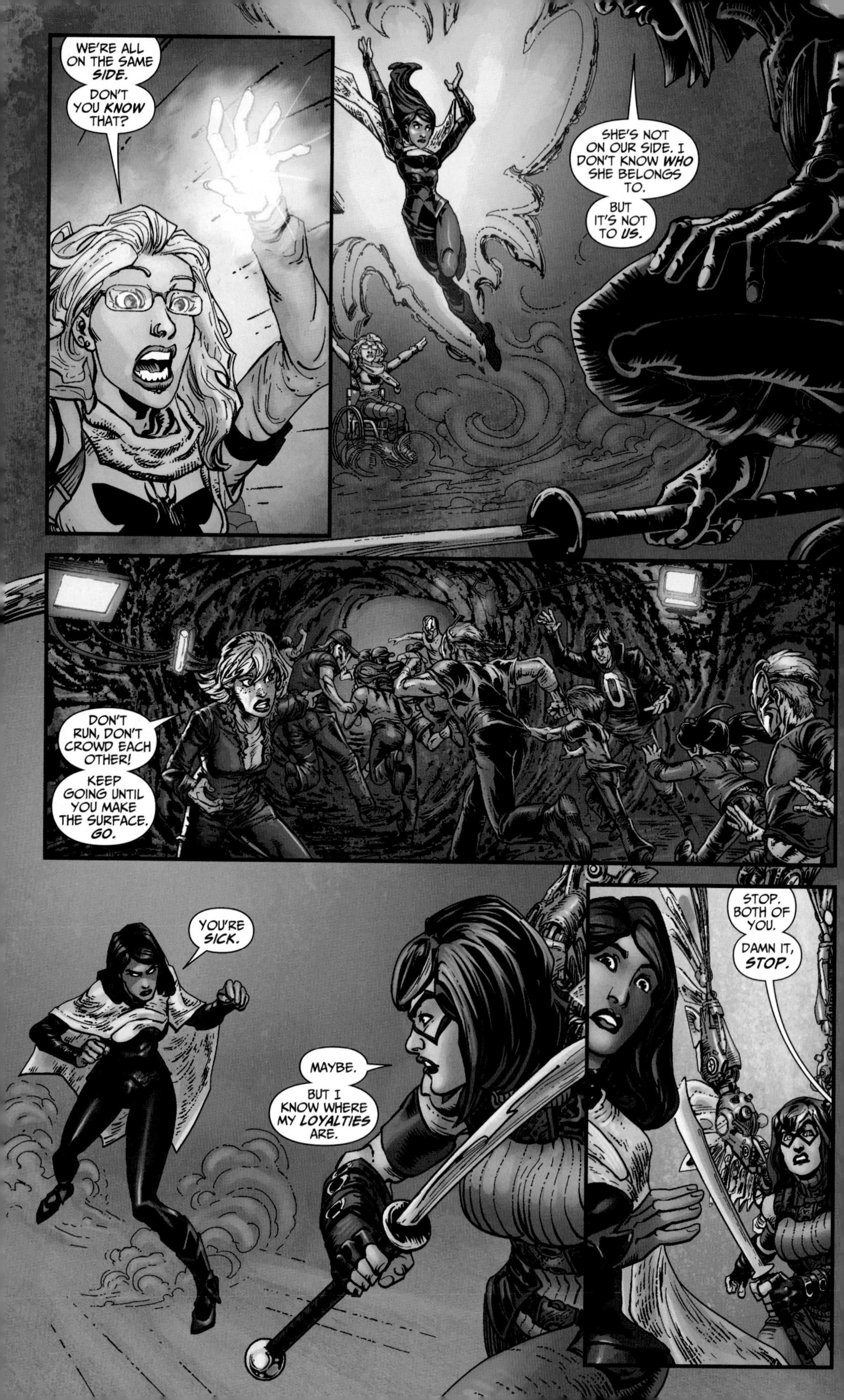
WE'RE ALL ON THE SAME SIDE.
DON'T YOU KNOW THAT?
SHE'S NOT ON OUR SIDE. I DON'T KNOW WHO SHE BELONGS TO.
BUT IT'S NOT TO US.
DON'T RUN, DON'T CROWD EACH OTHER!
KEEP GOING UNTIL YOU MAKE THE SURFACE. GO.
YOU'RE SICK.
MAYBE.
BUT I KNOW WHERE MY LOYALTIES ARE.
STOP. BOTH OF YOU.
DAMN IT, STOP.

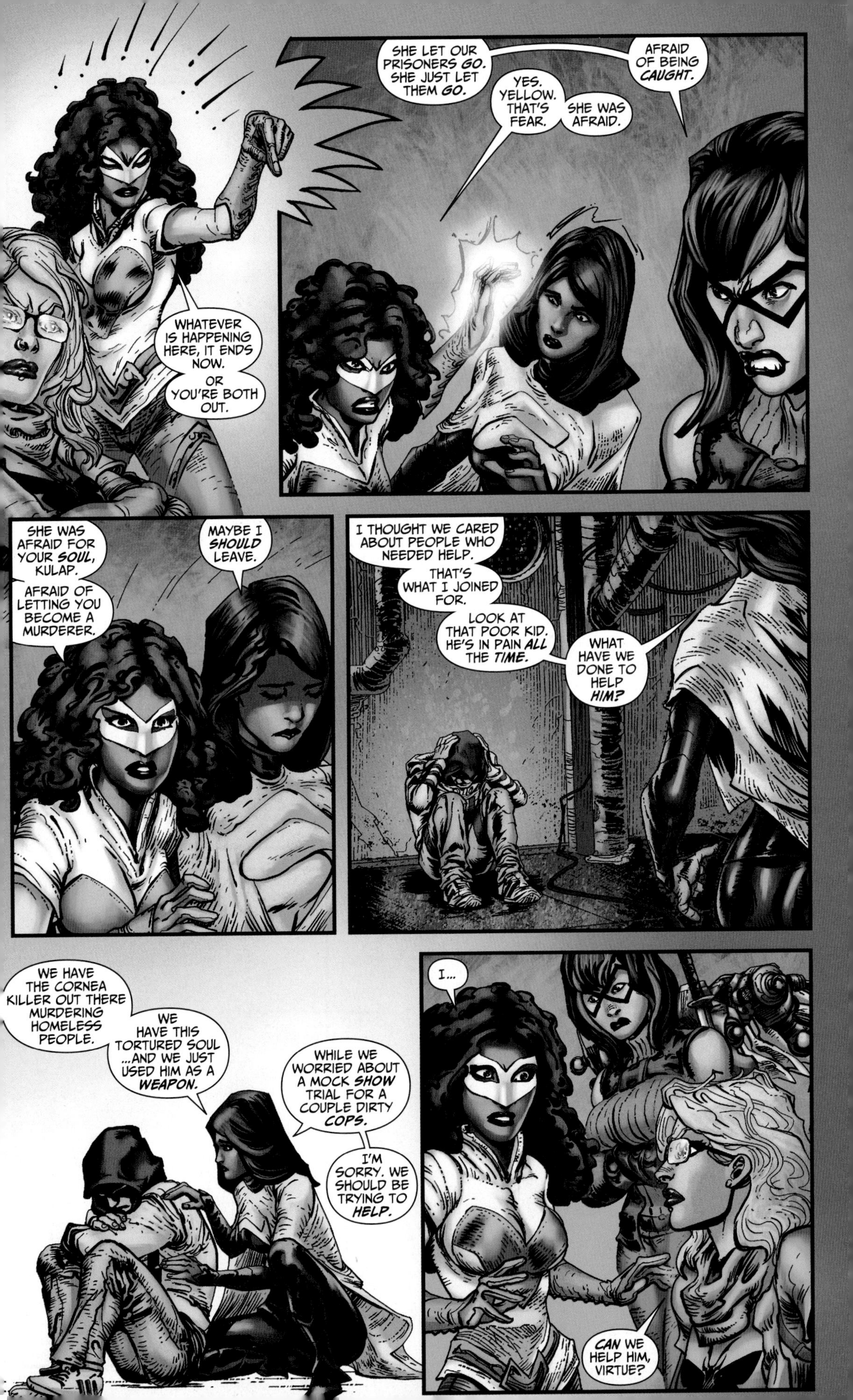
WHATEVER IS HAPPENING HERE, IT ENDS NOW.
OR YOU'RE BOTH OUT.
SHE LET OUR PRISONERS GO. SHE JUST LET THEM GO.
YES. YELLOW. THAT'S FEAR.
SHE WAS AFRAID.
AFRAID OF BEING CAUGHT.
SHE WAS AFRAID FOR YOUR SOUL, KULAP.
AFRAID OF LETTING YOU BECOME A MURDERER.
MAYBE I SHOULD LEAVE.
I THOUGHT WE CARED ABOUT PEOPLE WHO NEEDED HELP.
THAT'S WHAT I JOINED FOR.
LOOK AT THAT POOR KID. HE'S IN PAIN ALL THE TIME.
WHAT HAVE WE DONE TO HELP HIM?
WE HAVE THE CORNEA KILLER OUT THERE MURDERING HOMELESS PEOPLE.
WE HAVE THIS TORTURED SOUL ...AND WE JUST USED HIM AS A WEAPON.
WHILE WE WORRIED ABOUT A MOCK SHOW TRIAL FOR A COUPLE DIRTY COPS.
I'M SORRY. WE SHOULD BE TRYING TO HELP.
I...
CAN WE HELP HIM, VIRTUE?

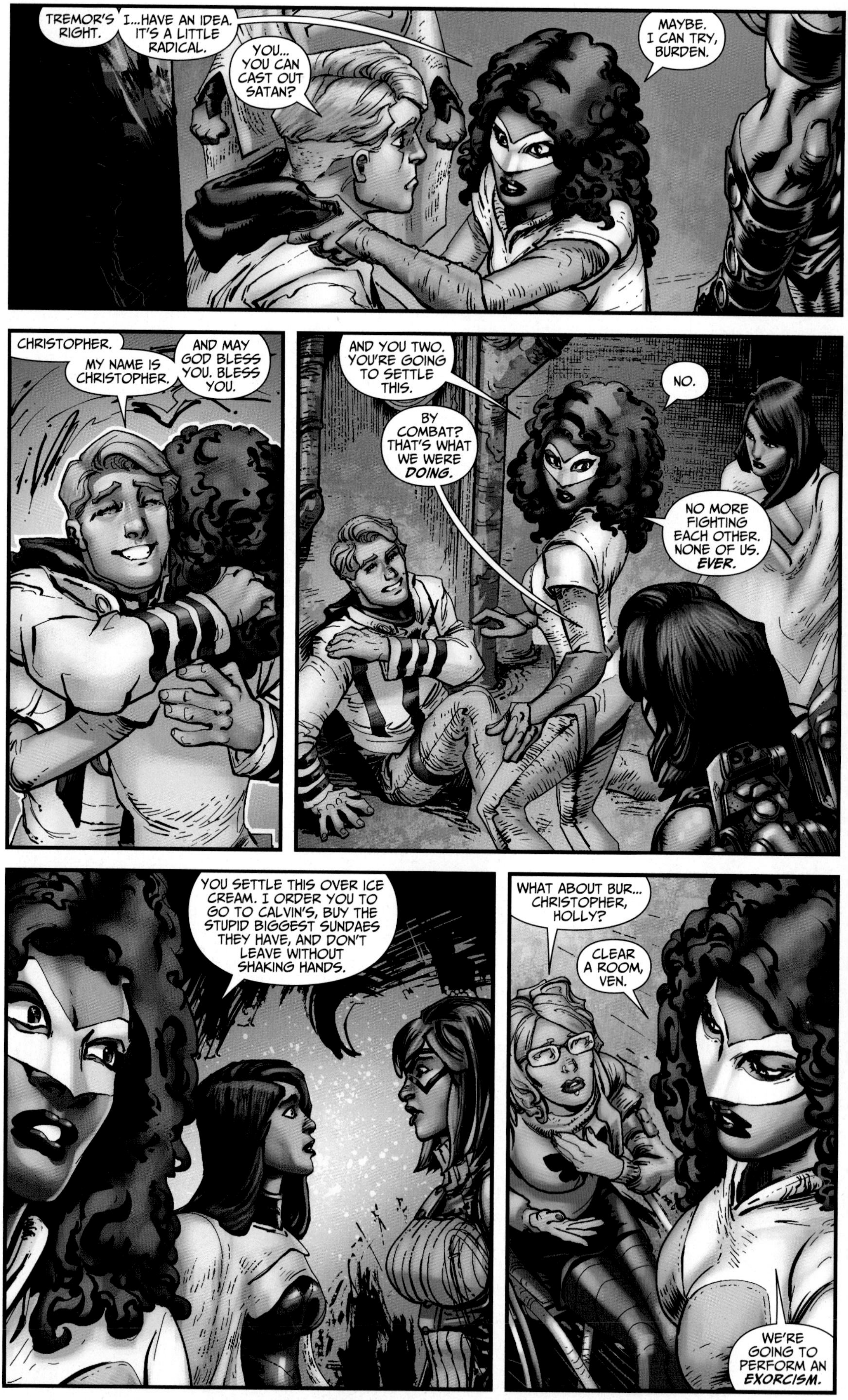
TREMOR'S RIGHT.
I...HAVE AN IDEA. IT'S A LITTLE RADICAL.
YOU... YOU CAN CAST OUT SATAN?
MAYBE. I CAN TRY, BURDEN.
CHRISTOPHER.
MY NAME IS CHRISTOPHER.
AND MAY GOD BLESS YOU. BLESS YOU.
AND YOU TWO. YOU'RE GOING TO SETTLE THIS.
NO.
BY COMBAT? THAT'S WHAT WE WERE DOING.
NO MORE FIGHTING EACH OTHER. NONE OF US. EVER.
YOU SETTLE THIS OVER ICE CREAM. I ORDER YOU TO GO TO CALVIN'S, BUY THE STUPID BIGGEST SUNDAES THEY HAVE, AND DON'T LEAVE WITHOUT SHAKING HANDS.
WHAT ABOUT BUR... CHRISTOPHER, HOLLY?
CLEAR A ROOM, VEN.
WE'RE GOING TO PERFORM AN EXORCISM.

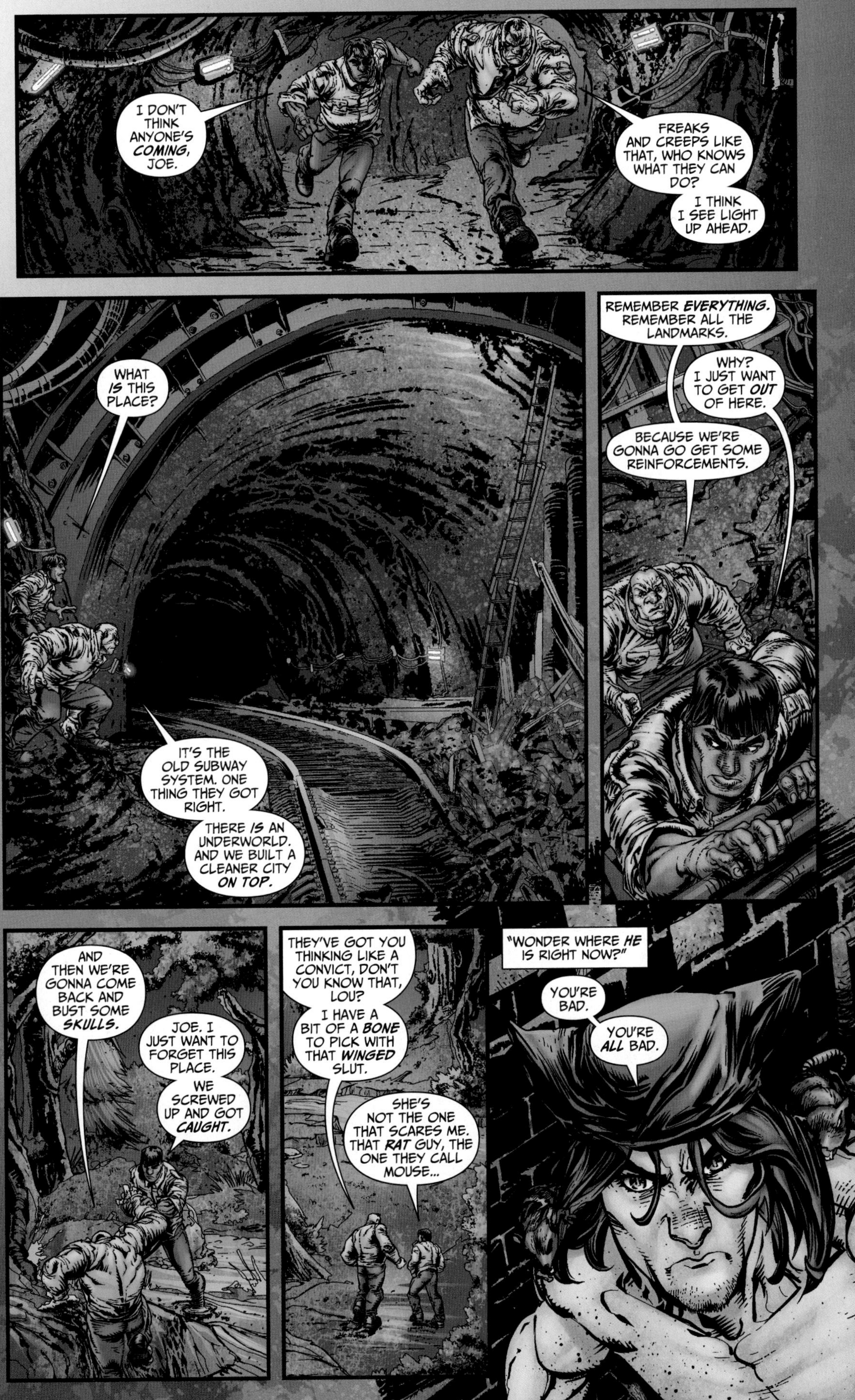
I DON'T THINK ANYONE'S COMING, JOE.
FREAKS AND CREEPS LIKE THAT, WHO KNOWS WHAT THEY CAN DO?
I THINK I SEE LIGHT UP AHEAD.
WHAT IS THIS PLACE?
IT'S THE OLD SUBWAY SYSTEM. ONE THING THEY GOT RIGHT.
THERE IS AN UNDERWORLD. AND WE BUILT A CLEANER CITY ON TOP.
REMEMBER EVERYTHING. REMEMBER ALL THE LANDMARKS.
WHY? I JUST WANT TO GET OUT OF HERE.
BECAUSE WE'RE GONNA GO GET SOME REINFORCEMENTS.
AND THEN WE'RE GONNA COME BACK AND BUST SOME SKULLS.
JOE. I JUST WANT TO FORGET THIS PLACE.
WE SCREWED UP AND GOT CAUGHT.
THEY'VE GOT YOU THINKING LIKE A CONVICT, DON'T YOU KNOW THAT, LOU?
I HAVE A BIT OF A BONE TO PICK WITH THAT WINGED SLUT.
SHE'S NOT THE ONE THAT SCARES ME. THAT RAT GUY, THE ONE THEY CALL MOUSE...
"WONDER WHERE HE IS RIGHT NOW?"
YOU'RE BAD.
YOU'RE ALL BAD.

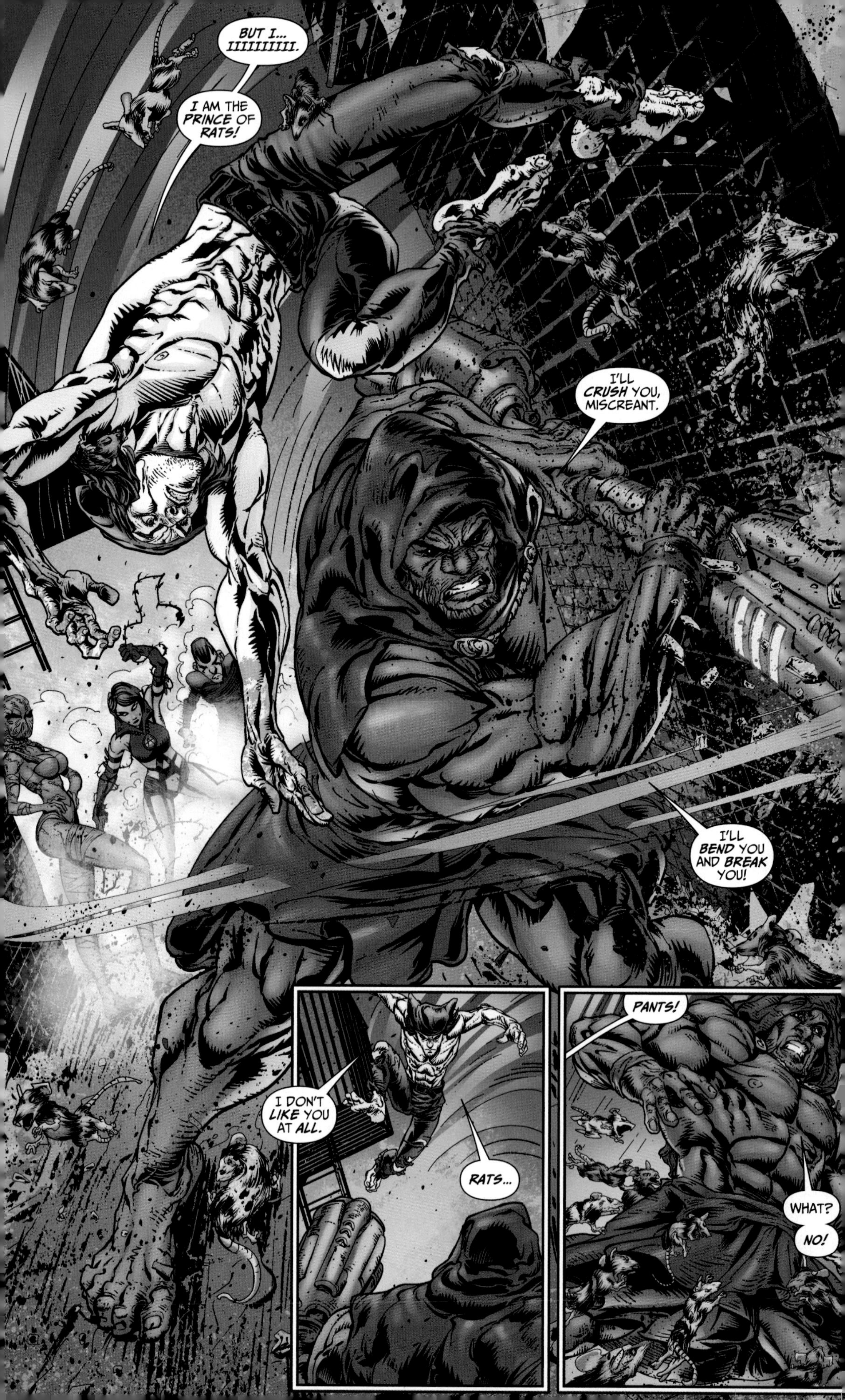
BUT I... IIIIIIIIII.
I AM THE PRINCE OF RATS!
I'LL CRUSH YOU, MISCREANT.
I'LL BEND YOU AND BREAK YOU!
I DON'T LIKE YOU AT ALL.
RATS...
PANTS!
WHAT?
NO!

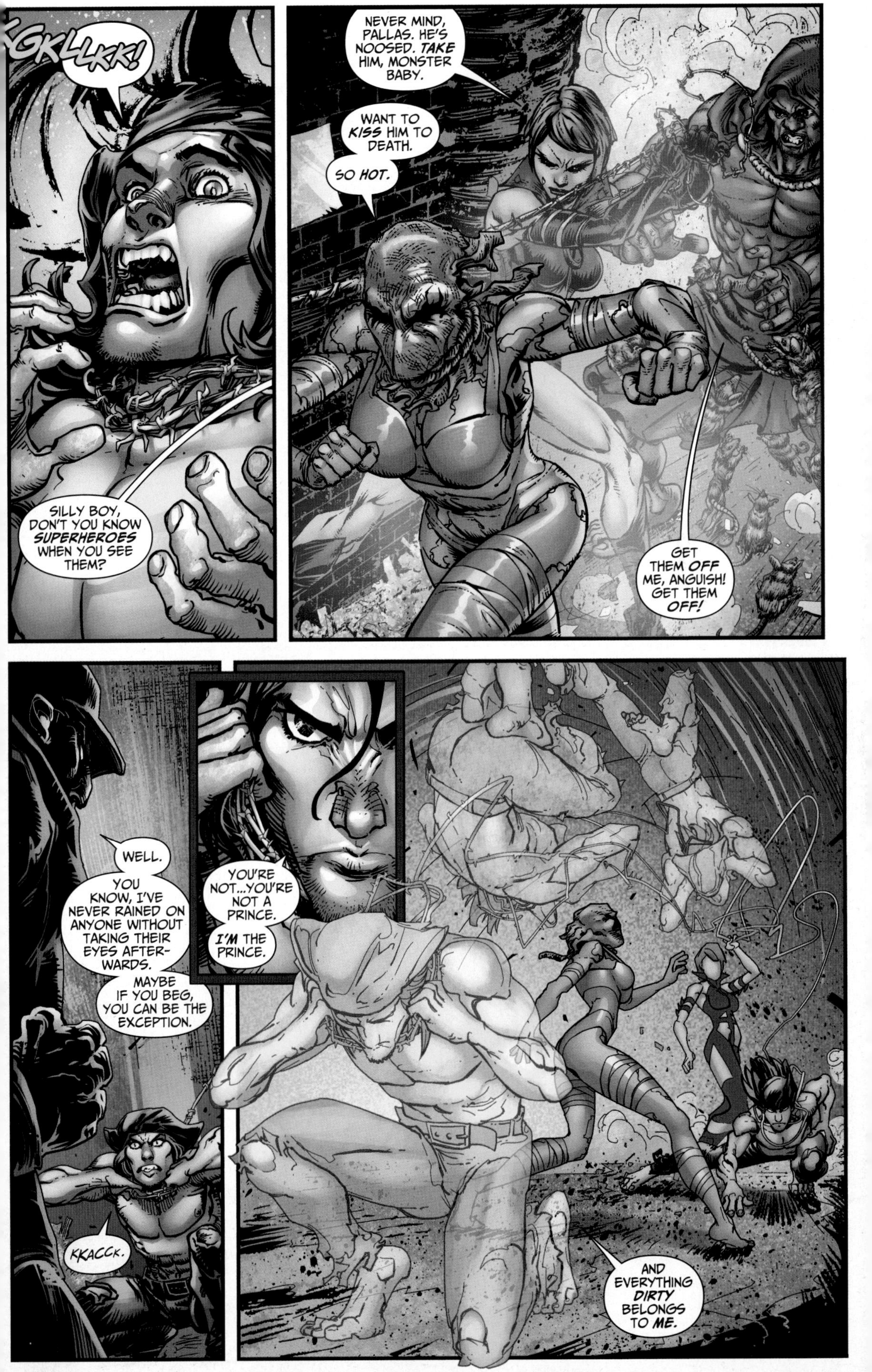
GKLLKK!
SILLY BOY, DON'T YOU KNOW SUPERHEROES WHEN YOU SEE THEM?
NEVER MIND, PALLAS. HE'S NOOSED. TAKE HIM, MONSTER BABY.
WANT TO KISS HIM TO DEATH.
SO HOT.
GET THEM OFF ME, ANGUISH! GET THEM OFF!
WELL.
YOU KNOW, I'VE NEVER RAINED ON ANYONE WITHOUT TAKING THEIR EYES AFTER-WARDS.
MAYBE IF YOU BEG, YOU CAN BE THE EXCEPTION.
KKACCK.
YOU'RE NOT...YOU'RE NOT A PRINCE.
I'M THE PRINCE.
AND EVERYTHING DIRTY BELONGS TO ME.

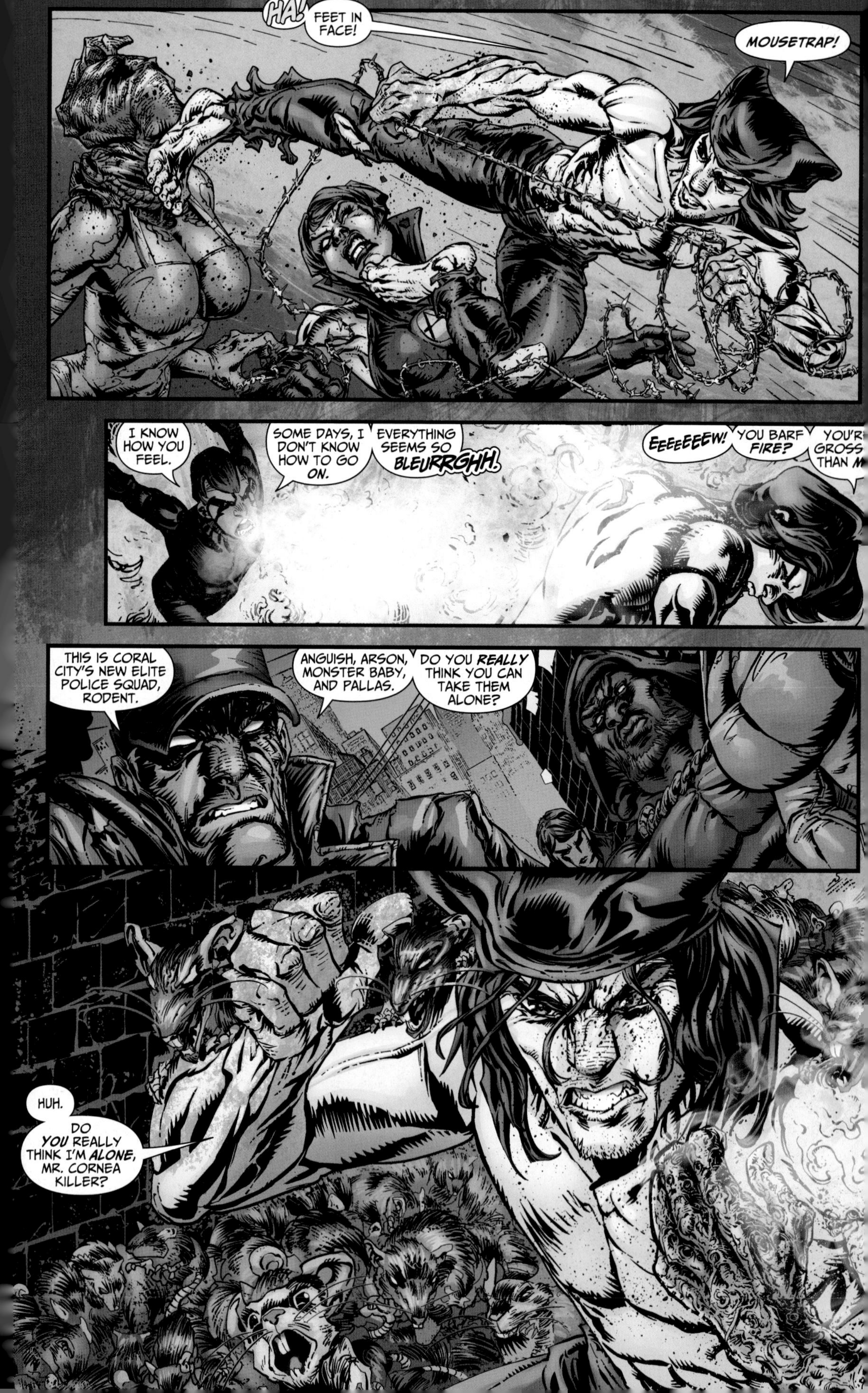
HA!
FEET IN FACE!
MOUSETRAP!
I KNOW HOW YOU FEEL.
SOME DAYS, I DON'T KNOW HOW TO GO ON.
EVERYTHING SEEMS SO BLEURRGHH.
EEEEEEEW!
YOU BARF FIRE?
THIS IS CORAL CITY'S NEW ELITE POLICE SQUAD, RODENT.
ANGUISH, ARSON, MONSTER BABY, AND PALLAS.
DO YOU REALLY THINK YOU CAN TAKE THEM ALONE?
HUH.
DO YOU REALLY THINK I'M ALONE, MR. CORNEA KILLER?

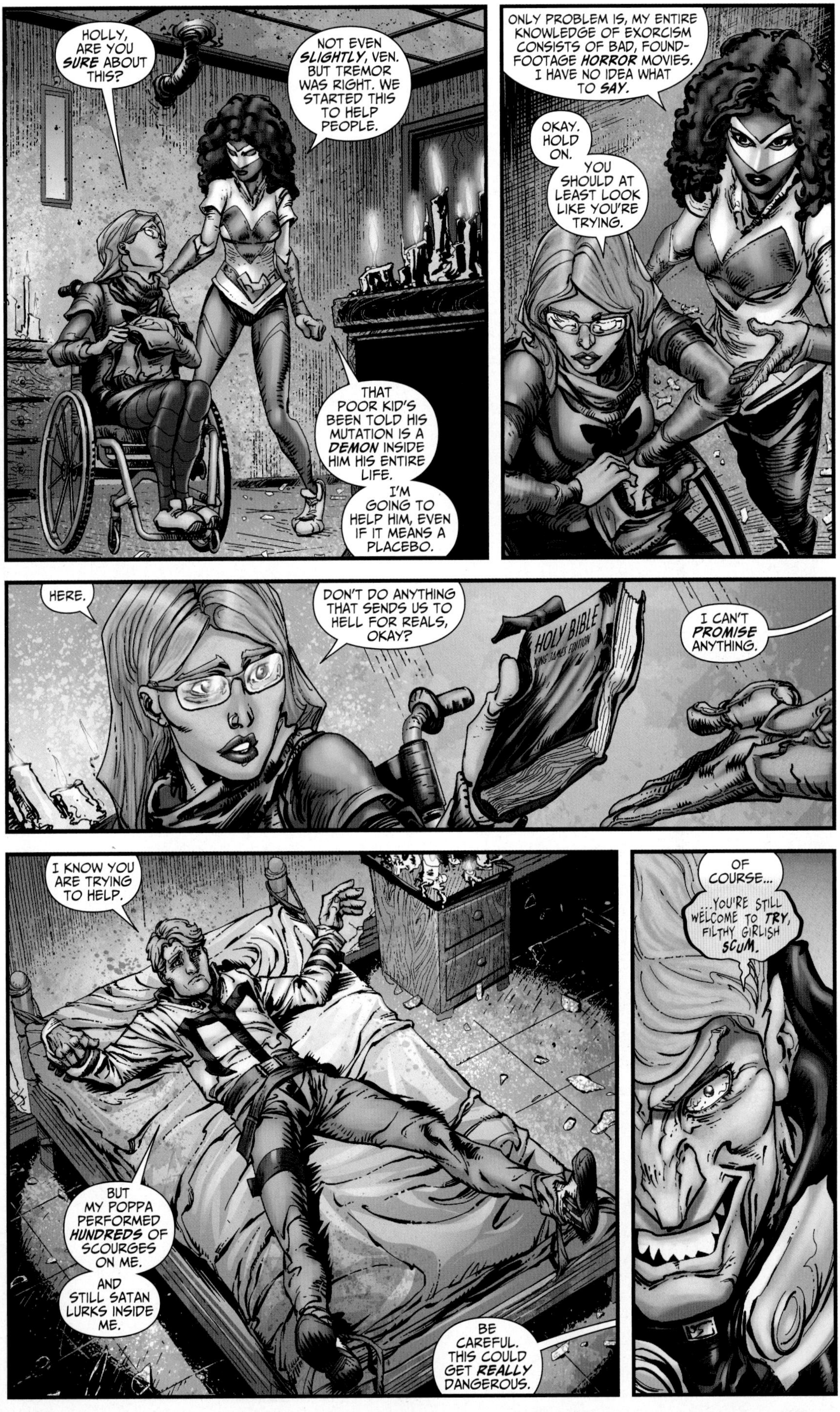
HOLLY, ARE YOU SURE ABOUT THIS?
NOT EVEN SLIGHTLY, VEN. BUT TREMOR WAS RIGHT. WE STARTED THIS TO HELP PEOPLE.
THAT POOR KID'S BEEN TOLD HIS MUTATION IS A DEMON INSIDE HIM HIS ENTIRE LIFE.
I'M GOING TO HELP HIM, EVEN IF IT MEANS A PLACEBO.
ONLY PROBLEM IS, MY ENTIRE KNOWLEDGE OF EXORCISM CONSISTS OF BAD, FOUND-FOOTAGE HORROR MOVIES. I HAVE NO IDEA WHAT TO SAY.
OKAY. HOLD ON.
YOU SHOULD AT LEAST LOOK LIKE YOU'RE TRYING.
HERE.
DON'T DO ANYTHING THAT SENDS US TO HELL FOR REALS, OKAY?
HOLY BIBLE
KING JAMES EDITION
I CAN'T PROMISE ANYTHING.
I KNOW YOU ARE TRYING TO HELP.
BUT MY POPPA PERFORMED HUNDREDS OF SCOURGES ON ME.
AND STILL SATAN LURKS INSIDE ME.
BE CAREFUL. THIS COULD GET REALLY DANGEROUS.
OF COURSE...
...YOU'RE STILL WELCOME TO TRY, FILTHY GIRLISH SCUM.

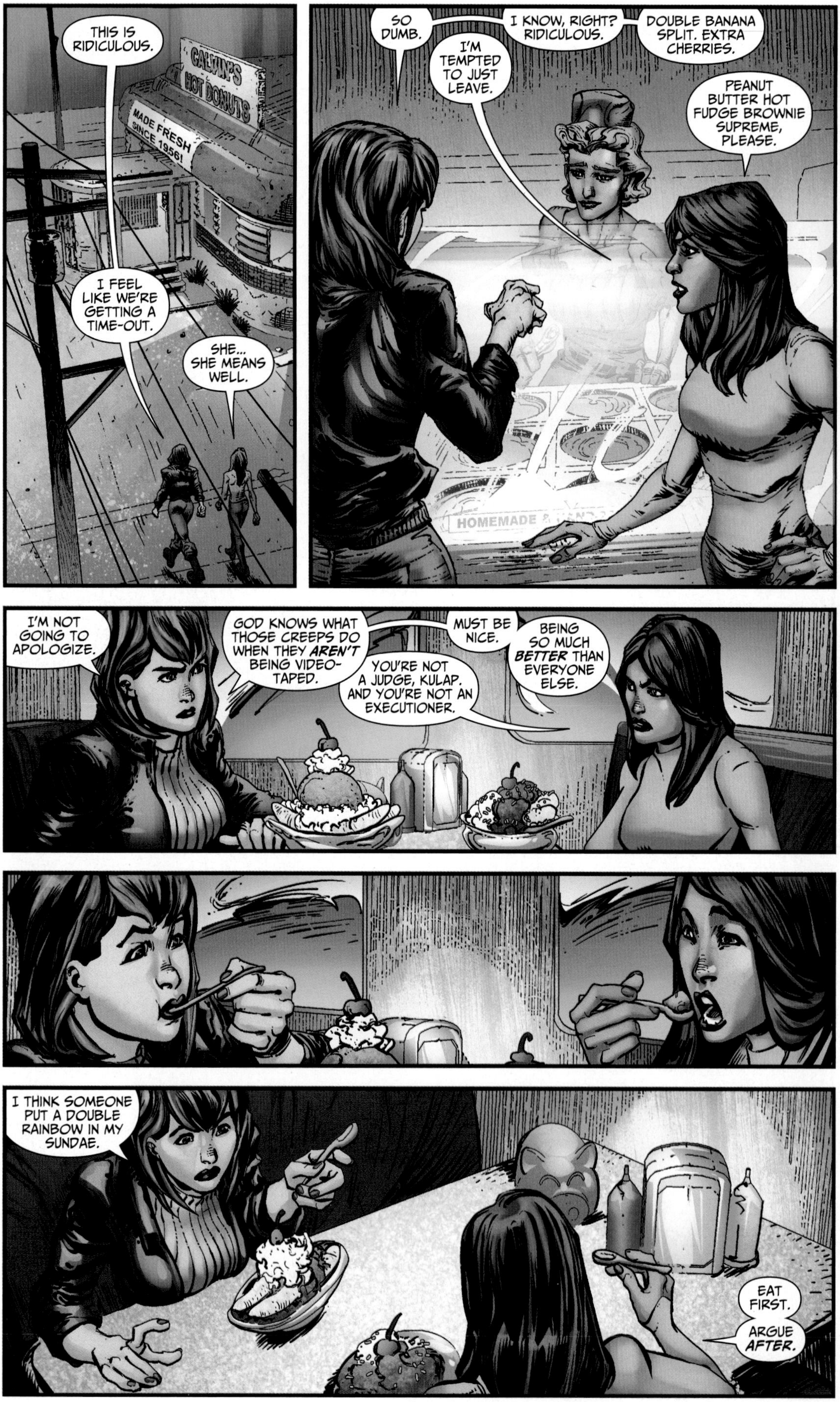
THIS IS RIDICULOUS.
CALVIN'S HOT DONUTS
MADE FRESH SINCE 1956!
I FEEL LIKE WE'RE GETTING A TIME-OUT.
SHE... SHE MEANS WELL.
SO DUMB.
I KNOW, RIGHT? RIDICULOUS.
DOUBLE BANANA SPLIT. EXTRA CHERRIES.
I'M TEMPTED TO JUST LEAVE.
PEANUT BUTTER HOT FUDGE BROWNIE SUPREME, PLEASE.
HOMEMADE &
I'M NOT GOING TO APOLOGIZE.
GOD KNOWS WHAT THOSE CREEPS DO WHEN THEY *AREN'T* BEING VIDEO-TAPED.
MUST BE NICE.
BEING SO MUCH *BETTER* THAN EVERYONE ELSE.
YOU'RE NOT A JUDGE, KULAP. AND YOU'RE NOT AN EXECUTIONER.
I THINK SOMEONE PUT A DOUBLE RAINBOW IN MY SUNDAE.
EAT FIRST.
ARGUE *AFTER*.

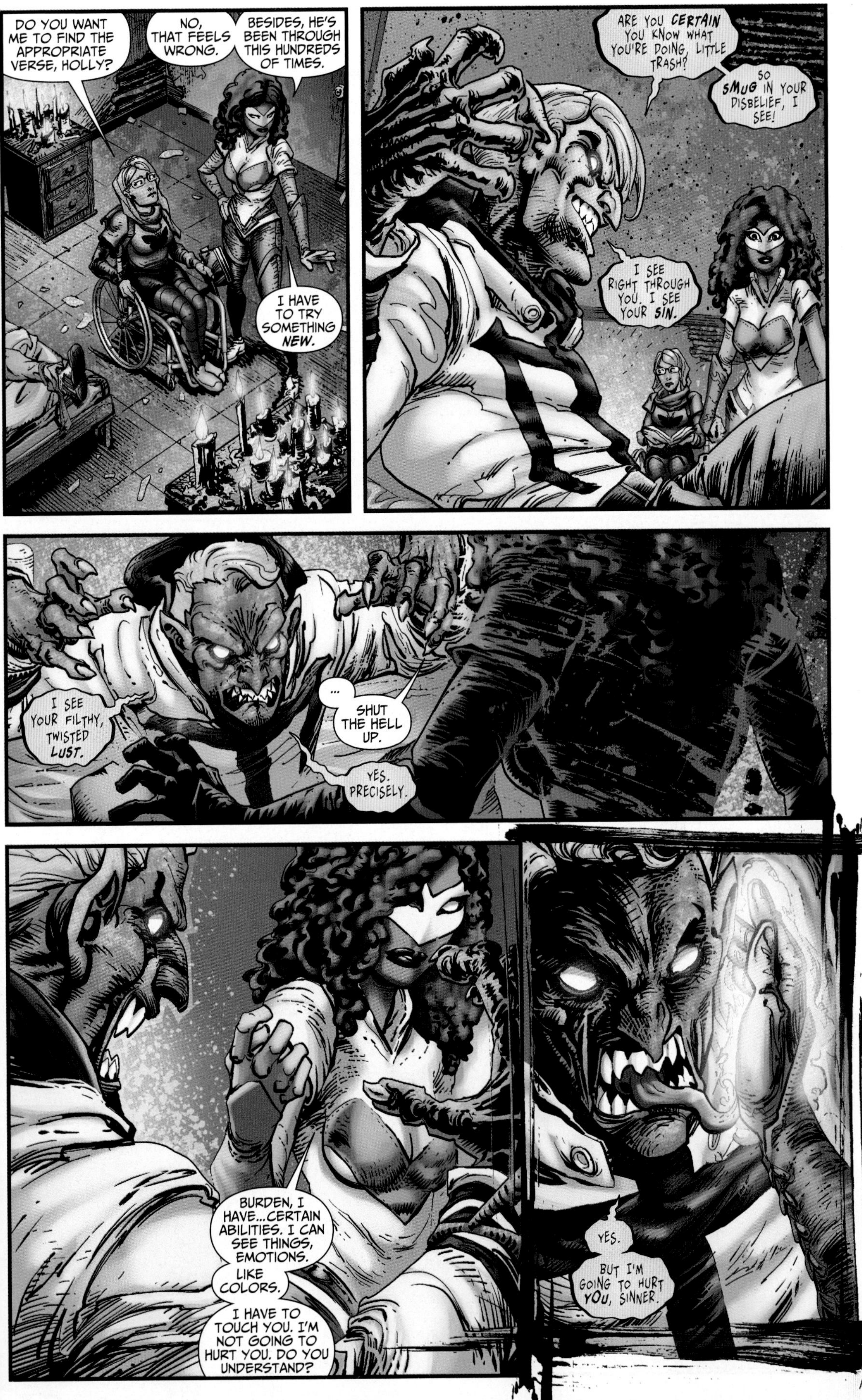
DO YOU WANT ME TO FIND THE APPROPRIATE VERSE, HOLLY?
NO, THAT FEELS WRONG.
BESIDES, HE'S BEEN THROUGH THIS HUNDREDS OF TIMES.
I HAVE TO TRY SOMETHING NEW.
ARE YOU CERTAIN YOU KNOW WHAT YOU'RE DOING, LITTLE TRASH?
SO SMUG IN YOUR DISBELIEF, I SEE!
I SEE RIGHT THROUGH YOU. I SEE YOUR SIN.
I SEE YOUR FILTHY, TWISTED LUST.
...
SHUT THE HELL UP.
YES. PRECISELY.
BURDEN, I HAVE...CERTAIN ABILITIES. I CAN SEE THINGS, EMOTIONS.
LIKE COLORS.
I HAVE TO TOUCH YOU. I'M NOT GOING TO HURT YOU. DO YOU UNDERSTAND?
YES.
BUT I'M GOING TO HURT YOU, SINNER.

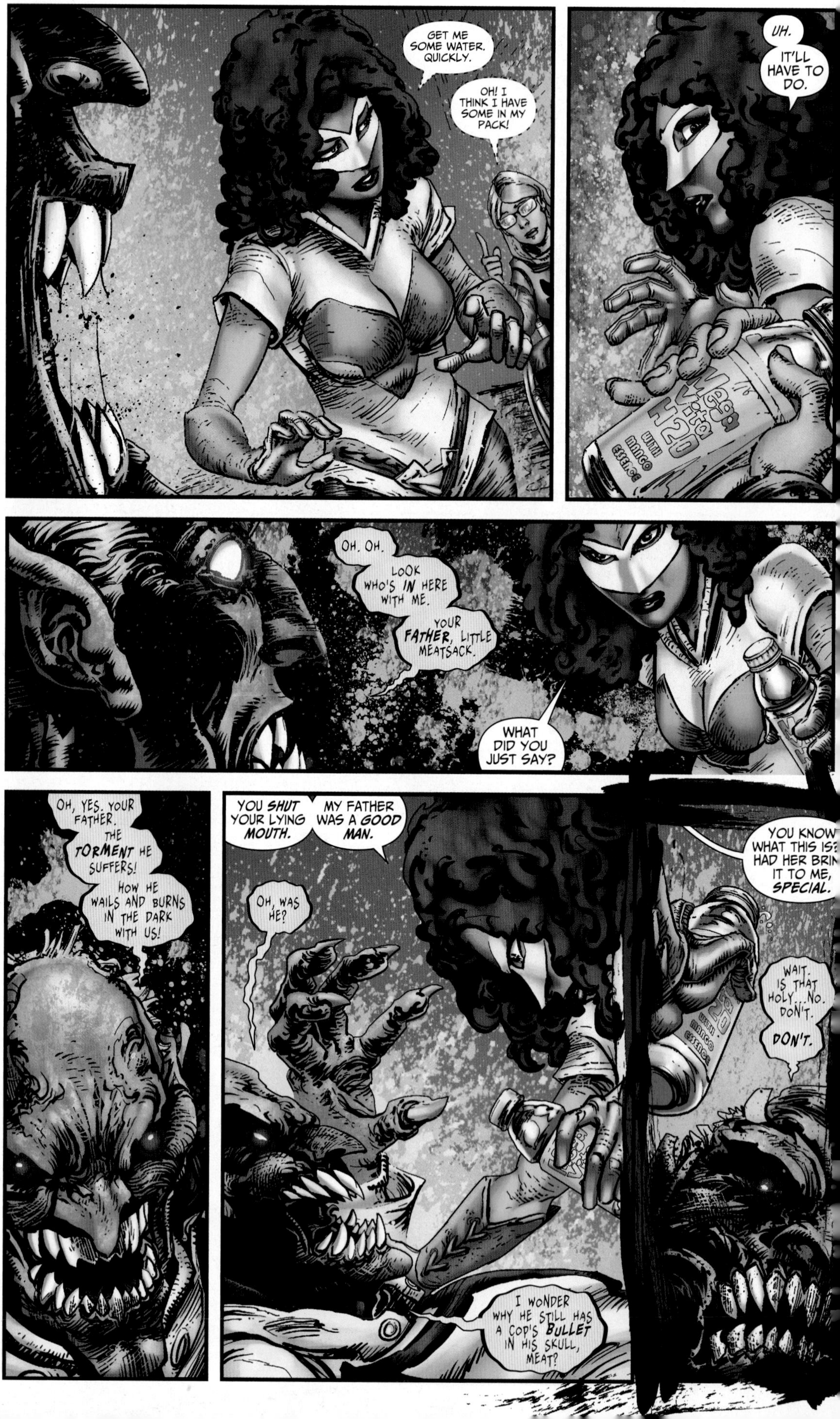
GET ME SOME WATER. QUICKLY.
OH! I THINK I HAVE SOME IN MY PACK!
UH.
IT'LL HAVE TO DO.
Mega Vita H2O with mango essence
OH. OH.
LOOK WHO'S IN HERE WITH ME.
YOUR FATHER, LITTLE MEATSACK.
WHAT DID YOU JUST SAY?
OH, YES. YOUR FATHER.
THE TORMENT HE SUFFERS!
HOW HE WAILS AND BURNS IN THE DARK WITH US!
YOU SHUT YOUR LYING MOUTH.
MY FATHER WAS A GOOD MAN.
OH, WAS HE?
I WONDER WHY HE STILL HAS A COP'S BULLET IN HIS SKULL, MEAT?
YOU KNOW WHAT THIS IS? HAD HER BRIN IT TO ME, SPECIAL.
WAIT. IS THAT HOLY... NO. DON'T.
DON'T.

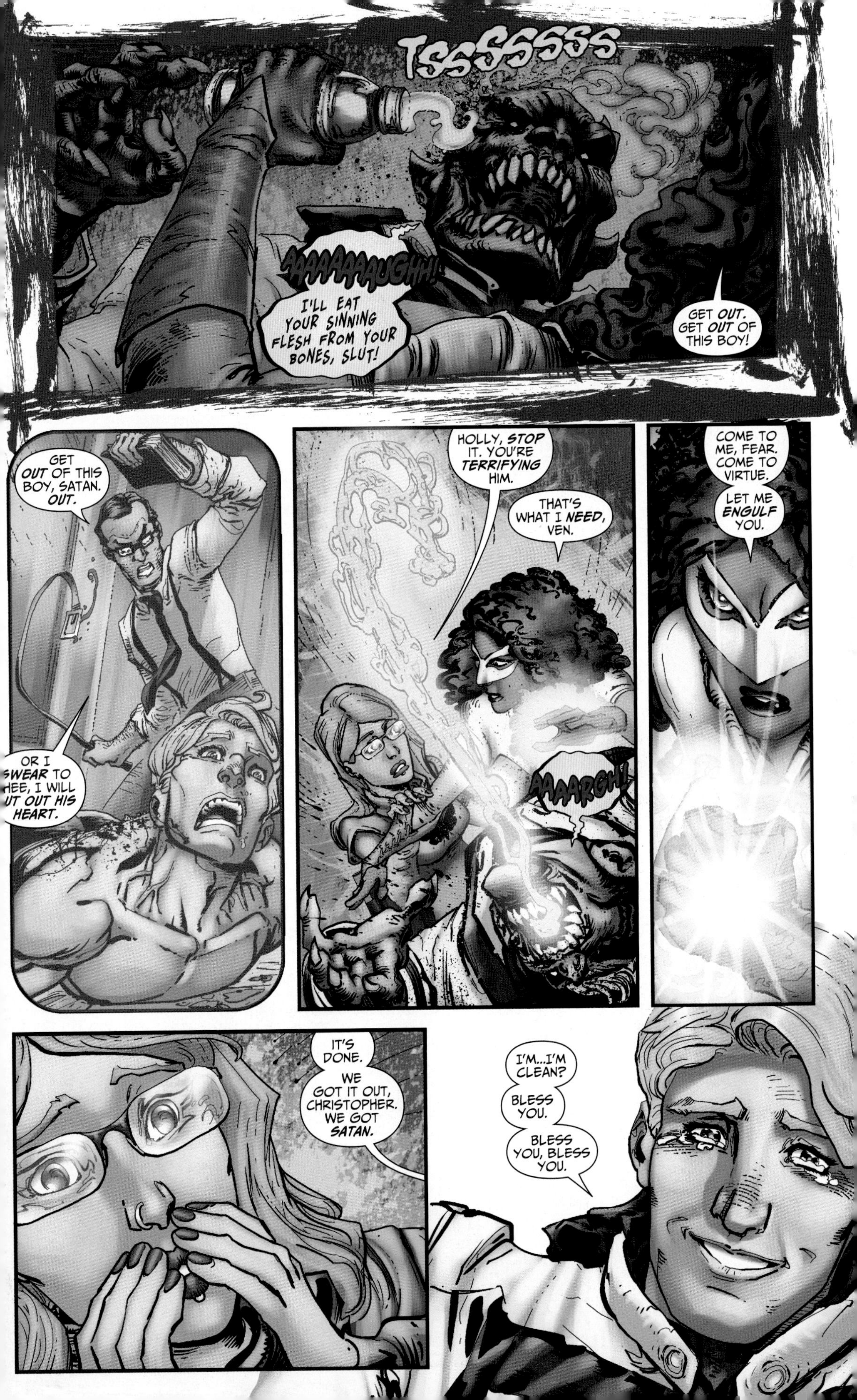
TSSSSSSS
AAAAAAAAUGHH!
I'LL EAT YOUR SINNING FLESH FROM YOUR BONES, SLUT!
GET OUT. GET OUT OF THIS BOY!
GET OUT OF THIS BOY, SATAN. OUT.
OR I SWEAR TO HEE, I WILL UT OUT HIS HEART.
HOLLY, STOP IT. YOU'RE TERRIFYING HIM.
THAT'S WHAT I NEED, VEN.
AAAARGH!
COME TO ME, FEAR. COME TO VIRTUE.
LET ME ENGULF YOU.
IT'S DONE.
WE GOT IT OUT, CHRISTOPHER. WE GOT SATAN.
I'M...I'M CLEAN?
BLESS YOU.
BLESS YOU, BLESS YOU.

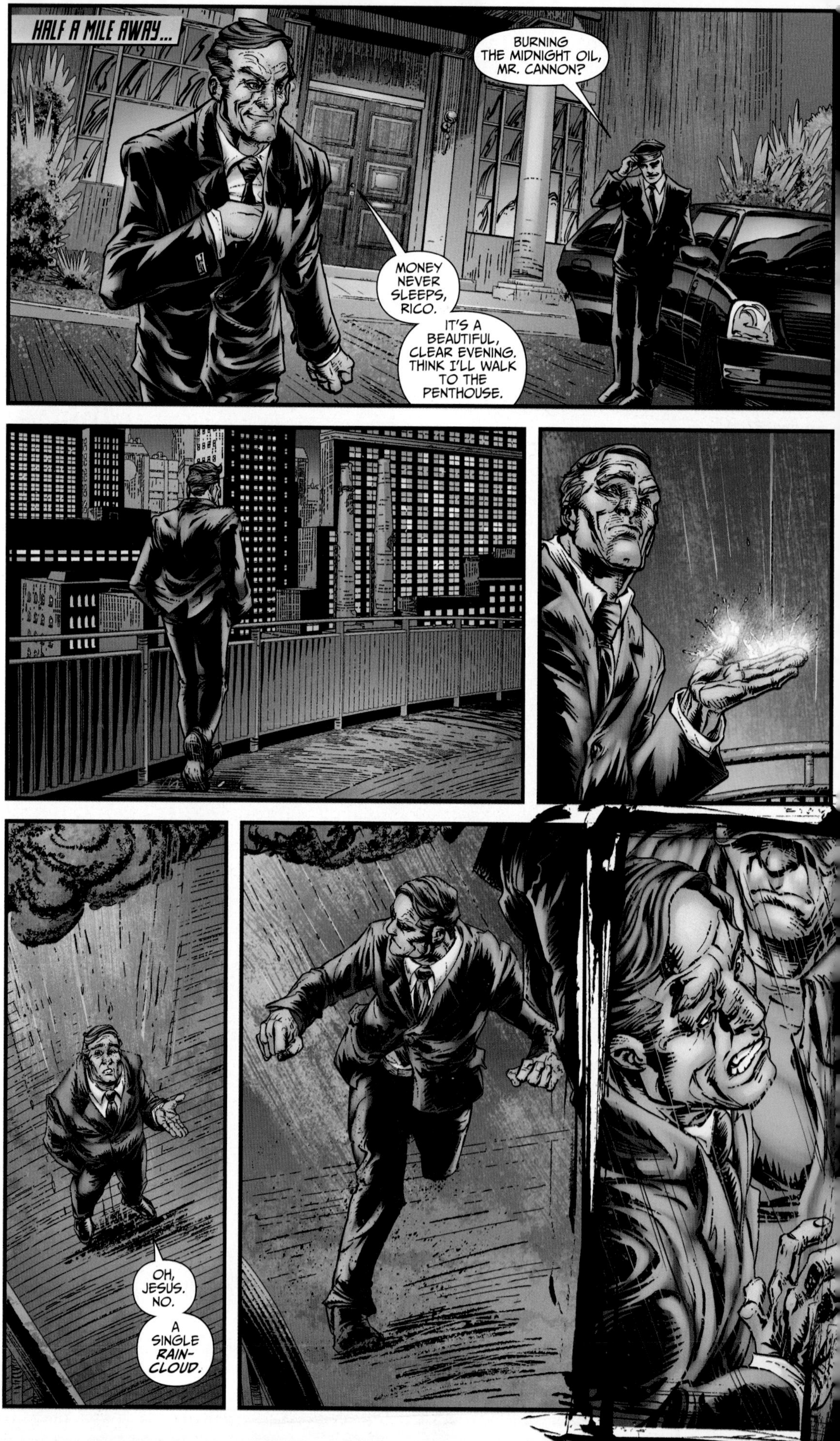
HALF A MILE AWAY...
BURNING THE MIDNIGHT OIL, MR. CANNON?
MONEY NEVER SLEEPS, RICO.
IT'S A BEAUTIFUL, CLEAR EVENING. THINK I'LL WALK TO THE PENTHOUSE.
OH, JESUS. NO.
A SINGLE RAIN-CLOUD.

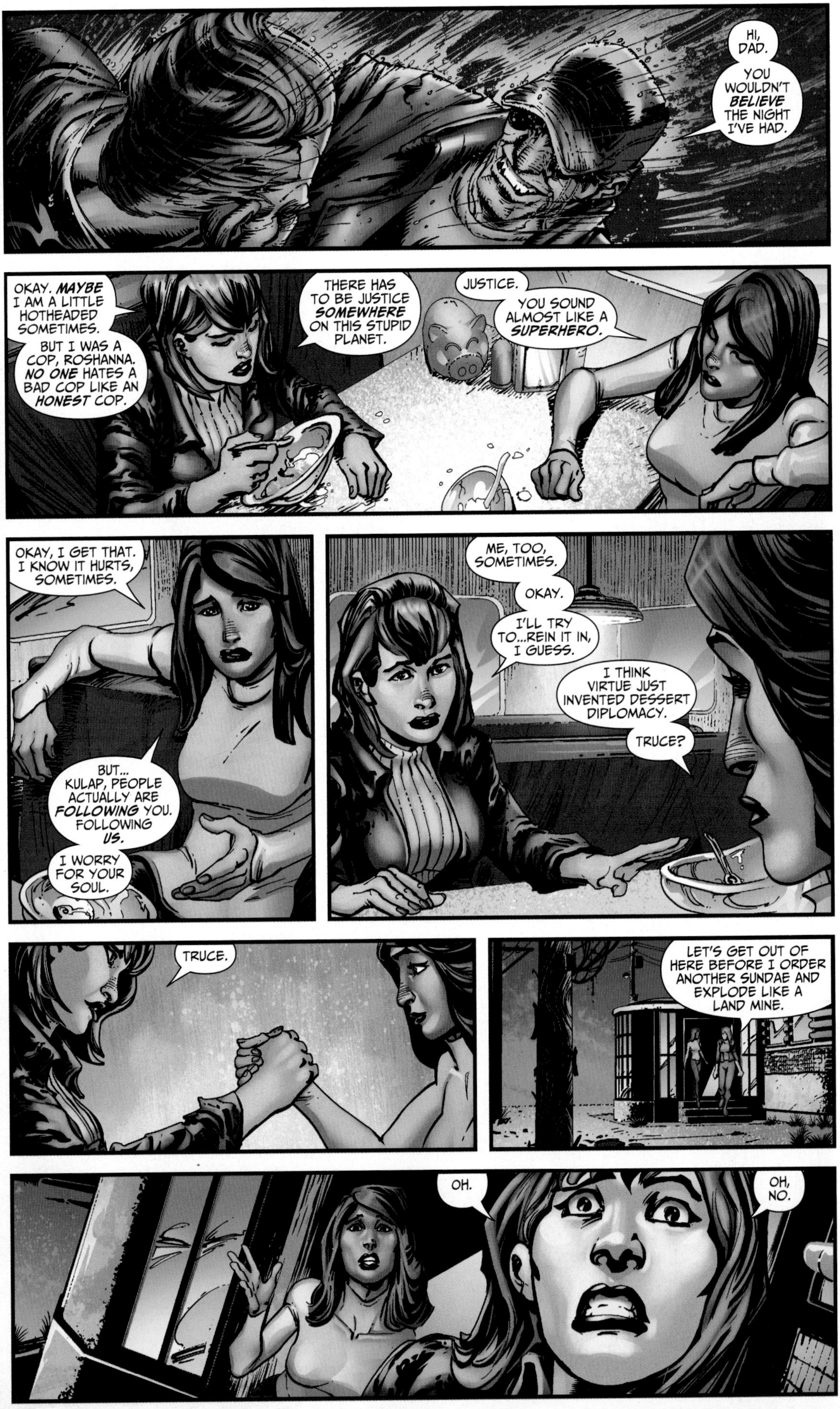

HI, DAD.
YOU WOULDN'T BELIEVE THE NIGHT I'VE HAD.
OKAY. MAYBE I AM A LITTLE HOTHEADED SOMETIMES.
BUT I WAS A COP, ROSHANNA. NO ONE HATES A BAD COP LIKE AN HONEST COP.
THERE HAS TO BE JUSTICE SOMEWHERE ON THIS STUPID PLANET.
JUSTICE.
YOU SOUND ALMOST LIKE A SUPERHERO.
OKAY, I GET THAT. I KNOW IT HURTS, SOMETIMES.
BUT... KULAP, PEOPLE ACTUALLY ARE FOLLOWING YOU. FOLLOWING US.
I WORRY FOR YOUR SOUL.
ME, TOO, SOMETIMES.
OKAY.
I'LL TRY TO...REIN IT IN, I GUESS.
I THINK VIRTUE JUST INVENTED DESSERT DIPLOMACY.
TRUCE?
TRUCE.
LET'S GET OUT OF HERE BEFORE I ORDER ANOTHER SUNDAE AND EXPLODE LIKE A LAND MINE.
OH.
OH, NO.

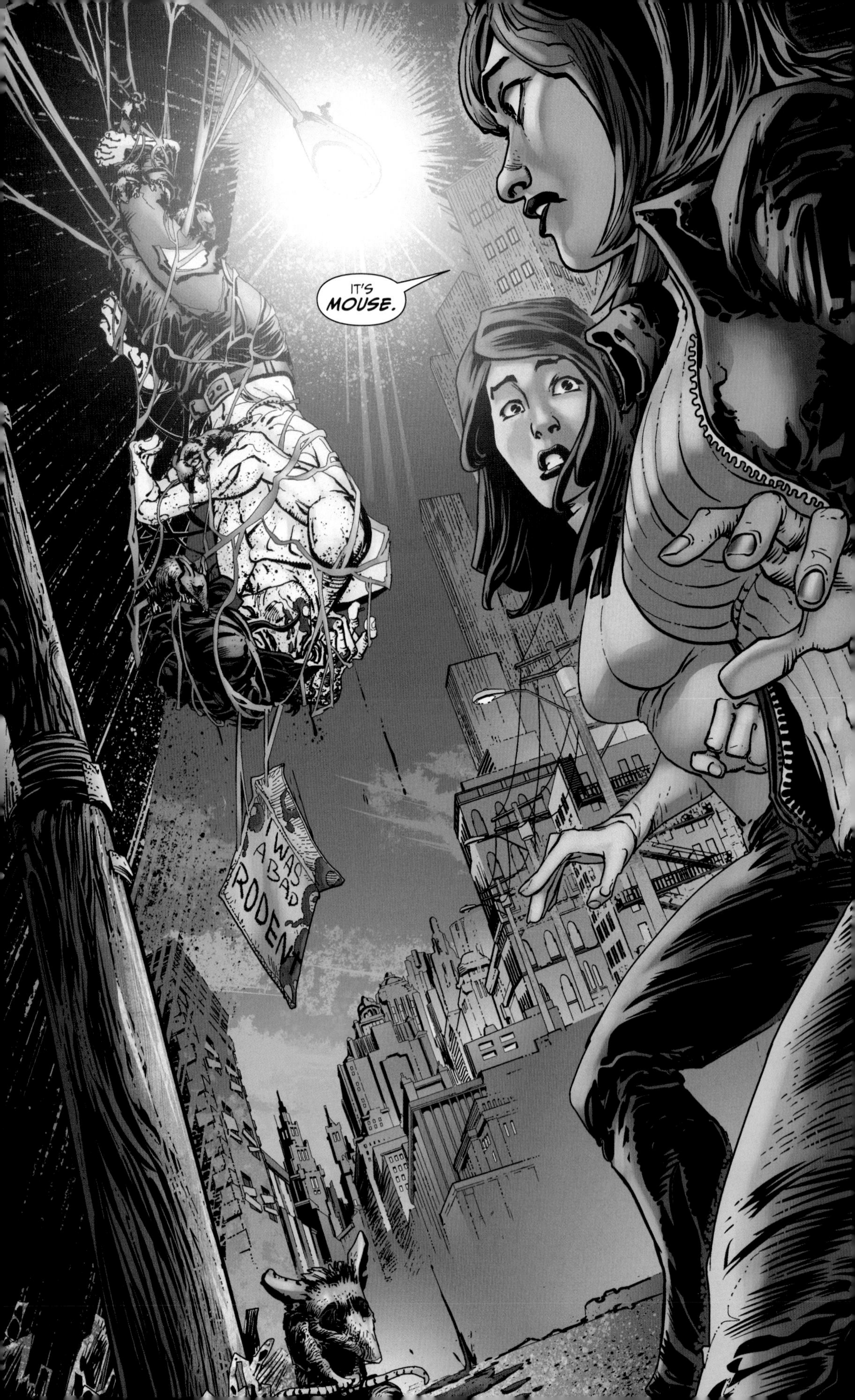
IT'S MOUSE.
I WAS A BAD RODEN

THE MOVEMENT

ART BY FREDDIE E. WILLIAMS II

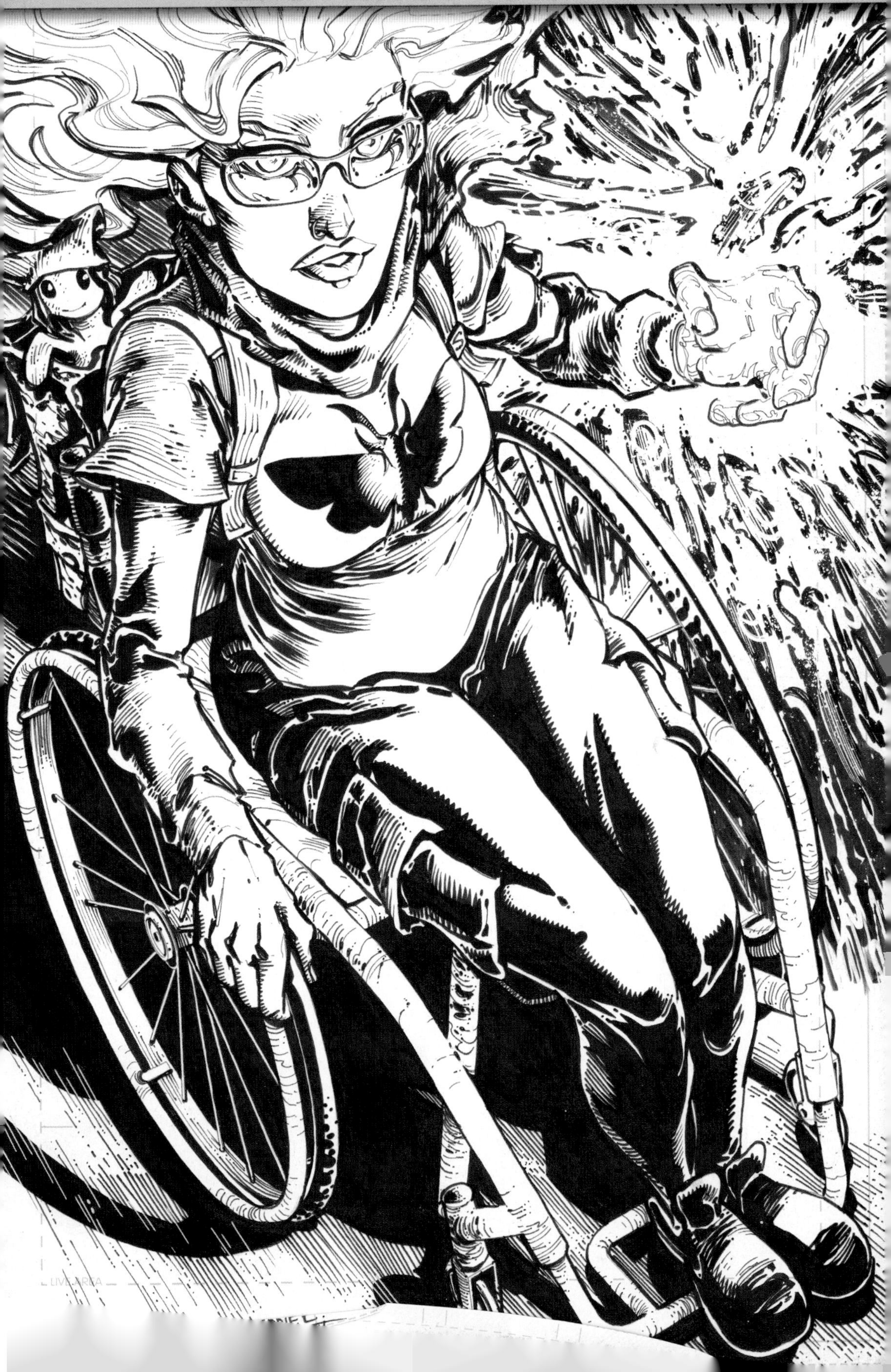

LONG FEATHERS

EYES C

METAFORICLY STRAPPING HIMSELF PAYING PENANCE

SHACKLES CHAINS

SPAWN-LIKE CHAINS

A LOT OF "V"s

LONG SHIRT

PRIEST LIKE ROBE

HEAD TOE LEA ARM

LACES = "V"s

ONLY THAT FE A "SUP

VIRTUE

BURDEN

KATH

REFLETIVE LIKE SUN GLASS

I'D LIKE TO NOT SEE NORMAL EYES IN THE MASK

SHINY GASS OVER EYES?

NO EXPRESSIO

TITLE THE MOVEMENT character Lineup ISSUE # MONTH INTERIORS

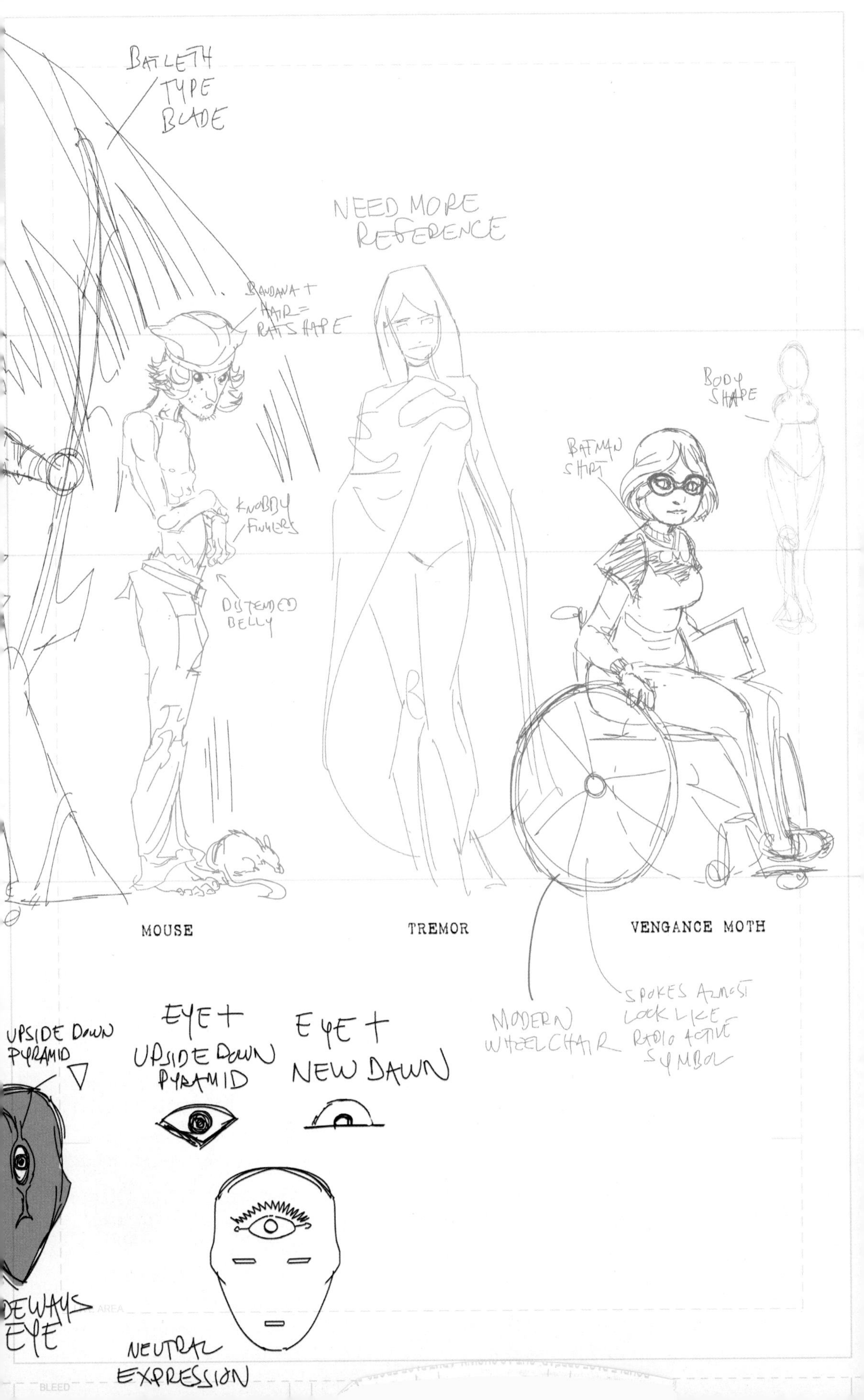

BATLETH TYPE BLADE
NEED MORE REFERENCE
BANDANA + HAIR = RAT SHAPE
KNOBBY FINGERS
DISTENDED BELLY
BODY SHAPE
BATMAN SHIRT
MOUSE
TREMOR
VENGANCE MOTH
MODERN WHEELCHAIR
SPOKES ALMOST LOOK LIKE RADIO ACTIVE SYMBOL
UPSIDE DOWN PYRAMID
EYE + UPSIDE DOWN PYRAMID
EYE + NEW DAWN
DEWAYS EYE
NEUTRAL EXPRESSION

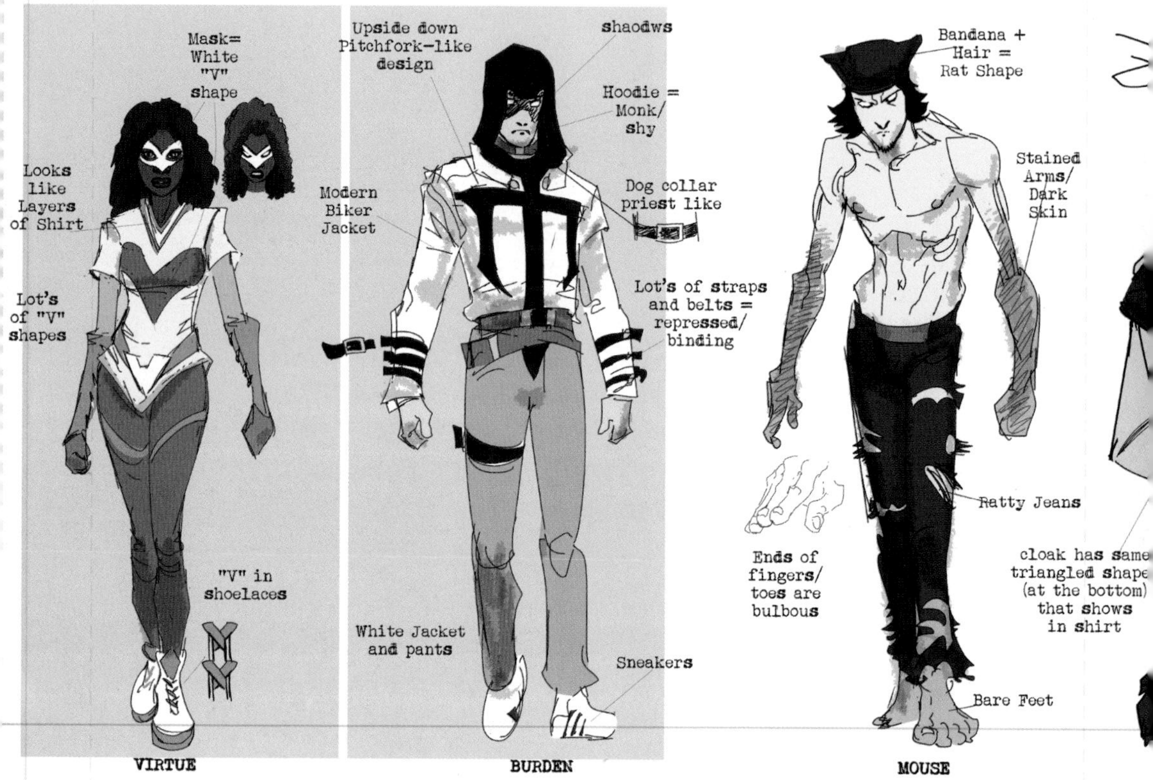
Mask=
White
"V"
shape
Looks
like
Layers
of Shirt
Lot's
of "V"
shapes
"V" in
shoelaces
VIRTUE
Upside down
Pitchfork-like
design
shaodws
Hoodie =
Monk/
shy
Modern
Biker
Jacket
Dog collar
priest like
Lot's of straps
and belts =
repressed/
binding
White Jacket
and pants
Sneakers
BURDEN
Bandana +
Hair =
Rat Shape
Stained
Arms/
Dark
Skin
Ratty Jeans
Ends of
fingers/
toes are
bulbous
Bare Feet
MOUSE
cloak has same
triangled shape
(at the bottom)
that shows
in shirt

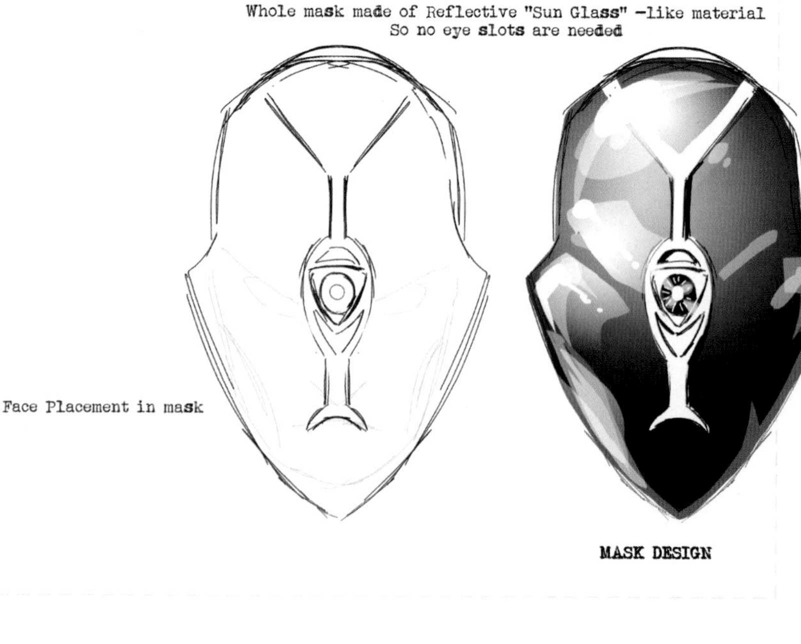
Whole mask made of Reflective "Sun Glass" -like material
So no eye slots are needed
Face Placement in mask
MASK DESIGN

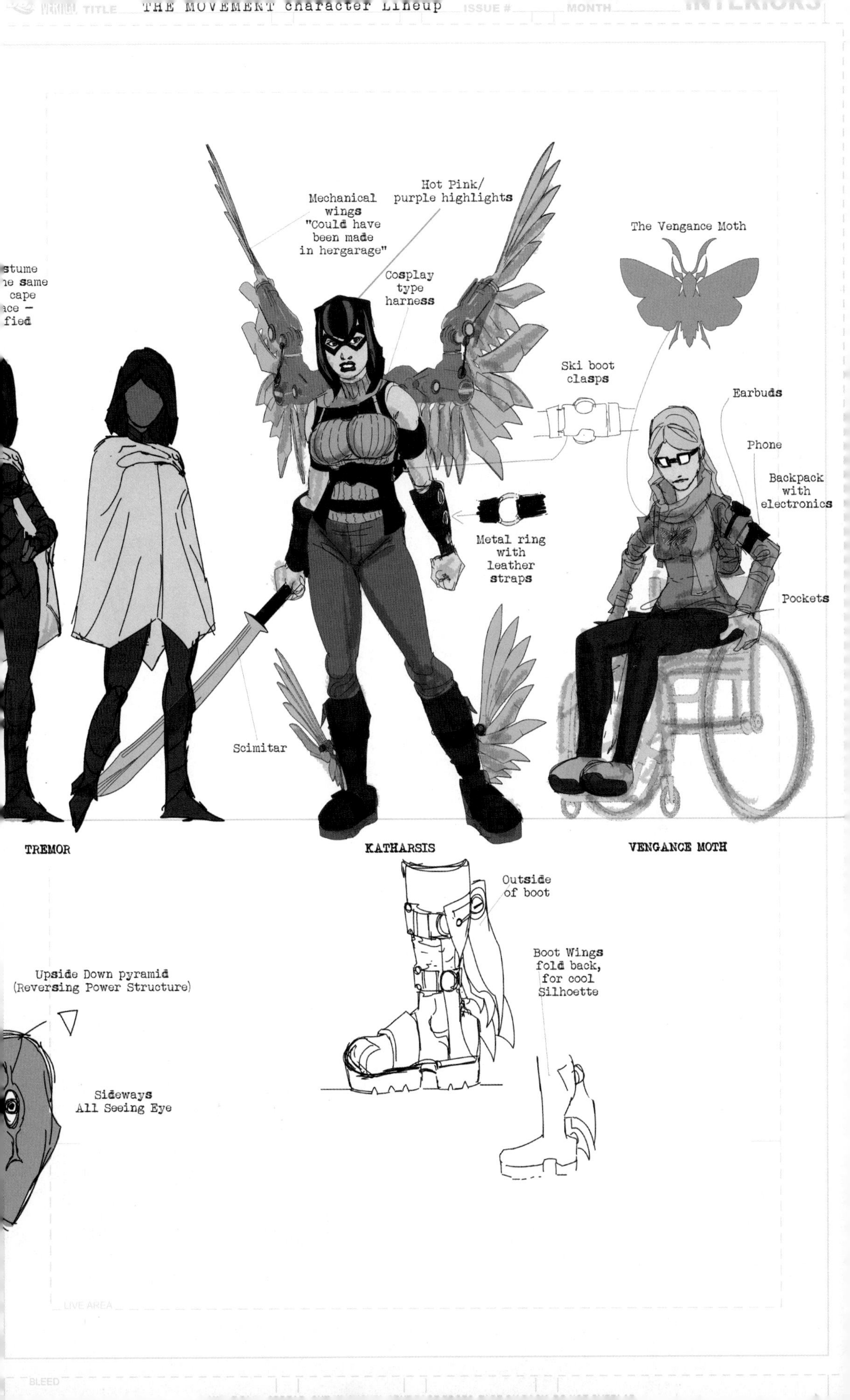
TITLE THE MOVEMENT character Lineup
ISSUE #
MONTH
stume
e same
cape
ce –
fied
Mechanical wings "Could have been made in hergarage"
Hot Pink/ purple highlights
Cosplay type harness
The Vengance Moth
Ski boot clasps
Earbuds
Phone
Backpack with electronics
Metal ring with leather straps
Pockets
Scimitar
TREMOR
KATHARSIS
VENGANCE MOTH
Outside of boot
Boot Wings fold back, for cool Silhoette
Upside Down pyramid (Reversing Power Structure)
Sideways All Seeing Eye
LIVE AREA
BLEED

"Simone and artist Ardian Syaf not only do justice to Babs' legacy, but build in a new complexity that is the starting point for a future full of new storytelling possibilities. A hell of a ride."
—IGN

START AT THE BEGINNING!

BATGIRL VOLUME 1: THE DARKEST REFLECTION

BATWOMAN VOLUME 1: HYDROLOGY

RED HOOD AND THE OUTLAWS VOLUME 1: REDEMPTION

BATWING VOLUME 1: THE LOST KINGDOM

GAIL **SIMONE** ARDIAN **SYAF** VICENTE **CIFUENTES**

"Drips with energy."
—IGN

"Grade A."
—USA TODAY

START AT THE BEGINNING!

TEEN TITANS VOLUME 1: IT'S OUR RIGHT TO FIGHT

LEGION OF SUPER-HEROES VOLUME 1: HOSTILE WORLD

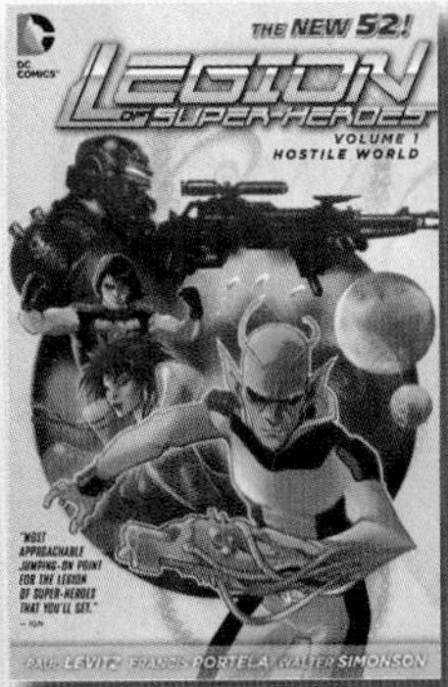
THE NEW 52!
LEGION OF SUPER-HEROES
VOLUME 1
HOSTILE WORLD

LEGION LOST VOLUME 1: RUN FROM TOMORROW

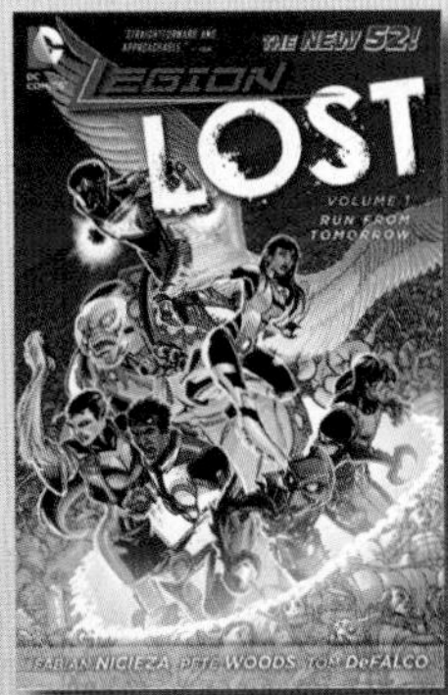
THE NEW 52!
LEGION LOST
VOLUME 1
RUN FROM TOMORROW

STATIC SHOCK VOLUME 1: SUPERCHARGED

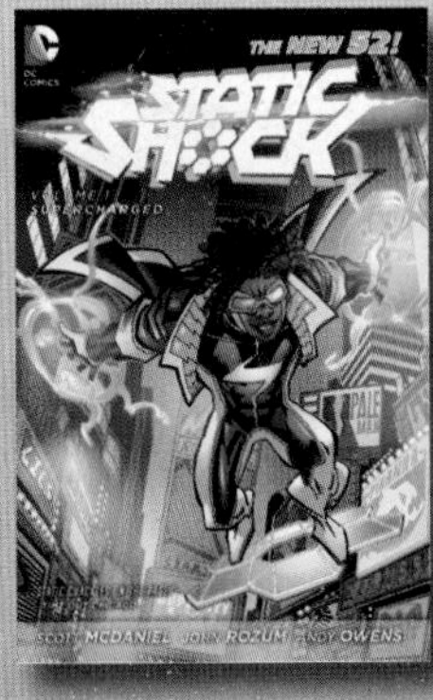
THE NEW 52!
STATIC SHOCK

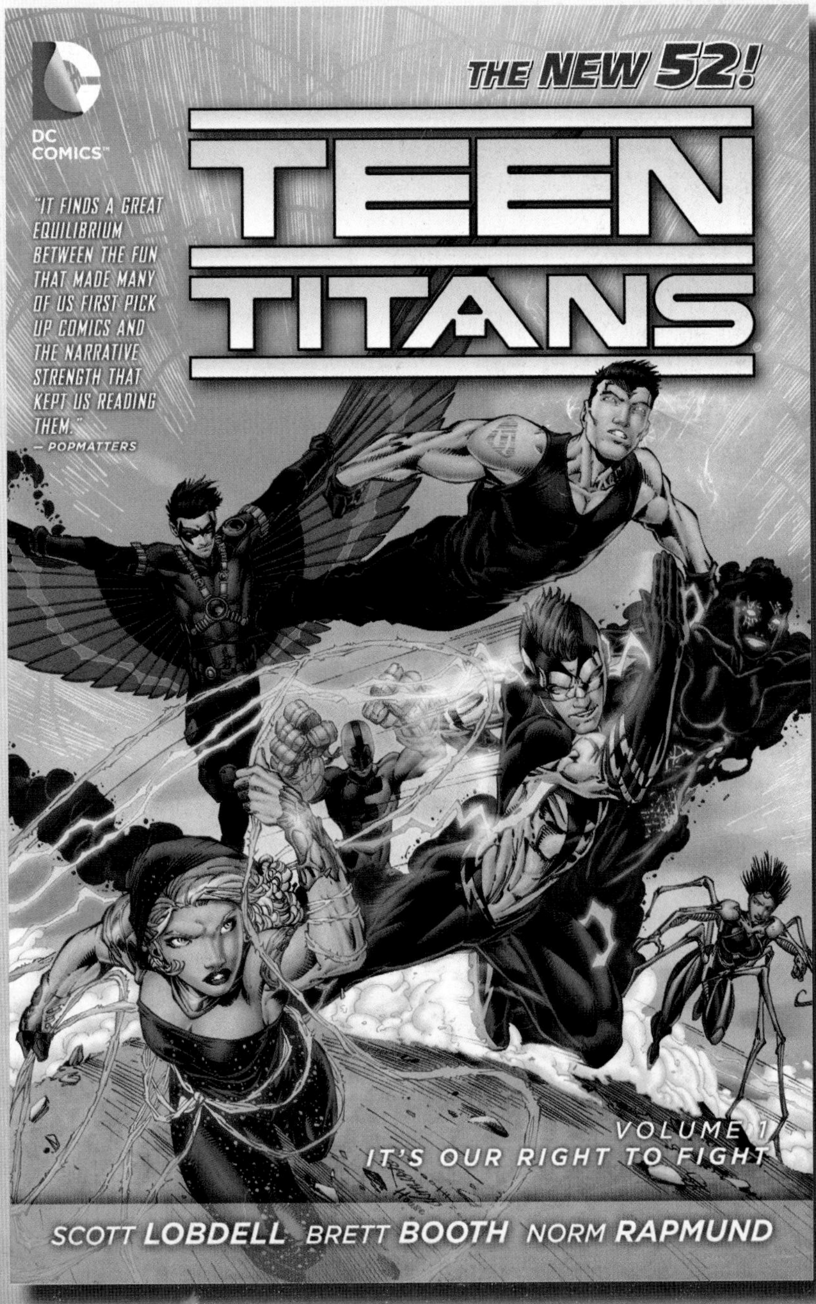
DC COMICS
THE NEW 52!
TEEN TITANS
"IT FINDS A GREAT EQUILIBRIUM BETWEEN THE FUN THAT MADE MANY OF US FIRST PICK UP COMICS AND THE NARRATIVE STRENGTH THAT KEPT US READING THEM."
— POPMATTERS
VOLUME 1
IT'S OUR RIGHT TO FIGHT
SCOTT LOBDELL BRETT BOOTH NORM RAPMUND

START AT THE BEGINNING!
THE FLASH
VOLUME 1: MOVE FORWARD

JUSTICE LEAGUE
INTERNATIONAL
VOLUME 1: THE
SIGNAL MASTERS

O.M.A.C.
VOLUME 1:
OMACTIVATE!

CAPTAIN ATOM
VOLUME 1:
EVOLUTION

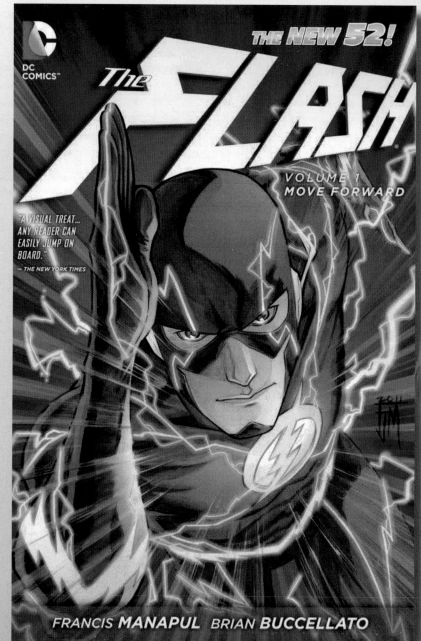

FRANCIS MANAPUL **BRIAN BUCCELLATO**